Diary of a Professional
Commodity Trader

Diary of a Professional Commodity Trader

Lessons from 21 Weeks of Real Trading

PETER BRANDT

WILEY

John Wiley & Sons, Inc.

Published by John Wiley & Sons, Inc., Hoboken, New Jersey.
Published simultaneously in Canada.

For general information on our other products and services or for technical support, please contact our Customer Care Department within the United States at (800) 762-2974, outside the United States at (317) 572-3993 or fax (317) 572-4002.

Wiley also publishes its books in a variety of electronic formats. Some content that appears in print may not be available in electronic books. For more information about Wiley products, visit our web site at www.wiley.com.

ISBN 978-0-470-52145-8 (cloth); ISBN: 978-0-470-94724-1 (ebk); 978-0-470-94725-8 (ebk); 978-0-470-94726-5 (ebk)

Printed in the United States of America

10 9 8 7 6 5 4 3 2 1

This book is dedicated to my wife, Mona, and my children, who for more than 30 years have tolerated the ups and downs of the life of a commodity trader.

Also to some very dear folks I refer to as the Factor family, about two dozen fellow commodity traders who, since 1980, have served as a sounding board as I developed my trading plan and honed my craft.

Contents

Acknowledgments

I owe a debt of real gratitude to my friend Dave Forbes, CEO of Petra Financial in Colorado Springs, who allowed me to use his office and staff to prepare this book.

I am also in debt to Glen Larson and his awesome team at Genesis Financial Technology, who provide me with assistance in preparing the charts for this book. I use the Genesis data and charting platform, Trade-Navigator, in my own trading and have found Glen and his team to be real partners in my market operations.

Dan Chesler, President of Chesler Analytics (a firm providing technical market research to energy traders) originally suggested that I write this book. Dan and I go back several decades as peers. If you have ever written a book, you will understand it when I say that I don't know whether to thank Dan or curse at him for encouraging me.

Finally, I want to thank Meg Freeborn and Kevin Commins of John Wiley & Sons for hanging with me during this process. I started this book in early 2009, but for health reasons I was sidetracked for nearly nine months. Meg and Kevin demonstrated great patience and guidance to get this project back on track.

Diary of a Professional Commodity Trader

Foundations of Successful Trading

Is trading an art, or is it a science? Or is it some combination of the two? I am not sure of the answers to these questions. I am not sure it is necessary to know the answers. I view trading as a craft. A successful trader is a craftsman, applying his or her skills in the same way as a baseball pitcher who has perfected throwing a knuckleball, or a welder specializing in joining together exotic metals, or a software engineer who overcomes complex problems to design new chip technology.

All craftsmen undergo apprenticeships. An apprenticeship is not some specified period of time in a specified classroom or training grounds. Rather, an apprenticeship is a composition of personal, professional, and proprietary experiences that lead to the knowledge and skills to perform a craft.

Part I of this book relates my apprenticeship as a trader and provides context and background to all that follows in the book. Part I contains two sections:

1. An Introduction to my background and history as a trader, the reasons I decided to write this book, a road map to the book, and what I hope this book accomplishes
2. A brief overview of classical chart principles, the foundation of my trading approach

Part I lays the foundation for the architectural design of my trading plan, which is detailed in Part II.

Introduction

O ne of the first things I check out in a new book is the number of pages prior to Chapter 1—long book introductions put me to sleep. I will assume that most of you are like me—you want to cut to the chase. The last thing I wanted to do was write a book with a lengthy introduction, but my opinion has changed now that I'm on the author's side of the equation. It turns out introductions can be useful in providing necessary context and perspective for a book. And so, please forgive me for committing the sin I have always disliked—I think it will be worth it.

This is a book about me as a trader of commodity and forex markets and how I use price charts in my craft. I think of it as a mosaic: eventually the parts of this book will tie together in the same way that a good mosaic becomes visible only in its entirety. Piece by piece or section by section, a mosaic makes no sense. Only at a distance and in its fullness does a mosaic gain clarity and perspective. The concept of a mosaic describes how this book will unfold. First, a bit about how I got started in the business.

The Invention of a Commodity Trader

In 1972, shortly after graduating from the University of Minnesota with a degree in advertising, I moved to Chicago to work for one of the nation's largest ad agencies. A neighbor was a trader at the Chicago Board of Trade (CBOT). Through our conversations and my visits to see him on the trading floor, I became captivated by the futures markets. In commodity trading I saw the opportunity to earn a good living, work for myself, and be challenged in a very exciting field. In short, I became hooked.

Everybody started in the commodity field at the bottom. Being hired at a sizable salary was not a reality of the business. I needed a plan B if I were to quit advertising and enter the commodity field. So, I asked the president of the advertising agency if he would hire me back at a 30 percent increase in salary if I quit, tried the commodity business for a year unsuccessfully, and reapplied for my old job. He agreed to the deal.

I entered the commodity business in 1976 when I was in my 20s with the singular goal of trading my own personal account. But I needed to learn the ropes first.

When I entered the business, most traders at the CBOT (as well as the Chicago Mercantile and the New York commodity exchanges) started at or near the bottom of the pecking order. The same thing exists to this day. An "MBA fast track" has never really existed in the trading pits. The learning curve is steep—the washout rate is high.

I learned the business by working for Continental Grain Company and Conti, its futures market brokerage operation. At the time Continental Grain was the second largest grain exporter in the world next to Cargill. Continental sold its grain merchandising business to Cargill in 1999.

During my time in the advertising field I had been working on the accounts of McDonald's and Campbell's Soup Company. It became a very fortunate coincidence that both companies were huge users of agricultural products.

Processors of agricultural commodities, such as Campbell's Soup, had become accustomed to decades of oversupply conditions and stable commodity prices. But a number of events in the early 1970s, including global crop failures, led to massive bull markets in the price of agricultural products and nearly every raw material. In a matter of months the price of some commodity goods doubled. Figures I.1 and I.2 show gold and wheat prices as proxies for raw material prices.

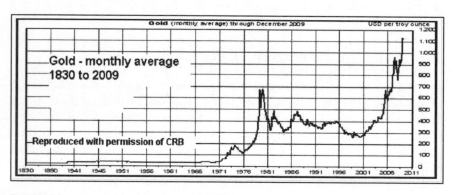

FIGURE I.1   Spot Gold Prices, 1830–2009.

Food companies were not prepared for the price explosions taking place. Top management and purchasing executives of these companies were desperate for solutions. Few food processors had any experience with forward pricing in either the cash or futures markets.

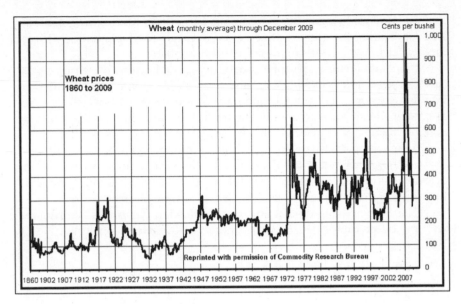

FIGURE I.2   Soft Wheat Prices, 1860–2009.

This was the environment when I switched careers from advertising to commodities.

Immediately upon joining Conti, I approached the president of Campbell's Soup Company with a proposal. I thought perhaps the futures markets could be a way for Campbell's Soup to hedge its forward purchases.

I suggested that the company appoint a senior purchasing executive to relocate to Chicago for a time to determine if commodity contracts might be a beneficial management and purchasing tool. I further proposed that the designated purchasing executive and I would then submit a formal proposal to top management—and the proposal could just as likely nix as recommend the idea of futures contracts.

In the end, we recommended that the corporation could strategically use futures contracts in cocoa (Campbell's Soup owned Godiva Chocolate at the time), corn and soybean meal (to grow chickens for its various frozen and canned products), soybean oil, iced broilers (then actively traded at the CBOT), live cattle and hogs (depending on the price relationship between the cuts of meats used by the company and the price of live animals on the hoof), and the three major wheat contracts traded in the U.S. (Campbell's Soup made noodles by the ton and owned Oroweat and Pepperidge Farms bakeries).

Campbell's Soup saw the wisdom in the use of commodity futures contracts. My consulting role with the company covered my business overhead and my family's living expenses while I learned the futures business. Had I begun trading for myself immediately, I would have likely been forced rapidly back into advertising or another career path.

After learning the ropes for a couple of years, I began trading proprietary funds around 1980, starting with less than $10,000. Initially, my personal trading was not successful, although not disastrous. I tried just about every approach I heard or read about. The traders around me at the CBOT were making money, but I just couldn't seem to find a niche that worked.

Then a friend introduced me to the book *Technical Analysis of Stock Market Trends*, written in the 1940s by John Magee and Robert Edwards. The book was—and still is—considered the bible of classical charting principles. I consumed the book in a weekend and have never looked back.

Chart trading offered me a unique combination of benefits not available with the other approaches I had attempted or considered, including:

- An indication of market direction
- A mechanism for timing
- A logical point of trade entry
- A means to determine risk
- A realistic target for taking profits
- The determination of a risk/reward relationship

I have been a chart trader ever since. More specifically, I trade breakouts of classical chart formations such as head and shoulders tops and bottoms, rectangles, channels, triangles, and the like. I focus on weekly and daily chart patterns that form over a period of four weeks to many months. Even though my focus on charts is longer term, my actual trading tends to be short term, with trades lasting anywhere from a day or two (in the case of losses) to a month or two.

Since 1981, my principle occupation has been trading proprietary funds, although off and on through the 1980s I sold trading research to other traders. In the late 1980s and early 1990s I traded some hedge funds for a couple of big money managers such as Commodities Corp. (since bought by Goldman Sachs). A number of the best hedge fund traders in the world have worked for Commodities Corp. (I do *not* pretend to be in their league.)

As a result of market burnout and an interest in nonmarket opportunities, in the early 1990s I began to distance myself from day-to-day contact with the markets and granted power of attorney over my own funds to another trader. It was not a successful experiment. From the mid-1990s through 2006 I pursued some personal non-profit interests (social causes) and did little or no trading at all. I started to employ my former trading plan again in January 2007.

In 1990, I cowrote a book with a since-deceased friend, Bruce Babcock, titled *Trading Commodity Futures with Classical Chart Patterns*, discussing in very general terms my approach to trading. That book sparked a desire to someday write a book providing much more detail on my trading operations. This book is the product of that desire.

My Proprietary Trading Record

For the active trading years of 1981–1995 (including four years when I granted power of attorney to another trader) and again starting in 2007, my average annual rate of return for proprietary funds has been 68.1 percent (annual Value Added Monthly Index [VAMI] method). I experienced one losing year during the time I was the sole trader for my proprietary funds (–4.7 percent in 1988). The numeric average of my worst annual month-ending drawdowns has been 15.4 percent. The performance capsule of my proprietary trading is shown in Figure I.3. Please read the disclaimers and discussion of my proprietary trading in the Author's Note at the end of the book. Past performance is not necessarily indicative of future results.

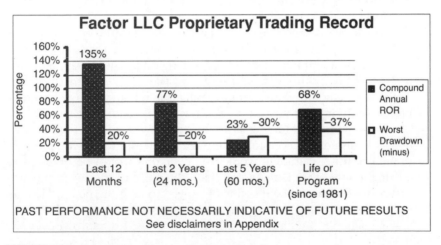

FIGURE I.3   Factor LLC Proprietary Trading Record.

Why I Wrote This Book

In the business of commodity trading books, advisory services, seminars, and computerized trading programs, there is a lot of junk being peddled. There are numerous books written each year about speculating in stocks and commodities. Does the investment world really need another book?

Given my low opinion of most trading and investment books, it is ironic that I am even writing this book. Specifically, I have had a general disdain for books approaching technical trading on a hypothetical basis. In contrast,

I love the *Market Wizards* series by Jack Schwager because it presents the human side of real-life traders who use their ingenuity to make money by outsmarting the markets. If you have never read these books, then you have really missed out on some great insight into market speculation. I also loved two books by Michael Lewis, *Liar's Poker* and *The Big Short: Inside the Doomsday Machine* because both offer a real look at the real lives of smart traders.

I accepted this book challenge because John Wiley & Sons and I shared a vision for a book that would be a diary of my real-time trading operations during the course of a set time frame.

This book contains a combination of seven characteristics that I believe are unique among commodity trading books:

1. I am a real trader who trades real markets in real time with real money. I am not an academician or a person who relies on the sale of books to pay my mortgage. I am not selling a trading system or subscriptions to an advisory web site. I am just a trader trying to make money from the markets.

2. This book will catalog real-time trading signals and endeavors, not some arbitrary set of optimized rules form fit to last year's charts. This book will be a real-time diary of my trading on a day-by-day, trade-by-trade, thought-by-thought, mistake-by-mistake, victory-by-victory, and emotion-by-emotion basis. I am stepping out in faith that I will even be profitable during the next 21 weeks. But traders take risks.

3. This book will reveal trading as an upstream swim against human emotions. Consistently successful trading is a tough job. I make no pretense to the opposite. If trading were easy, everyone would be doing it for a living. Some other authors can share the glory of their constant successes. I will discuss the emotions involved to take the next trade after eight straight losing trades. Successful speculation can lead to hair-graying, sleep-losing, and dog-kicking emotions. I hope to convey the same.

4. I will attempt to show that successful speculation is mostly about managing risks. In fact, good traders view themselves first and foremost as risk managers. Just like "Texas Hold-Em," how one plays his or her cards is more important than the cards themselves. Money management has not been given the attention it deserves.

5. I will attempt to kill a really sacred cow whose death is long overdue—the idea that it is possible to be right on 70 or 80 percent of one's trades. This cow really needs to die. Perhaps I can strike a successful blow.

   Novice traders spend 90 percent of their time and money pursing methods to identify trades. In my own experience, "Trade identification" is the *least* important component of a consistently profitable trading operation. In fact, the method by which a trader identifies the markets to trade is of very little importance. I make no contention that the method I use is the best or is even above average. More to the point, how I select trades just does not matter at the end of the day. I believe that novice traders who chase systems that claim success on 80 percent of trades do so because they don't have the stomach for losing trades. But a strong stomach for losers and a miniature pride on the need for winners are necessary for consistently profitable trading operations.

6. I have absolutely no desire in this book to show how I can turn a small fortune into a large one. Books that talk about turning $10,000 into a million dollars may be good marketing, but let's get real! A person who can achieve this type of performance would possess all of the world's currency within a decade. Do the math!

   I am risk averse. My goal in 2010 is an 18 to 24 percent return. I would be in hog heaven if commodity futures and forex markets could perpetually provide for me an average two or so percent monthly return—with a minimum amount of capital volatility. I will leave it to other authors to disclose their secrets to big fortunes. If you are looking for a book on how to convert a small account into a million dollars, this book is not for you. If you want a book that details a comprehensive process for speculation aimed at exploiting an edge, then keep reading.

7. Charting has been good to me. I know it may sound a lot nobler than it really is, but I would like to share what I have learned over the years about the craft of trading chart patterns. In hindsight, it is easy to imagine how a market should have been traded. But in real time the chickens come home to roost. I believe that I can add to the body of practical knowledge on chart trading. Perhaps I can spare others the torment of the learning process.

In the end, my goal is to display the actions and emotions of a professional trader—and this involves a whole lot more than a way to identify the next trade.

This Book's Audience

I am writing this book to:

- Professional commodity and forex traders
- The general investment public (especially Baby Boomers who are now concerned about their retirement assets)

■ Novice commodity "wannabe" traders who have never really gained traction in their trading

Professional Commodity/Forex Traders

You will not learn a single thing from this book, although if you are a chartist, hopefully I can add something to your body of knowledge. Nor should you be reading this book to learn anything about my approach and niche. You are successful because you know precisely what your own game plan is. But you may get a kick out of some of the anecdotes I share as I attempt to exploit my "edge" in the markets. You understand that successful speculation is primarily a human endeavor as we attempt to "swim upstream" against our emotions.

My hat is off to you. You are absolutely the best traders in the world. The global financial meltdown of 2007 and 2008 would have never taken place if professional commodity traders were in charge things of things. As a group, you can be proud that you did not contribute to the global economic woes of recent years.

As professional commodity and forex traders, you have a lot to be proud of. Table I.1 takes a look at the performance of the top 20 professional futures and forex trading operations during the past five years (measured by risk-adjusted rates of return).

TABLE I.1 Performance of the Top 20 Commodity/Forex Trading Operations from 2005 through 2009

Commodity and Forex Trading Firms	Avg. Annual ROR*	Avg. of Worst Drawdowns*	Avg. ROR During 2008 Meltdown*	% of Years Profitable in Past 5 Years (avg. of worst losing year, if applicable)*
Top 5 firms	20.5%	−8.9%	22.5%	88% (+.03%)
Firms 6–10	12.8%	−11.3%	27.0%	80% (−1.8%)
Firms 11–15	10.2%	−10.9%	20.6%	84% (−1.4%)
Firms 16–20	8.2%	−11.1%	11.7%	76% (−4.7%)
Composite* (unweighted)	12.9%	−10.5%	20.0%	82% (−1.9%)

*Commodity trading advisors managing at least $10 million with drawdowns no greater than 15% were considered for the list of the top 20 CTAs and were ranked based on average annual rate of return (ROR).
Source: Managed Account Research Inc. web site.

Of the top 20 professional commodity-trading firms during the past five years, 19 made money in 2008 as the rest of the financial world lost billions in the global meltdown. Of these top 20 firms, the average five-year compounded rate of return (ROR) was 12.9 percent. Seven did not have a single losing year in the past five years. The average worst peak-to-valley losing spell was only –10.5 percent. The average worst year among the 20 firms was –1.9 percent. Compare this to the roller-coaster ride called the stock market.

I believe that there are four principal reasons why the community of professional commodity traders is profitable year in and year out:

1. Most commodity and forex traders started trading with proprietary money. You were not just handed a multimillion-dollar pool because you had your MBA in finance or your PhD in quantum physics. In fact, you are just as likely to be a college dropout, a European history or theology major, or a former air traffic controller.
2. You understand risk because you trade leveraged markets. You know the high price to be paid for being stubborn with a losing trade. You know that small losses have a way of becoming large losses, and large losses can sink a ship. You would have never let a massive pile of worthless mortgage paper dig too deeply into your pockets.
3. You trade transparent markets that have instant and real price discovery mechanisms. The instruments you trade get marked to the market every day based on real values. You can determine the liquidation value of your portfolio to the penny at any given time—and if you need to scramble for cover, you can do so within minutes. You just laugh to yourself when you think about AIG, Lehman, and the mortgage instruments that nearly sunk the global economy. How in the world did the major financial houses put billions of dollars into instruments that could not accurately be valued at the end of every day? Imagine that some of the world's largest financial firms of their type were staking their future on financial derivative instruments they did not even understand, and when they failed, the government bailed them out. And after the government bailed them out, the executives of these firms paid themselves billions in bonuses. Nice gig if you can get it! Frankly, I think the entire bunch needs to be taken out behind the woodshed.
4. You know that a key to successful trading deals with how you handle losing trades, not in always being right. You understand that profits have a way of taking care of themselves if losses can be managed.

Average Investors

If you are like most "investors," you have experienced an "asset disappearing act" during the past several years as the value of your stocks, hedge funds, and real estate has tanked, at worst, or violently vacillated at best. Your assets have been on a wild ride.

Yet it is possible to generate consistent double-digit returns with a minimum amount of capital volatility in the commodity futures and forex markets. But you need to know that to do so is not easy work if you undertake the challenge on your own. Consistently successful trading requires diligence beyond easy description. There is not a simple golden egg.

You probably grew up hearing repeatedly that commodity markets were for speculators and that real estate and stocks were for investors. Hopefully, you now know that the traditional concept of an "investment" has no basis in reality. With the exception of T-bills, everything is speculation. Perhaps we may find out in the next few years that even U.S. government debt instruments are not a safe bet. It may even be that 30-year T-bonds will be the next bubble.

Like it or not, buy-and-hold strategies are a joke. Every decision you make in life represents a trade-off. Everything is a trade. Everything is a gamble.

You have also probably heard that commodity and foreign exchange markets represent "rags to riches" or "riches to rags" speculation because of the large leverage contained in the instruments traded.

Under the right hands, commodity futures and forex trading can be a rather conservative venture. As of March 2010, a total of $217 billion was being managed by professional commodity traders who attempt to provide their clients with consistently above-average RORs with a minimum of asset volatility.

If I sound like a cheerleader for managed futures, it is because I am. Research has shown that having a managed commodity portfolio decreases the volatility of a balanced stock and bond portfolio. Figure I.4 compares the Barclay Commodity Trading Advisor Index to the S&P 500 Index dating back to the early 1980s. You decide which roller coaster you would have rather ridden. I will allow this graph to speak for itself.

Novice "Wannabe" Traders

For you, I have some stark words! You have been duped! You have wasted your money buying expensive "black-box" trading systems, attending seminars promising you riches, thinking that the next great trading platform will solve your problems, or subscribing to the services of online trade pickers/scammers. And it is your own fault. It is your fault because you want to find an approach that overcomes your emotional inability to take trading losses in stride. Your ego and pride are too entangled with your trading.

You have had your share of profitable trades. In fact, perhaps you have even had some profitable years. But you have never become a consistently profitable performer because you spend the majority of your time, money,

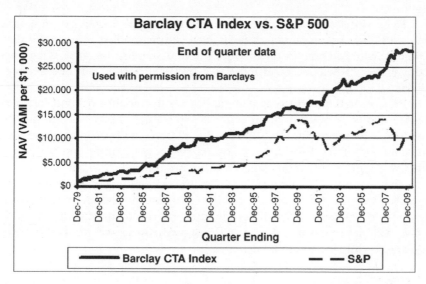

FIGURE I.4 The Barclay CTA Index versus S&P 500 Index, 1980–2010.

and energy seeking for a way to overcome your psychological ineptitude. Playing off the name of the song by Dolly Parton, you have been "looking for success in all the wrong places."

You have spent 90 percent of your effort on the least important of trading components: trade identification. I will explore all of the trading components I believe are necessary for consistent success later in this book, but trade identification is the least important of all. In my opinion, learning the importance of managing losing trades is the single most important trading component.

Years ago, while at the CBOT, I conducted an unscientific survey among about a dozen or so consistently profitable professional traders. Over the years I have asked the same question to trading novices. The question I asked was:

> *You have your choice—two different trading approaches. Both performed equally in recent years; one was profitable 30 percent of the time, and the other was profitable 70 percent of the time. Which approach would you be more apt to adopt?*

Professional traders choose the 30 percent right approach by a two-to-one margin. Novice traders overwhelmingly choose the 70 percent approach. Why the difference?

Professional traders recognize something that the novices may not comprehend. There is no margin of error in the approach that needs to be right 70 percent of the time in order to produce its expected results. What happens if the 70 percent approach has a bad year (50/50 ratio of losers to winners)?

Professional traders recognize the inherently superior risk management profile of the 30 percent approach. The 30 percent approach intrinsically has a built-in margin for error. In fact, the 30 percent approach assumes that most trades will be losers. Every approach has good times and bad times. The expectation of bad times needs to be built into the equation.

There is an old adage that "it is easy to make money in the commodity markets, but just try to keep it." There is a lot of wisdom in this adage. Keeping the money is a function of money and risk management. The good times will never occur unless a trader figures out a way to keep capital together during the tough times.

The Book's Road Map

This book is about using price charts to trade the commodity and forex markets. More specifically, this book will simply examine how I use charts for market speculation.

I make no pretense that chart trading is superior to any other form of trading, or that my use of charts for trading is superior to how other traders use charts in their trading operations. In fact, I know that my trading approach has weaknesses. I uncover new weaknesses every year. I will uncover weaknesses during the course of writing this book.

The six major points that I want you to remember as you read *Diary of a Professional Commodity Trader* are:

1. Consistently profitable commodity trading is not about discovering some magic way to find profitable trades.
2. Consistently successful trading is founded on solid risk management.
3. Successful trading is a process of doing certain things over and over again with discipline and patience.
4. The human element of trading is enormously important and has been ignored by other authors for years. Recognizing and managing the emotions of fear and greed are central to consistently successful speculation. I make no pretense that I have this aspect of trading mastered.
5. It is possible to be profitable over time even though the majority of trading events will be losers. "Process" will trump the results of any given trade or series of trades.
6. Charting principles are not magic, but simply provide a structure for a trading process.

I will emphasize and reemphasize these six points throughout the book.

This is a book about how I trade the commodity markets using price charts. I do not want to oversell this book as anything else. I will simply relate what I have learned about trading with charts since 1980. I have picked up some major lessons along the way. I have made every mistake possible—some of them numerous times. I have eaten humble pie over and over again. I have never gained a taste for it.

Diary of a Professional Commodity Trader is a book about price charts, so I feel the obligation to provide some historical background on the subject. Chapter 1 briefly discusses the history and underlying theory of classical charting principles. However, this book assumes that you already have a working knowledge about charting. Chapter 1 ends with a discussion of what I believe to be the inherent and serious limitations of a trading approach based on charting techniques.

Trading is a business—and all successful businesses need a business plan to guide decisions and operations. Over the years, I have come to the conclusion that all consistently profitable approaches to commodity market speculation are based on certain common denominators.

In Chapters 2 through 7, I explain the basic building blocks that have evolved within my own approach. All of my specific trading decisions flow from these building blocks. Other professional traders may have completely different building blocks or similar building blocks they refer to with different names. I have grouped the important elements of my own trading approach into three different categories:

- Preliminary Components (Chapter 2)
- Trading Components (Chapters 3–5)
- Personal Components (Chapter 7)

Chapter 6 provides a case study anatomy of my trading in three markets during the past year, detailing how trades were entered, how protective stops were initially set and then advanced, how profits were taken, and how much leverage and risk were taken in each trading event.

Chapters 8 through 12 could be summarized with the phrase, "Let the games begin!" These chapters will be a real-time, day-by-day, week-by-week, and month-by-month diary of my actual trading from December 2009 through April 2010. These months were not cherry-picked based on performance. Sidebars and subsections will be included on just some of the following:

- Observations on market behavior
- The personality of different markets and different patterns
- Trading continuation versus reversal patterns
- The use of intraday charts

- Commentaries on trading
- Lessons learned (and relearned)
- Missed trades
- The human element exposed

These chapters will be rich with charts showing the evolution of patterns and the execution details of the Factor Trading Plan. You need to know that these chapters were written each day in real time without the benefit of hindsight. The chapters will reflect my trades—the good, the bad, and the ugly—as well as my thinking process and the feelings in my gut. Even as I am writing this draft in early December 2009, I have no idea if my trading will be profitable.

Chapter 13 will be a summary, statistical analysis, and discussion of the trading months represented by this book. Chapter 14 will present the "Best Dressed List" of the best examples of classical charting principles for 2009 and the period covered by the trading journal. Hopefully, the Factor Trading Plan will have taken advantage of the most outstanding market situations. My profitability during the five months will depend on my real-time ability to recognize and properly implement my trading tactics in any market situation.

The appendices contain tables highlighting the trading operations of the period covered by this book. Appendix A contains the trading record covered by the journal. This table details the markets traded, the dates of entry and exit, leverage taken, pattern recognized, type of trading signal, trading result, and rules used for exiting the trade. Appendix B is a guide to the charts contained in the book, cross-referencing them based on the classical chart patterns identified and on the signal categories and trade management techniques used in my trading plan. Appendix C lists the books, web sites, and trading platforms I recommend.

If this book could accomplish one thing, it would be to show that successful market speculation is a craft, requiring an extensive and ongoing apprenticeship in studying the markets in the school of hard knocks. Successful speculation is a process that must address many aspects of market behavior and self-knowledge and mastery.

I have several hopes for the readers and the trading community as a whole through this book. First, I want to honor the difficult task undertaken by professional traders to achieve consistently successful performance. Trading is tough work that involves the mind, the spirit, and all of our emotions. Promoters that sell easy-money and quick-fix systems and approaches as a means to easy profits are a dishonor to the real-life challenges of trading.

Second, I want to communicate to nontraders and traders still early in their journey to consistent profitability that trading requires a comprehensive approach addressing far, far more than simply having a belief that a certain market is going to advance or decline. Trading is a business that must address a wide variety of decisions and contingencies.

Third, I want to pay homage to the field of classical charting principles as a trading tool. Chartists are inappropriately criticized for their "hocus-pocus" approach to understanding the markets when charting should never be understood as anything but a trading tool, not a method for price forecasting.

Fourth, and finally, the human factor is seldom mentioned in books on trading, yet it is the single most important component of consistently profitable market operations. I want to address this underdiscussed aspect of market speculation.

CHAPTER 1

The History and Theory of Classical Charting Principles

S peculators have used charts to make trading decisions for centuries. It is generally believed that candlestick charts in their earliest form were developed in the 18th century by a legendary Japanese rice trader named Homma Munehisa. Munehisa realized that there was a link between the price of rice and its supply-and-demand factors, but that market price was also driven by the emotions of market participants. The principles behind candlestick charts provided Munehisa a method to graphically view the prices over a period of time and gain an edge over his trading competitors. An edge is all that a speculator can ever expect.

In the United States, Charles Dow began charting stock market prices around 1900. The first exhaustive work on charting was published by Richard W. Schabacker (then the editor of *Fortune* magazine) in 1933. Under the title *Technical Analysis and Stock Market Profits*, Schabacker provided an organized and systematic framework for analyzing and understanding a field now known as "classical charting principles."

Schabacker believed that the stock market was highly manipulated by large operators who tended to act in concert. He observed that the activities of these large players could be detected on price charts showing the opening, high, low, and closing price for each trading session.

He further observed that prices, when plotted on a graph, were either in periods of consolidation (representing accumulation or distribution by the large operators) or sustained trends. These trends were known as periods of price "markup" or "markdown." Finally, Schabacker noted that periods of consolidation (as well as some trending periods) tended to display certain geometric formations—and that, depending on the geometry, the direction and magnitude of a future price trend could be predicted.

Schabacker then identified the form and nature of a number of these geometric patterns. These included such traditional patterns as:

- Head and shoulders (H&S) tops and bottoms
- Trend lines
- Channels
- Rounding patterns
- Double bottoms and tops
- Horns
- Symmetrical triangles
- Broadening triangles
- Right-angled triangles
- Diamonds
- Rectangles

The pioneering work of Schabacker was picked up in 1943 by Robert Edwards and John Magee in the book *Technical Analysis of Stock Trends*, commonly referred to as the bible of charting.

Edwards and Magee took Schabacker's understanding to the next level by specifying a number of trading rules and guidelines connected with the various chart patterns. Edwards and Magee made the attempt to systematize charting into trading protocols. *Technical Analysis of Stock Trends* has remained the standard reference book for more than three generations of market speculators who use charts in some manner for their trading decisions.

My Perspective of the Principles

As a trader, classical charting principles represent my primary means for making decisions. I maintained all of my charts by hand in the days before sophisticated computer programs and trading platforms. Now there are numerous computerized and online charting packages and trading platforms.

I continue to rely solely on high/low/close bar charts in daily, weekly, and monthly form. I pay no attention to the myriad of numerous indicators have been developed in the past 20 years, such as stochastics, moving averages, relative strength indicators (RSIs), Bollinger bands, and the like (although I do use the average directional movement index [ADX] to a very limited degree).

It is not that these methods of statistical manipulation are not useful for trading. But the various indicators are just that—statistical manipulations and derivatives of price. My attitude is that I trade price, so why not study price directly? I can't trade the RSI or moving average of soybeans. I can only trade soybeans.

I am not a critic of those who have successfully incorporated price derivatives into their trading algorithms. I am not a critic of anyone who can consistently outsmart the markets. But for me, price is what I trade, so price is what I study.

Three Limitations of the Principles

Three important limitations of classical charting should be understood by market operators who use charts or are considering the use of charts.

First, it is very easy to look at a chart and call the markets in hindsight. I have seen unending examples in books and promotional materials of charts marked up retroactively to make magnificent trends look like "easy money." Unfortunately, in order to emphasize some charting principles, this book may commit this very sin.

It is the dominant and gargantuan task of a chart trader to actually trade a market in real time in a manner even closely resembling how a market would have been traded in look-back mode. Significant and clear chart patterns that produce profitable trends are most often comprised of many small patterns that failed to materialize. Charts are organic entities that evolve over time, fooling traders repeatedly before yielding their real fruit.

Second, charts are trading tools and not useful for price forecasting. Over the years, I have been extremely amused by "chart book economists" who are constantly reinterpreting the fundamentals based on the latest twists and turns of chart patterns.

There is a huge difference between being short a market because of a chart pattern and being "bearish" on the fundamentals of a market because of the same chart pattern. Charts represent a trading tool—period. Any other use of charts will only lead to disappointment and often net trading losses. The idea that chart patterns are reliably predictive of future price behavior is foolhardy at best. Charts are a trading tool, not a forecasting tool.

As a trader who has used charts for market operations for 30 years, I believe I am permitted to make this statement. I am an advocate for charting—not a critic. But I am a critic of using charts in the wrong way. In my opinion, it is wrong-headed to use charts for making price forecasts, and especially for making economic predictions.

You may know trading advisory services that use charts to make predictions on the economy. They let you know when they are right. They make excuses or become silent when they are wrong. I think it is a much more honest position to just admit that I never know where any given market is going, whether or not the chart seems to be telling a story.

The third limitation is that emotions cannot be removed from the trading equation. It is impossible to study and interpret price charts separate from the emotional pull of fear, price, hope, and greed. So it is foolish to pretend that charts provide an unbiased means to understand price behavior. The bias of a trader is built into his chart analysis.

Summary

Classical charting principles provide a filter to understand market behavior and a framework for building an entire approach to market speculation. In the chapters to follow, I will display the construction of a comprehensive approach to market speculation using these charting principles—an approach I call the Factor Trading Plan. I will then proceed to apply the Factor Trading Plan, using classical charting principles as the foundation, to actual commodity and forex speculation for a period of about 21 weeks.

Characteristics of a
Successful Trading Plan

L ike any sound business, a trading operation needs a business plan—a comprehensive business plan that accounts for all variables to one degree or another. During my 30-plus years of trading, I have developed a set of guidelines, rules, and practices that direct my trading decisions. I refer to these components in their composite as the Factor Trading Plan.

The Factor Trading Plan has evolved over the years based on trading experience and results, and continues to evolve as the behavioral nature of the markets changes. I acknowledge that the construction of other professional traders' plans may be quite different than mine, but many common themes will hold true. In fact, I strongly believe some common characteristics are by nature necessary for successful market speculation.

Part II explains the basic building blocks of my trading approach. The Factor Trading Plan is governed by three pillars under which reside 10 major components, as shown in Figure PII.1. The broad pillars include:

- The preliminary components—dealing with matters of personality and temperament, available speculative capital, and philosophy toward risky ventures.
- The components of the trading plan itself—dealing with how markets are analyzed, how trades are made, and how trades and risk are managed.
- The personal components—dealing primarily with the characteristics and habits of a successful trader.

Chapter 2 will cover the pillar for the preliminary components. The pillar for the trading plan itself is the most complicated and is covered in Chapters 3 through 5. Then, Chapter 6 provides case studies showing

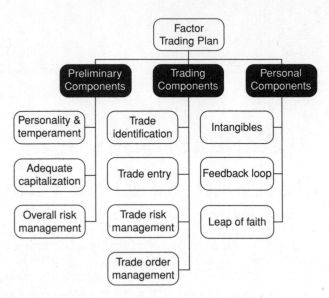

FIGURE PII.1   Pillars and Components of the Factor Trading Plan.

the trading plan in action. Finally, Chapter 7 deals with the pillar discussing the personal characteristics and habits required for successful market speculation.

Refer to Figure PII.1 as an overview of the pillars and components of the Factor Trading Plan. It should serve as your road map in the chapters directly ahead. You can refer back to this road map to understand each section in the proper context.

Building a Trading Plan

The preliminary components of a trading operation deal with issues to be addressed before a single trade is even considered. I believe that many people have failed at trading in the commodity and forex markets because they jumped into trading without laying down a proper foundation. The preliminary components must be taken into consideration as essential to consistently profitable speculation.

These components, as shown in Figure 2.1, the road map to this chapter, include trader personality and temperament, proper capitalization, and a keen view of risk management.

Trader Personality and Temperament

Commodity and leveraged forex markets are volatile and highly leveraged. Commodity trading is not for the faint of heart. Individuals who choose to trade commodity and forex markets or choose to place their funds with a professional manager must understand the volatility involved.

For those individuals who choose to trade their own accounts, no more than 10 to 20 percent of liquid investment assets should be designated to commodities—and only if a substantial portion of these funds can be lost without jeopardizing a present or future standard of living.

Individuals who elect to trade for themselves should also be aware of several factors unique to commodity trading. Commodity markets trade nearly 24 hours per day. The markets close for a brief time late each afternoon in the United States to determine a closing price and then immediately reopen for a new day of trading. Seamlessly (and on computer trading platforms), trading rotates the earth from the United States to Asia to Europe and back to the United States—from late afternoon on Sunday in the United States until late afternoon on Friday. Nonstop! Week after week! The beat goes on!

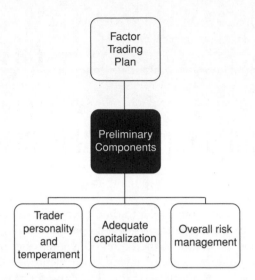

FIGURE 2.1   The Preliminary Components of a Trading Plan.

Commodity contracts are highly leveraged, often by as much as 100 to 1. This means that $1,000 of account assets can control as much as $100,000 of a commodity or foreign currency transaction. It also means that a 1 percent adverse price change in a commodity unit can result in a complete loss of the funds used to margin that commodity or forex transaction.

It is not unusual for even a lightly exposed commodity trader to experience 2 to 3 percent daily equity fluctuations.

There are some excellent books on commodity trading. It is not my intent to provide the basics of commodity or forex trading in this book. For novice traders, I recommend *Trading for a Living* by Alexander Elder and several other books listed in Appendix C.

There is a *very* significant factor of commodity and forex trading that novice traders should understand—and this factor represents a marked difference from trading in government securities, real estate, collectables, or stocks.

For every long in the commodity and forex markets, there is a short bet on the other side of the trade. In the stock market, the "short interest" (percentage of trading volume on the New York Stock Exchange, or NYSE, traded as a short sale) is normally around 3 percent and is seldom more than 5 percent. In contrast, there is a short seller in 100 percent of trades in the commodity and forex markets.

The nature of a short for every long is known as the "zero-sum" game. There is a dollar lost for every dollar gained. Actually, commodity and forex markets are less than a zero-sum game because brokerage commissions and fees are charged on every transaction.

In the stock market, nearly everybody is rewarded by a rising market. But the zero-sum feature of commodities and forex is significant because novice traders must beat professional traders and commercial interests in order to be profitable. The commodity markets represent a gigantic game of pockets being picked.

Certain personality types are incompatible with the realities of the commodity and forex markets. While other professional traders may disagree, I warn three types of novice investor types to avoid the commodity markets:

1. Day traders
2. "Balance checkers"—people who want to know their account balances frequently during a trading day
3. The emotionally unfit—individuals whose emotional makeup has led to frequent life troubles

Day Traders

Day traders have the odds stacked squarely against them in the commodity markets because transaction costs must be covered to be profitable. Let's assume that a day trader in the forex markets gets in and out of one trading unit of the euro and U.S. dollar currency crossrate pair (expressed as EUR/USD) five times during the course of each day (with each trading unit being 100,000 euros). The trader would be able to conduct this trading with as little as $2,000 in margin money (this varies according to the dealer or broker used, the size of an account, and ever-changing regulatory rules).

Commissions are very low or nonexistent in forex trading, but day traders must maneuver a two- to four-"pip" bid/offer spread in each transaction. The banks and dealers make their money in this bid/offer spread. For example, at the instant of this writing the EUR/USD is bid at $1.4559 and offered at $1.4561, the difference being two "pips."

The spread means that banks and dealers are buying the euro for $1.4559 and selling it for $1.4561, a two-pip advantage. Inversely, it means that the speculative public is buying the euro at $1.4561 and selling it for $1.4559, a two-pip disadvantage. Very large speculative traders, such as professional trading operators, qualify for a narrower bid/offer spread (perhaps a single pip) while smaller speculators using heavily advertised forex web platforms might pay a three-pip disadvantage on every transaction.

But for the sake of this discussion, I will use the two-pip spread. Over the course of five round turns in a trading day, a day trader would need to make 10 pips just to break even (two pips in and out of each trade times five round-turn trades). Ten pips equal $100 (or more depending on the forex pair traded).

Over the course of two weeks the transaction costs would amount to $1,000 (10 pips per day for 10 days, or 100 pips at $10 each on a trading unit of 100,000 euros). Thus, the $2,000 of margin money used to trade the EUR/USD spread would be wiped out by transaction fees every four weeks—meaning that the day trader would need to make a 100 percent return each month just to avoid the depletion of margin funds.

Balance Checkers

In my experience, traders who are obsessed with the value of their accounts during the course of a trading day are destined for failure in the commodity and forex markets. The reason deals with the nature of the leveraged markets. Undue concern with one's account value will override market judgment and lead to defensive trading. Defensive trading never works.

To be successful in the commodity markets a trader needs to focus on trading the markets (not his or her equity balance) within a framework of proper money and trade management (these subjects will follow). Trading commodity and forex markets is not for you if you would need to check your account balance frequently.

The Emotionally Unfit

The commodity markets take no prisoners. If a person has a major character or emotional defect, the commodity markets will uncover and exploit it.

Successful trading is an upstream swim or uphill run against human nature. It is fair to say that consistently profitable market operations *require* that a trader learn to overcome strong emotional pulls. In fact, most professional traders can relate how many of their most successful trades required action in direct opposition to emotional urges.

Individuals whose emotions have led them into troubled financial decisions, personal habits, or relationships should avoid commodity trading at all costs. Trading commodity and forex markets are hard enough without carrying a load of emotional baggage.

Summary

The Factor Trading Plan—or any other organized and logical approach to market speculation—assumes that a trader is able to manage his emotions. This does not mean that you will *not* experience strong emotional temptations to act counter to a game plan. It also does *not* mean that you will be 100 percent successful in preventing emotions from influencing periodic trades. And it certainly does *not* mean that you will become emotionless in market operations. It *does* mean that you are able to recognize emotions (fear, anxiety, unrealistic hopes, greed, stress, or self-doubt) for what they are, come to understand that emotions are normal but not reliable, and develop techniques for overcoming the pull of emotions to dictate trading decisions.

Proper personality and temperament within the Factor Trading Plan (or any other successful trading operation) requires two things:

1. Financial ability to experience prolonged periods of unprofitable trading
2. Ability to manage emotions—at least most of the time—and not allow them to override trading rules and guidelines.

Adequate Capitalization

In 1980, I founded Factor Trading Company and began trading with less than $10,000. To have seriously believed I could be successful with such a limited amount of capital was absolutely insane. It was nothing short of a miracle that I did not wash out. It was three steps forward, two steps back until I bet the entire wad on a Swiss Franc trade in 1982 (see Figure 2.2).

FIGURE 2.2   Long Swiss Franc: The Factor's First Big Trade.

It was only after this currency move that I had enough capital to consider myself to be in the game. But it was at that point my trading principles began to form. Just for fun, I am including the chart of the trade that launched my account to a level of capitalization at which I could take trading seriously. It scares me today to think of how much leverage I employed in that trade. I risked in the magnitude of 20 times the leverage I use today.

I have often been asked by friends how much money one needs to trade the commodity and forex markets. There is no easy answer to this question because there are so many variables. I can answer the question based only on my own trading approach.

The Factor Trading Plan requires multiples of $100,000 to take all of the signals. It is not that $100,000 is needed to cover the margin requirements of the signals generated by the plan. Rather, the capitalization level is based on the interplay between expected (hoped for!) profits and likely periods of capital drawdown.

Historically, my average annual rate of return has been a multiple of two to three times my worst annual drawdown. There are several acceptable methods to express the relationship between return and risk (including the Sterling ratio, the Calmar ratio, the Sortino ratio, and the MAR ratio). For any given year, my modified Calmar ratio (the annual return divided by worst month ending drawdown) has been all over the map, ranging from a negative number to as high as 30 to 1.

The $100,000 asset increment is based on my desire to limit my expected worst-case drawdown each year to 10 percent of trading capital. This does not mean that my drawdowns will never exceed 10 percent—or that I will even be profitable, for that matter. The point is that my unit of capitalization is based on risk parameters, not on factors often used by novice traders in making decisions about their trading operations. I have actually heard novice traders say something like the following: "I have a $25,000 account and the margin for a soybean contract is $2,500; therefore I can afford to buy or sell 10 contracts." As a general rule, I will trade no more than a single contract of soybeans per $100,000 of capital.

My guess—and it is only a guess—is that many other professional traders consider a capital unit to be at least $100,000. Some of the better-known commodity trading advisors accept accounts capitalized by no less than $500,000 or even $1 million. These amounts obviously represent their standard trading unit.

Overall Risk Management

Successful trading operations are dictated primarily by how risk is managed. Many novice commodity traders assume each trade will be a winner.

Professional traders manage their trading to assume that each trade may be a loser. Obviously, there is a major difference between the two perspectives.

The Factor Trading Plan operates with several global assumptions, including:

- I have no idea where any given market is headed. I may think I know, but in reality I do not know. History has shown that my degree of certainty about a given market's direction is inversely correlated with what actually happens. In fact, I think a trader with excellent money management practices could take the other side of trades in which I have a strong belief and make money consistently.
- About 30 to 35 percent of my trades over an extended period of time will be profitable.
- The probability of my very next trade being profitable is less than 30 percent.
- As many as 80 percent of my trades over shorter periods of time will be unprofitable.
- There is a high probability each year that I will incur eight or more losing trades in a row.
- There will be losing weeks, losing months, and even losing years in my trading operations.

Important risk management guidelines have been incorporated into the Factor Trading Plan to address these global assumptions. The primary guideline is that the risk on any given trade is limited to 1 percent of trading assets, and preferably closer to half of 1 percent of assets.

Because I think in incremental units of $100,000, this means that my risk per trade per unit of $100,000 is a maximum of $1,000. My trading assets committed to margin requirements rarely exceed 15 percent. I don't recall ever receiving a margin call for the account used to trade my full program.

If I risk 1 percent of assets per trade and am wrong eight straight trades at least once each year, it means that I will experience a drawdown of at least 8 percent with certainty, at least on a closed trade basis.

A 15 percent drawdown is about as much as I can emotionally handle. I have encountered a drawdown of at least 15 percent in 9 out of every 10 years I have operated a fully implemented trading program.

I find myself more risk intolerant as I grow older. At the present time, my risk management protocol attempts to limit the maximum annual drawdown to 10 percent (measured from week-ending peak to week-ending valley). I attempt to ignore intraday equity spikes because I have no desire to catch the bottom of each day's high or low, and I do not want to waste energy in even thinking about it. In fact, as I will discuss in this book, I think it is unwise to pay attention to account equity levels on a day-to-day basis.

I consider correlation between markets when determining risk. For example, a bearish trend by the U.S. dollar against the euro is also likely to be accompanied by U.S. dollar losses against the Swiss franc and British pound. A bull market in soybeans is likely to be accompanied by advances in soybean oil or soybean meal. In composite positions of highly correlated markets (grains, interest rates, stock indexes, currencies, precious metals, industrial commodities), I attempt to limit my risk to 2 percent of assets. All successful trading operations must be built on a foundation of overall risk management.

Points to Remember

- The commodity and forex markets are highly leveraged.
- Unlike stocks and bonds, trading commodities and forex markets is a zero-sum game. For you to be profitable, someone else must lose money.
- Do you have adequate capital to trade commodities, and can you afford to lose it?
- Can you understand and manage the emotional swings of market speculation?
- Do you have the emotional or psychological need to be right on your trades? Can you accept an approach to trading that is wrong on the majority of trading decisions?
- Would your primary focus in trading be to find winning trades or to manage losing trades? Risk management must be given priority over trade identification to achieve consistently successful performance.

CHAPTER 3

Identifying the Trades and the Trading Vocabulary

I will now move to the mechanics of the Factor Trading Plan. The trading plan attempts to answer such questions as:

- What markets should I trade?
- Should I be long or short?
- Should I get in now or wait—and if I wait, what exactly should I wait for?

These practical and tactical questions, and more, are answered by the components within the trade identification pillar of the Factor Trading Plan, as shown in Figure 3.1.

This is an appropriate point to reemphasize that I have no pretention that my approach to trading is the best for everybody or that my trading operations cannot be improved. In fact, as you read through this book you will no doubt see many warts on my trading plan.

The primary point I want to make by describing in detail the Factor Trading Plan is not that my trading is particularly clever, but that a comprehensive plan covering all of the important aspects is necessary for consistently successful trading operations. The process of trading is an important part of consistent success. A trader needs to anticipate as many contingencies as possible in his speculative maneuvers.

The Factor Trading Plan is based upon the following set of assumptions:

- The likely direction of any given market cannot be determined by studying charts.
- Charts are a trading tool, not a predictive tool. Charts can provide traders with a slight edge, but should not be used to make price forecasts.

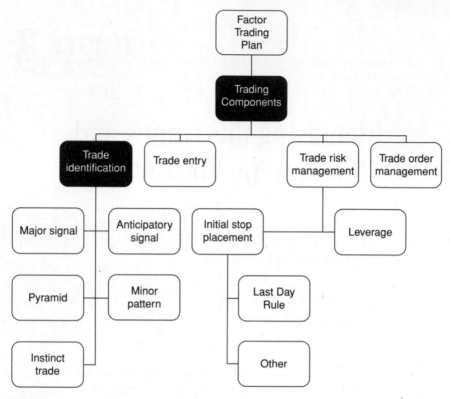

FIGURE 3.1   The Trade Identification Pillar.

- Charts should not be used to maintain a constant opinion or position in any given market.
- Do not assume that the next trade will be profitable.
- More often than not a market will defy what its chart structure implies.
- Markets make enormous moves that can't be explained by classical charting principles.

With these assumptions in mind, Chapters 3 through 5 cover how the Factor Trading Plan works, focusing on the trading components. This chapter lays down the general concept used to identify trades and defines the terminology or "shop talk" used by the trading plan. Chapter 4 shows examples of the ideal types of trades sought by the plan. Chapter 5 details the types and frequency of trades engaged by the trading plan, discusses how trades are entered and exited, and explains the logistics of how the entire plan is managed.

Trade Identification

There are numerous methods used by traders to define a trade. The important point is that a trader must be able to know what is or is not a trading signal, event, or moment. This is true whether a trader uses a mechanical or discretionary technical approach, a supply-and-demand fundamental approach, or an economic model. Lack of certainty if a market is or is not setting up a trade is a cardinal sin. This is why I recommend that novice traders paper-trade or trade a small trial account for a year or two prior to placing real skin in the game.

The Factor Trading Plan is based on a technical approach to market analysis. Technical trading approaches study price behavior itself to identify candidate trades and generate trading signals. In contrast, fundamental trading approaches are based on the supply-and-demand factors of a market and general overall economic conditions. It is not within the scope of this book to delve any deeper into different approaches to market analysis or trading.

The technical approach used by the Factor Trading Plan falls into a category known as *discretionary* (as opposed to the *mechanical* approach used by many technical traders). A discretionary trading plan requires that the trader makes certain subjective judgment calls from one trade to the next, whereas a mechanical (some market operators use the term *black box*) system is programmed to generate precise entry and exit instructions in order to eliminate day-to-day human decision making.

Using a discretionary approach is a personal preference, not in any way an indictment against mechanical systems. In fact, some of the more frustrating aspects of my own trading could possibly be resolved if I used a mechanical system. But, in general, I believe that a discretionary approach better fits my personality and understanding of price behavior and dynamics.

More specifically, the Factor Trading Plan uses classical chart patterns as the basis for all trading decisions. A discussion of classical charting principles can be found in Chapter 1.

Vocabulary of the Factor Trading Plan

All industries and companies have their own shop talk to describe concepts and practices inherent in their business operations. While definitions of terms often appear in the appendix of a book, I believe it is very important to lay out the operating and tactical terms of the Factor Trading Plan at this point of the book. Understanding certain terms will enable you to follow my discussion of charts and trades during the remainder of this manuscript.

The terms and definitions are not listed alphabetically but in the order I think through things during actual trading operations.

Trading Unit

As a trader, I think in units of $100,000. When I calculate risk and leverage, it is always in relationship to $100,000 blocks of capital. Thus, if I am trading a $500,000 block of money, I think about it as five trading units.

Position Unit

A position unit is the number of contracts or size of a position taken per $100,000 and determines the risk assumed on a trade. The risk is normally about six-tenths to eight-tenths of 1 percent. I refer to a position with less risk as an underleveraged position and positions with more risk as extended-leverage positions.

Position Layering

Often, I attempt to build a position by entering into a trade on multiple dates and at different prices. For example, if I establish a position in anticipation of a future breakout, I consider myself to have established the first layer. If I establish another position at the breakout of a major pattern, I become two layers deep. Perhaps a near-zero-risk opportunity to extend leverage develops at a retest; then I could become three layers deep. Now if I can find a pyramid opportunity, I will end up with a four-layer position. I do not add to a losing position, but put on layers only as earlier layers are profitable. Even in a multiple-layer position, my combined risk in a market rarely exceeds 1 percent.

Multiple-layer trades are not the norm.

Breakouts

I am a breakout trader. But I define a breakout in two ways. First, all patterns have boundary lines that define the exact geometry of the patterns. Some traders and market analysts draw boundary lines precisely with a fine-point pen. I draw boundary lines roughly, often cutting through some highs and lows in order to provide the best fit of an area of price activity to a geometric pattern. I also use thick lines, not a fine-point pen, to establish the boundary. Of course, there are instances when I call a breakout too closely—and I often pay the price for doing this.

Robert Edwards and John Magee considered a breakout to be a price penetration equal to or greater than 3 percent of the value of a stock. This is far too generous when trading commodities. For example, a 3 percent breakout in $1,000 gold would be $30 per ounce.

A breakout is more complicated than simply penetrating a pattern boundary. All patterns are comprised of minor or intermediate high and low points. These high and low points define the parameters of the boundary lines. To be a valid breakout, I also want to see a market penetrate the most recent high or low price that defined the boundary. And to be most comfortable with a trade, I want to see a market penetrate the highest or lowest price within the completed boundary. Figure 3.2 show these chart points on a weekly graph of the British pound/U.S. dollar (GBP/USD).

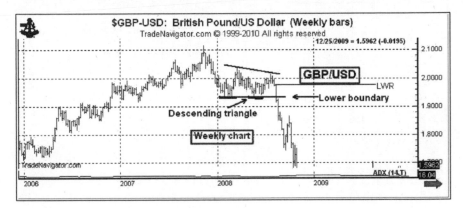

FIGURE 3.2 Pattern Breakout in the British Pound.

Ice Line

I use the terms *ice line* and *boundary line* interchangeably. The concept of the ice line is that once a market moves through the boundary of a pattern, that boundary line ideally should separate all the price action that preceded the breakout from the price behavior following the breakout. The ice line is analogous to a sheet of ice on a lake in the winter. The ice supports a person or vehicle from dropping into the water. But once the person breaks through the ice, the ice sheet then becomes a barrier to survival. Figure 3.3 shows the ice line in GBP/USD. Figure 3.4 displays the same concept in platinum.

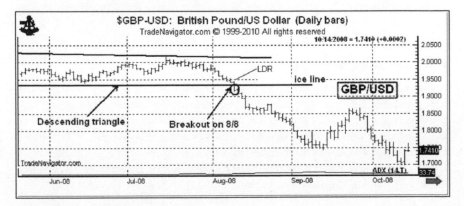

FIGURE 3.3 Ice Line in the British Pound.

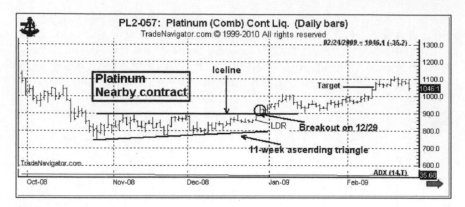

FIGURE 3.4   Ice Line in Platinum.

Out-of-Line Movement

Drawing boundary lines on chart patterns is not an exact science. The reality is that a market does not care where I draw a boundary line. There is nothing magic about geometric boundaries. It is great when the minor or intermediate lows or highs of a market provide a perfect demarcation for boundary lines, but this is the exception and not the norm. A boundary line should be drawn to best fit to an area of price congestion even if it means that the boundary line is drawn through some of the price bars.

There are occasions when a daily price bar significantly penetrates a boundary line on an intraday basis, but then almost immediately returns back into the geometric pattern. Such price action was defined by Edwards and Magee as an out-of-line movement. While out-of-line movements can create some tactical challenges to trading, history will usually show the out-of-line price activity as just a one- or two-day freak incident. Boundary lines do not need to be redrawn to accommodate out-of-line movement. Figures 3.5 and 3.6 exhibit out-of-line movements in London sugar and New York sugar, respectively.

Premature Breakout

A premature breakout is different from an out-of-line movement in the sense that a premature breakout can close outside of a predrawn boundary line and even spend several days in breakout mode. Prices then return back to the geometric pattern. However, the initial breakout was only a harbinger of things to come, and within a few weeks a genuine breakout occurs. I call these subsequent breakouts *secondary breakouts* or *pattern recompletions*. Figure 3.7 shows this concept in cocoa.

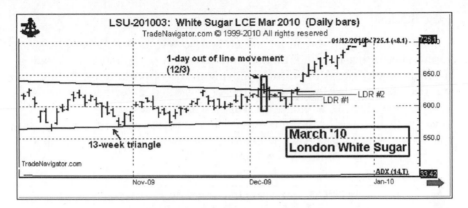

FIGURE 3.5 Out-of-Line Movement in London Sugar.

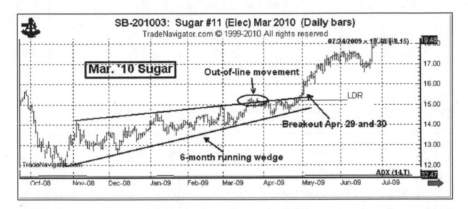

FIGURE 3.6 Out-of-Line Movement in March Sugar.

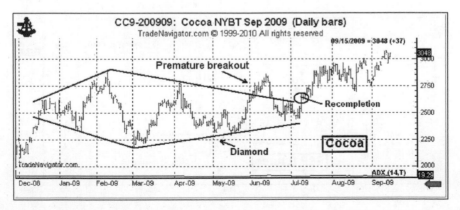

FIGURE 3.7 Premature Breakout in Cocoa.

False Breakout

Unlike the premature breakout, which is followed by a genuine breakout in the same direction, the false breakout results in prices either developing a much larger pattern or strongly moving in the opposite direction. Some traders refer to false breakouts to the downside as a *bear trap* and false upside breakouts as a *bull trap*. This means that traders who normally position themselves in the direction of the initial price thrust get stuck on the wrong side of the market. Figure 3.8 shows a false breakout in the German Deutscher Aktien Index (DAX).

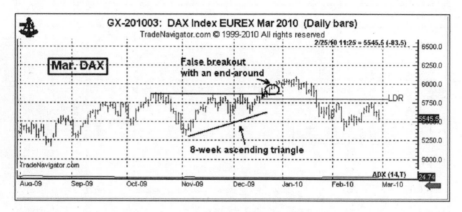

FIGURE 3.8   False Breakout and End-Around in the DAX.

In 2009, a great example of the false breakout occurred in the U.S. stock index markets. As shown in Figure 3.9, the Standard & Poor's (S&P) 500 futures completed a nine-week H&S pattern in July. Prices closed

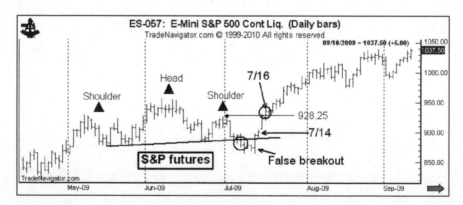

FIGURE 3.9   A False Breakout and Subsequent Buy Signal in the S&Ps.

below the neckline and remained in a breakout mode for five days before turning up sharply. The full price action of July 14 was above the neckline and indicated that a bear trap had been triggered. On July 16, the market rallied strongly above the previous right shoulder high, generating a very reliable buy signal.

Breakouts that are not genuine create a difficult trading dilemma. A trader who becomes positioned at the breakout does not know whether the subsequent return into the pattern represents a one-day out-of-line movement, a premature breakout or a false breakout. For this reason, I generally abandon any position that has a significant return to the pattern.

Horizontal versus Diagonal Patterns

I greatly prefer to trade a pattern that offers a horizontal or flat boundary, such as the boundaries of a rectangle, ascending triangle, H&S, etc. I consider such patterns to be horizontal. The reason these are superior patterns for trading is that the penetration of a boundary line most often occurs simultaneously with the violation of a major or minor high or low point within the pattern. An example can be seen in Figure 3.10, a rectangle that developed in gold in 2007. The decisive penetration of the upper boundary also penetrated the important April high, signaling a bull move.

FIGURE 3.10   Gold Displays a Horizontal Chart Pattern.

Diagonal patterns, by contrast, have slanted boundary lines. This creates three practical problems. First, my experience is that there are far more false or premature breakouts of slanted chart lines than in the case of horizontal boundaries.

Second, the penetration of a diagonal boundary may or may not violate a minor or major preceding high or low. Figure 3.11 shows a trendline in the EUR/USD, which was problematic in 2009.

FIGURE 3.11   Problematic Diagonal Chart Pattern in the Euro/U.S. Dollar Crossrate.

The trend line was violated in late October. The practical problem then becomes whether to redraw the trend line or deal with continued false trend-line violations, such as occurred later in November.

Third, the retest of the boundary of a diagonal pattern line would be progressively adverse to the position as days or weeks go on. Figure 3.12 shows a breakout of a falling wedge in gold followed by several days of retesting that put a breakout trade into a loss.

FIGURE 3.12   Diagonal Pattern in Gold.

The problems with the diagonal boundary become particularly acute when dealing with a trend line or a channel line. In fact, I normally do not consider a trend line to be a tradable event unless the market has tested the trend line numerous times.

Last Day Rule

The Last Day Rule is the principal method used in the Factor Trading Plan to determine the initial protective stop order once a position is entered.

If a pattern breakout is valid, then it logically follows that the day of the breakout is a significant event. Ideally, I establish a position at the point of a price breakout and use the low of an upside breakout day or the high of a downside breakout day to set my protective stop levels. This is called the Last Day Rule.

In cases when a market gaps through a boundary line or opens at or near a boundary line just prior to breaking out, I may elect the high or the low of the preceding day to determine the Last Day Rule.

Figure 3.13 shows a Last Day Rule in crude oil that remained unchallenged. In fact, the Last Day Rule nearly always remains unchallenged in valid chart pattern completions.

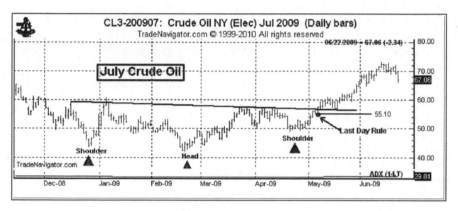

FIGURE 3.13   Last Day Rule in Crude Oil.

Figure 3.14 shows two Last Day Rules in silver, the first of which was breached, the second went unchallenged.

FIGURE 3.14   Two Last Day Rules in Silver—One Failed and One Worked.

Throughout the book, on as many charts as appropriate, I have noted the Last Day Rule with the designation LDR and a thin line and price.

Last Hour Rule

There are instances when a very large trading range occurs within a pattern on the day of a breakout. As a result, the Last Day Rule may represent a risk far exceeding the idealized four-fifths of 1 percent determined by money management guidelines. In such cases I may elect to use tighter protective stop placement. But rather than simply using some dollar amount I prefer to set a tighter stop using a chart point.

This tighter stop point may be determined by the high or low of the last hour spent within a pattern prior to the breakout, or the last 120 minutes, 240 minutes, or whatever time frame fits the risk and reward parameters I seek for a trade.

Ideally, if using the Last Day Rule offers an inappropriate risk level, I prefer to find a point on an intraday chart that represented a minor rally or reaction prior to the breakout. Of course, there are occasional trades when a money management stop is the best I can do. I conveniently use the phrase *Last Hour Rule* whether the stop is based on an hourly chart, two-hour chart, three-hour chart, or any other intraday time increment. Figure 3.15 shows a violation of the Last Hour Rule in the S&Ps.

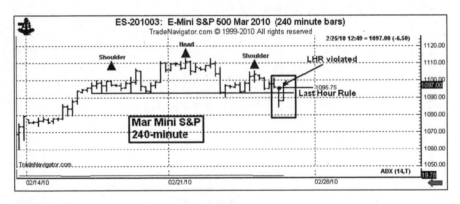

FIGURE 3.15   Last Hour Rule in March S&Ps.

The concept of the Last Day Rule also applies to weekly and even monthly charts. This risk management guideline will hold true for valid breakouts on charts of any time length.

Retest

My experience through the years is that the best trades break out cleanly, go almost immediately, and never look back. In fact, I believe that my net bottom line as a trader would have improved if I had exited every trade that closed at a daily loss. I wish I had the data to run such a simulation. But, often, a trade will hesitate following the initial breakout and retest the boundary within a few days to a week or so. Such a retest is normal and should not greatly concern a trader as long as the retest does not severely challenge the ice line. Retests in valid pattern breakouts normally do not penetrate the ice lines. Figure 3.16 displays a retest of a breakout in the Chicago Board of Trade (CBOT) rough rice market. Note that the retest itself took the form of an 18-day flag.

FIGURE 3.16 Retest of H&S Top in Rough Rice.

Hard Retest

A hard retest occurs when prices actually slice back into the completed pattern. While a hard retest can test the patience of a trader, it does not in and of itself mean that the pattern will fail.

I have been asked over the years if it would be wise not to take a trade at the breakouts, but instead attempt to establish a position upon the retest of the completed pattern. My answer to this question is an unqualified "NO!" Think about this matter logically. By not taking a trade at the point of a breakout, but instead waiting for some type of retest, a trader is eliminating trades that work immediately and do not look back, which are exactly the most desirable trades. A market that retests a pattern is inherently more likely to fail than a market that never has a retest. A hard retest is shown in the U.S. dollar/Canadian dollar (USD/CAD) in Figure 3.17.

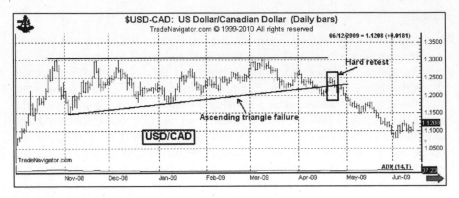

FIGURE 3.17   Hard Retest in USD/CAD.

Retest Failure Rule

A hard retest of a pattern allows me to adjust my stop using the high or low of the hard retest as a new protective stop point. Assuming that the initial stop was based on the Last Day Rule and a hard retest occurs, I can then advance a stop to just above the hard retest high in the case of a short position, or just below the hard retest low in the case of a long position. Figure 3.18 displays this concept on a weekly chart of November 2010 soybeans. Note the breakout of the 12-week week triangle the week of November 11 (letter A), the hard retest the week of December 25 (letter B), and the subsequent retest failure the week of January 15 (letter C).

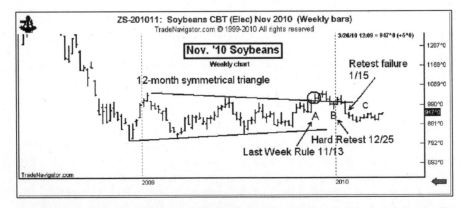

FIGURE 3.18   Retest Failure Rule on the Weekly Soybean Chart.

Target or Objective

Each chart pattern carries the implication for the magnitude of an ensuing trend. As a general rule, the minimum move following the completion of a chart pattern should be equal to the height of the pattern itself, although the exceptions to this rule are numerous and complex. In nearly every case, I take profits (partial or complete) when a market reaches its target. Figure 3.19 displays that the target in sugar is based on the principle that the distance from C to D should be equal to the distance from A to B, as shown. Figure 3.20 exhibits the same concept for the ascending triangle in the GBP/USD, where C to D should equal A to B.

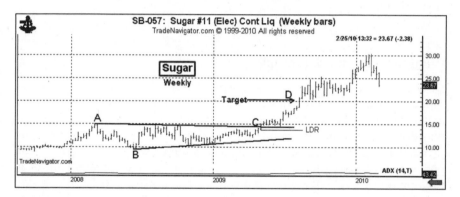

FIGURE 3.19 Price Target from Triangle in Sugar.

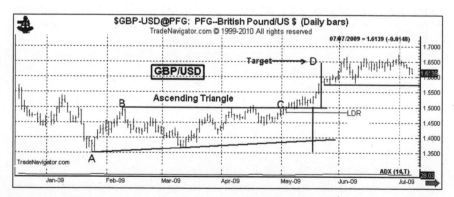

FIGURE 3.20 Price Target from Ascending Triangle in GBP/USD.

I use two other methods to determine price targeting. The first involves a technique known as *swing objectives*. The principle of a swing objective is that markets tend to advance or decline in legs that are of approximately equal distance.

Finally, I may periodically use point and figure (P&F) charts to calculate a longer-term target. P&F charts measure the amount of price action over a period of consolidation and are not time related. I use P&F counts several times each year when I believe that a period of consolidation (usually a large bottom or base) will produce a trend much more extended than indicated by the pattern target.

Important note: There is *no* guarantee that any market will reach its target. Traders need to be alert for markets that run out of steam prior to attaining a target.

Intervening Patterns and Pyramiding

During a sustained trend, a market frequently will experience a pause. These pauses often form smaller independent consolidation patterns. These patterns can be a continuation in form, meaning that another thrust in the direction of the dominant trend will be produced, or reversal in form, implying that the previous trend has come to a temporary or more permanent end. Continuation patterns offer the opportunity to both pyramid an initial position and to tighten up the protective stops on the initial position. Reversal patterns offer the opportunity to avoid riding the initial position back to the starting gates (or what I call a *popcorn* or *round-trip move*).

As a trader, I have mixed feelings toward continuation patterns—and my feelings differ based on the duration of the pauses within the main trend. Long pauses (more than three or four weeks) can wear down my patience. I much prefer shorter-duration pauses in a main trend, especially if the move coming into the pause was strong and the pause takes the form of a pennant or flag. Figures 3.21 and 3.22 display continuation patterns in Australian dollar/U.S. dollar (AUD/USD) during the same advance on the weekly and daily charts, respectively.

A continuation pattern during the course of a major trend allows me to advance my initial protective stop in the direction of a profitable trade. A breakout of a continuation chart will be accompanied by its own Last Day Rule. I may elect to move the protective stop from the initial Last Day Rule to the new Last Day Rule created by the continuation pattern.

It is also possible that a pattern implying a reversal of trend could develop prior to the attainment of an expected target. I may elect to move my protective stop in relationship to a pattern that carries trend implications counter to my position.

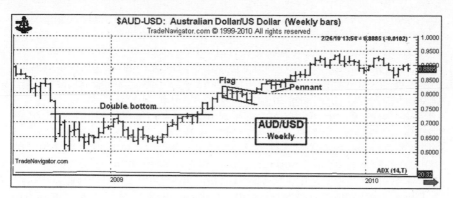

FIGURE 3.21 Continuation Patterns on the Weekly AUD/USD Graph.

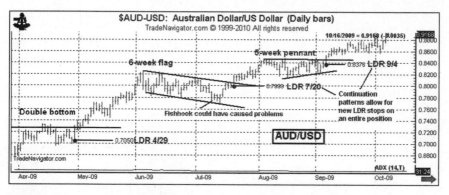

FIGURE 3.22 Continuation Patterns on the Daily AUD/USD Graph.

As previously discussed in this book, taking a profit before a target is reached can be very challenging to a trader. This area of my trading is most likely to be modified on an ongoing basis. All too often, unfortunately, my thinking is governed by the most recent trades. This type of optimization thinking is akin to a dog chasing its short tail—the short tail will always be moving just away from the dog's mouth.

Trailing Stop Rule

There was a time in my trading when I never moved my stops away from the Last Day Rule. A market would either reach its target or stop me out at the Last Day Rule.

There was an inherent risk management problem with this strategy. Assume, for example, that I entered a trade with a risk of $800 per $100,000 of capital and a target equal to $3,200 per trading unit. The initial relationship of reward to risk was four to one. Next, assume that the position went my way and reached a point where I had an unrealized profit of $2,400 per unit. This meant that I had $800 left to gain before taking profits. Leaving my stop at the original level meant that I was now risking $3,200 to the original Last Day Rule stop in order to gain the final $800.

This was insane money management, so I had to come up with some means to readjust my risk and reward parameters. For the sake of brevity, I will not take the time or space to discuss the popular concepts of a trailing stop based on a dollar amount or percentage retracement.

I developed a concept I call the Trailing Stop Rule. This trading guideline requires three days of price action to be implemented: the new high or low day, the setup day, and the trigger day.

Figure 3.23 shows the Trailing Stop Rule in action on a long position in the Dow Jones. The first step to the exit strategy is to identify the highest day of the move. Of course, it will change as new highs are made. The high day in the Dow was August 28. The setup day occurs on any day a market closes below the low of the high day. This occurred on August 31. The trigger and exit then takes place when the low of the setup day is penetrated. This occurred on September 1.

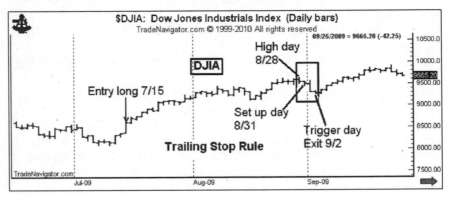

FIGURE 3.23   Trailing Stop Rule in DJIA.

I want to emphasize that there is nothing technically significant about the Trailing Stop Rule. It is simply a means to prevent a popcorn or roundtrip trade from occurring. Figure 3.24 shows the activation of the Trailing Stop Rule almost immediately after a pattern completion in GBP/USD.

Weekend Rule

The Richard Donchian Weekend Rule is a technique I may employ to extend the leverage in a trade. Donchian is considered to be the creator of the

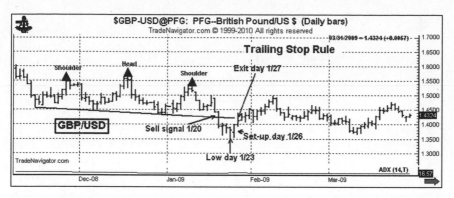

FIGURE 3.24 Trailing Stop Rule in GBP/USD.

managed futures industry and is credited with developing a systematic approach to futures money management. His professional trading career was dedicated to advancing a more conservative approach to futures trading. Donchian passed away in the early 1990s.

The Weekend Rule basically states that a market that decisively moves into new high or low ground on a Friday is very likely to continue the move on Monday and early Tuesday of the next week. The reasoning behind the Weekend Rule is that a decisive new high or low on Friday indicates the willingness of "strong hands" to take a position home for a weekend.

The Weekend Rule is even more valid when there is a long, three-day weekend.

For me, the Weekend Rule becomes most significant and useful when a pattern breakout (especially a weekly chart pattern) takes place on a Friday. In such cases, I may extend my risk from six-tenths to eight-tenths of 1 percent to a full 1 or 2 percent.

Figures 3.25 and 3.26 show major breakout days (all on Fridays) in the bull market in sugar in 2009.

Market Runs

The type of trend I most appreciate are straight-line market runs. Such runs are actually quite typical of strong trends. There are two types of straight-line moves, as shown by the accompanying examples.

Figure 3.27 of March soybean oil displays the first type of market run—a trend characterized by a series of continuous lower highs (or higher lows in the case of an advance). In this case, the market had 18 straight days of lower highs during a substantial drop. Nearly four weeks of lower lows is probably more than a trader can expect from a trend, but the point is that strong trends can be viciously persistent.

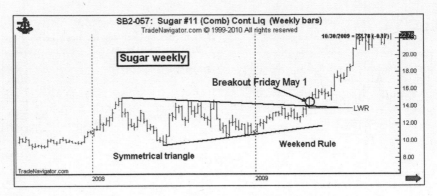

FIGURE 3.25   Weekend Rule Breakout in Sugar, May 2009.

FIGURE 3.26   Weekend Rule Breakout in Sugar, December 2009.

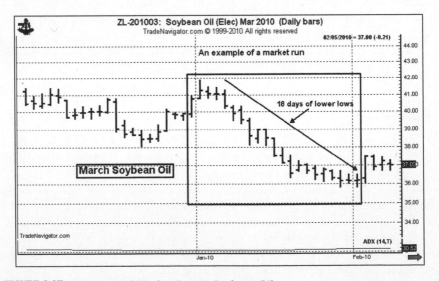

FIGURE 3.27   A Sustained Market Run in Soybean Oil.

The chart of the nearby contract of gold (Figure 3.28) displays the second type of market run. In this case the trend contained days with intraday lows beneath the previous days' lows, but in no case from October 29 through December 4 did the market close below the previous day's low.

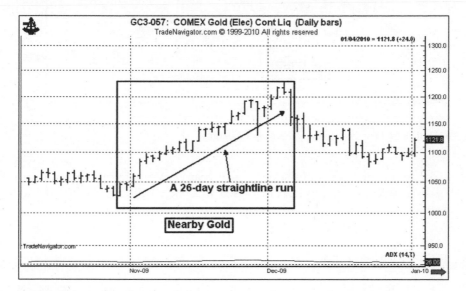

FIGURE 3.28 A Market Run in Gold.

Pattern Recompletion

I have discussed the concept of the premature breakout. A premature breakout assumes that there subsequently will be a genuine breakout. I refer to the secondary breakouts as pattern recompletions. Figure 3.29 is an extreme example of this idea. In July, the U.S. dollar/Japanese yen (USD/JPY) completed an H&S top pattern. After reentering the pattern in early August, the pattern was recompleted on August 27. The market then trended to the target at 86.20. For risk management, I used the Last Day Rule of the secondary completion at 94.58 (the August 26 high) to establish my protective stop level. As a general rule, I will attempt one pattern recompletion per major pattern. After that, I will count my losses and go shopping elsewhere.

It is easy for a discretionary trader to become obsessed with a particular market that has delivered a few straight losing trades, thinking that the market owes him something. This is a bad mental state to enter. Being compelled to recoup losses from a particular market in the same market is

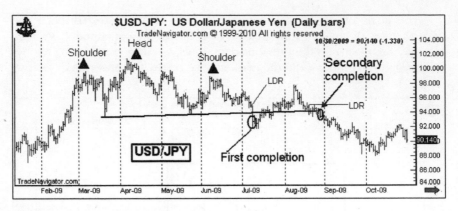

FIGURE 3.29   Pattern Recompletion in USD/JPY.

a dangerous practice. At least once each year I get caught up in this vicious cycle. I must constantly remind myself that there will always be another market at another time.

Points to Remember

- It is necessary to have an organized method to make the important decisions involved in trading, such as what market to trade, when to trade it, how to enter, how to set stops, how to exit, and what leverage to use.
- A trading plan must be based on the key assumption that it is impossible to know with certainty the direction of any given market at any given time.
- Classical charting can serve as the basis for creating a trading plan.
- Successful trading plans must have precise definitions of market behavior and trading actions.

CHAPTER 4

Ideal Chart Patterns

The technical approach I use is based on a subset within technical analysis known as classical charting principles (see Chapter 1). Specifically, I look for recognizable geometric patterns formed on high/low/close price bar charts to identify candidate trades. More specifically, I select candidate trades that meet the following criteria on price charts:

- For a major price trend, a continuation or reversal chart pattern of at least 10 to 12 weeks in duration visible on both a weekly and daily chart (although the daily and weekly charts may display slightly different geometric profiles).
- For a minor price trend continuation on a daily price graph only, a chart pattern of at least four to eight weeks in duration.
- For a minor price trend reversal on a daily price graph only, a chart pattern of at least six to 10 weeks in duration.
- For a pyramid opportunity within the context of a trend launched from a weekly chart, a very brief price pause (known as a flag or pennant) of one to four weeks in duration visible on a daily chart.

Chapter 5 will discuss in more detail the importance of understanding the whole idea of how many weeks it takes for a pattern to develop and why it is important to the Factor Trading Plan.

Just as bank tellers are trained to detect counterfeit currency by studying real money, it is important to exhibit examples of the genuine patterns sought by the Factor Trading Plan. Following are examples of "cherry-picked" chart patterns from 2008 and 2009. These charts exhibit the ideal types of trading situations.

I must emphasize at this point that it is easy to spot these patterns after the fact. The challenge of the chart trader is to identify and react to these types of chart configurations in real time. Nevertheless, laying down the best examples of chart formations is a great place to start.

As I point out elsewhere in this book, the types of patterns presented here are not typical of the trades I make on a regular basis—I only wish this were true! You will see plenty of my mistakes and examples of lack of patience in Part III of this book. But, for now, it is good to fix your mind on the ideal chart situation that I seek.

Reversal H&S Pattern in Copper

Figure 4.1 shows that copper completed a six-month H&S top pattern in early August 2008, followed in late August by a retest of the neckline. In the case of a valid chart pattern, it is unlikely that a retest, if any, can make much progress past the boundary line of the completed pattern. Normally, the boundary line acts as an "ice line" against any price movement back into a completed pattern. Notice that the retest did not violate the Last Day Rule of the August 4 pattern completion.

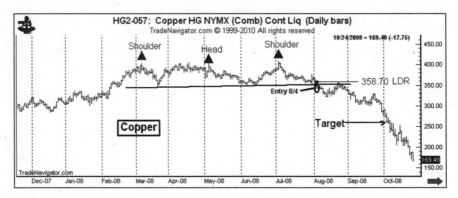

FIGURE 4.1   H&S Top Ends a Five-Year Bull Market in Copper.

Belabored patterns such as this have a way of wearing out the chart trader, who jumps the gun many times before the real trend begins. Traders that attempt to anticipate a pattern completion can become chopped up and become gun shy by the time the real breakout occurs. I know this from experience.

Reversal Rising Wedge in AUD/USD

In early August 2008, the AUD/USD (Australian dollar and U.S. dollar cross-rate) completed a 12-month rising wedge reversal pattern (Figure 4.2). As a general rule, prices decline sharply from rising wedges while breakouts of falling wedges back and fill, taking time for a new trend to get under way.

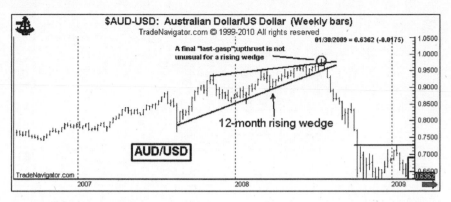

FIGURE 4.2 One-Year Rising Wedge in the Aussie Dollar Leads to a Waterfall Decline.

Continuation Wedge and Reversal Failure Top in Soybean Oil

Two charts are shown for this market. Soybean oil topped in March 2008. Following the March decline, the market staged a rally, finalized by a 15-week continuation wedge, completed on July 21 (Figure 4.3). If you look carefully, you will see that the final eight weeks of the wedge took the form of a symmetrical triangle. It is not unusual for large patterns to be launched by smaller patterns. For this reason, one of the trading signals I look for is a smaller pattern to become pre-positioned for a possible breakout of a larger pattern.

FIGURE 4.3 Eight-Week Triangle Caps Off a 15-Week Rising Wedge in Soybean Oil.

The decline on September 5 in soybean oil completed a massive failure (or double) top reversal pattern by penetrating the early April low (Figure 4.4). Note the retest in late September. This retest rally could not get back above the ice line. Recall that when the breakout day has very little

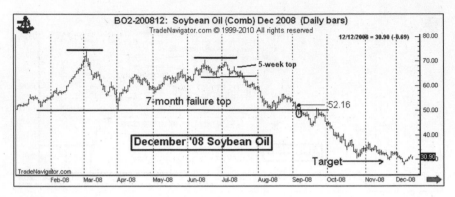

FIGURE 4.4   Seven-Month Failure Top Leads to Historic Drop in Soybean Oil Prices.

price activity within the completed pattern I will use the day previous to the breakout to establish the Last Day Rule. The breakout day was September 5, but the Last Day Rule was September 4. The target of 32 cents was met in late October.

Reversal Triangle Bottom in Sugar

Figure 4.5 shows that the rally in late December 2007 completed a six-month symmetrical triangle bottom in sugar.

FIGURE 4.5   Classic Six-Month Symmetrical Triangle in Sugar.

Continuation and Pyramid Patterns in USD/CAD

The chart of this market from 2008 displays two types of patterns (Figure 4.6). The advance in early August completed a continuation

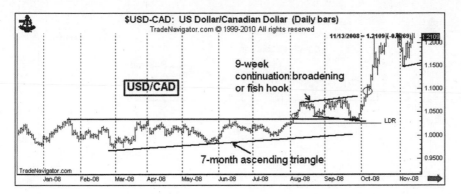

FIGURE 4.6   Major Advance in USD/CAD Began with a Seven-Month Ascending Triangle.

seven-month ascending triangle. The market retested the breakout in late August. A subsequent retest in late September made my life difficult and, in fact, forced me to lighten up my position. However, even this second retest had little ability to penetrate the completed triangle. The advance in the second week of October completed a nine-week continuation broadening pattern, providing the opportunity to pyramid the trade.

Reversal Top in Silver

The silver market is not for the faint of heart. This market can provide many fake-outs before rewarding a persistent trader. Note the very small three-week double top in March. I normally do not trade reversal patterns of such short duration. The market found a line of support in April, May, and June before starting a rally. This rally carried above the highs from April and May and really threw me a curve ball.

On September 11, I interpreted the price behavior as a three-month-plus rounding pattern and went long. It was a bull trap. The market quickly reversed and in early August completed a six-month failure top (Figure 4.7). Markets that generate a bull or bear trap prior to a real completion normally experience strong trends. The reason is that a trap prior to the real move locks traders into a losing position that it will not let them out of easily.

There is an important lesson in this chart. From late March through early July the market punished traders who bought strength or sold weakness with the expectation of holding a position for longer than a few days. This period of choppiness likely made traders very gun shy. It would have been very difficult for a chart trader to sell the August 7 breakout with the idea that silver was not being sold in the hole. Yet, selling the August 7 breakout,

FIGURE 4.7   Six-Month Failure Top in Silver.

even though the market was severely oversold, was the most profitable trade on the chart shown. Trades that are the emotionally toughest to execute are often the most financially rewarding.

Continuation H&S Pattern in the Russell 1000 Index

During the stock market collapse of 2008, the chart of the Russell 1000 formed an eight-month continuation H&S pattern (Figure 4.8). I have seen some chartists take too many liberties in identifying many patterns. One of the rules for an H&S pattern is that the right and left shoulders MUST overlap. The breakout of the neckline in mid September was very tricky because prices quickly traded back above the neckline. The initial breakout was premature. The breakout in late September was the real deal, and the market reached the target in November, finally bottoming out in March 2009.

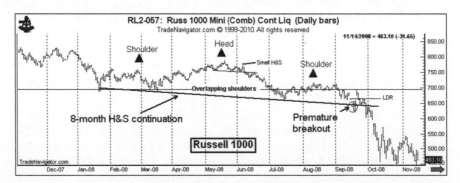

FIGURE 4.8   Continuation H&S Pattern Leads to Stock Market Collapse of Late 2008.

Notice that the head of the eight-month H&S took the form of a five-week H&S pattern.

When Is an H&S Pattern Not Real?

I am often amused by the interpretation of charts made by talking heads on CNBC and other financial media outlets. One of the patterns most bastardized by the "experts" is the traditional H&S pattern. As a general rule, genuine H&S tops and bottoms must be characterized by three features:

1. Remembering that an H&S pattern is most often a reversal pattern, there must be a trend to be reversed in order for an H&S interpretation to be valid.
2. The right and left shoulders must overlap—and the more overlap the better. If the right and left shoulders do not overlap, then there is no H&S pattern.
3. There must be some symmetry to the shoulders in terms of duration or height in order to validate an H&S pattern.

A final point: I greatly prefer a flat neckline or one that slants in the direction of the anticipated trend. I do not like upslanting necklines in H&S tops or downslanting necklines in H&S bottoms.

Continuation Rectangle in Kansas City Wheat

Following a strong bear trend from March through May 2008, the market consolidated in the form of a 14-week continuation rectangle. The completion of this rectangle in mid-September 2008 was followed by a weak retest of the lower boundary ice line. The market reached the target in early December. This rectangle is shown on the weekly and daily charts (Figure 4.9 and Figure 4.10 respectfully).

Continuation Rectangle and Pyramid Triangle in Crude Oil

During the historic price rise in crude oil ending in 2008, the market created a number of trading opportunities. The advance in February completed a four-month continuation rectangle. The hard retest in early March never closed back below the upper boundary ice line of the rectangle. The retesting process formed a three-week triangle that offered the opportunity to pyramid the market. The final target was achieved in early May (Figure 4.11).

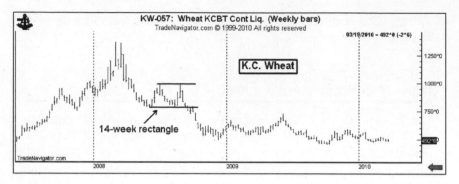

FIGURE 4.9   Weekly Chart Displays a Continuation Rectangle in Kansas City Wheat.

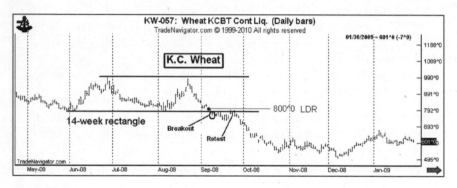

FIGURE 4.10   Daily Chart Counterpart of the Rectangle In Kansas City Wheat.

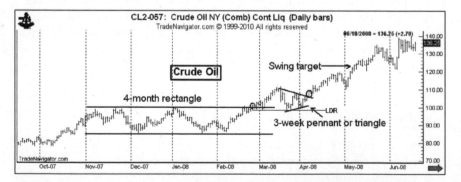

FIGURE 4.11   A Four-Month Rectangle and Three-Week Pennant in Crude Oil.

The breakout of the rectangle, while clean when viewed well after the fact, was extremely tricky at the time because of the hard retest in late March.

Continuation H&S Top in the Dow Utilities

Figure 4.12 exhibits the continuation three-month H&S top pattern (with a double head) that formed on the Dow Utilities chart in July during the great bear market of 2008.

FIGURE 4.12   A Three-Month H&S Top in the Dow Utilities Leads to the 2008 Meltdown.

Continuation Triangle, Reversal M Top, and Flag in the EUR/USD

Three charts are displayed for the euro/U.S. dollar (EUR/USD).

It is not unusual for a triangle to form in the late stages of an extended bull trend. Often, these late-stage triangles contain six contact points contrasted with midtrend triangles that normally contain only four contact points such as the triangle in the Kansas City wheat (refer back to Figure 4.10). The continuation triangle on the weekly graph in the EUR/USD met its target quickly (Figure 4.13). Note the six contact points of this triangle on the daily chart (Figure 4.14). The market then formed a five-month reversal "M" top (Figure 4.15). The new bear trend in EUR/USD formed a 10-day flag in September. Brief patterns such as flags and pennants offer an excellent opportunity to pyramid a trade.

FIGURE 4.13 Weekly Chart in the EUR/USD Crossrate Displays a Continuation Triangle and a Double (or "M") Top.

FIGURE 4.14 Daily Chart Shows the Three-Month Triangle in Early 2008 in the EUR/USD Crossrate.

FIGURE 4.15 A Five-Month Double Top and Two-Week Flag in the EUR/USD.

H&S Reversal Top and Three Continuation Patterns in the GBP/JPY

The weekly chart of the British pound/Japanese yen (GBP/JPY) during 2008 had it all—a major reversal top and a series of three bear market continuation patterns. Figure 4.16 is the weekly chart version of these chart formations. In early January, the market completed a 13-month H&S top. During January and February the market formed a five-week triangle pattern that was useful for increasing leverage (i.e., pyramiding). From the March low through early July a continuation rising wedge formed. As part of the massive drop from the July high to the early 2009 low the market formed a four-week flag, also useful for pyramiding a short trade. The daily chart showing these three continuation patterns is displayed in Figure 4.17.

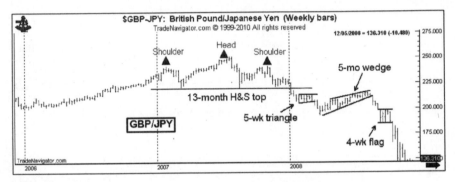

FIGURE 4.16   Textbook Bear Market on the GBP/JPY Weekly Chart.

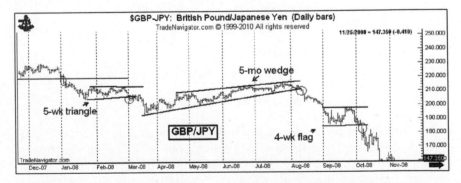

FIGURE 4.17   Daily Chart of GBP/JPY Shows a Series of Bear Market Patterns.

A Reversal Symmetrical Triangle in the AUD/JPY

Figure 4.18 exhibits the 14-month symmetrical triangle top completed in September 2008 on the weekly graph of the Australian dollar/Japanese yen (AUD/JPY). Again note the retest that occurred two weeks after the initial pattern completion. As is almost always the case with valid pattern breakouts, the retest was unable to make it back above the boundary ice line. This is a very common characteristic of major pattern completions. See Figure 4.19 for a daily chart version of these chart events.

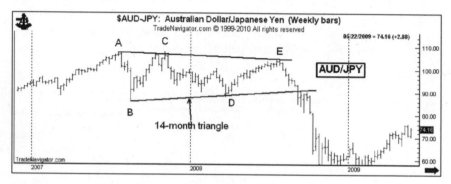

FIGURE 4.18   A 14-Month Symmetrical Triangle on the AUD/JPY Weekly Chart.

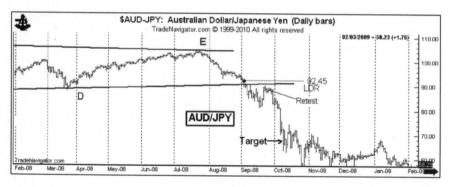

FIGURE 4.19   Daily Chart of the AUD/JPY Displays the Retest.

An additional point is worthy of note about the decline in the AUD/JPY. After building a top for 18 months, breaking out, and then experiencing a minor retest, the entire move down took only a couple of weeks. In fact, the majority of the decline after the late September retest was represented by a handful of days. It is a very awkward trading experience to wait 18 months for a pattern to be completed, only to have the move over in a matter of weeks.

Two Continuation Patterns in GBP/CHF

The bear market of 2008 in the GBP/CHF (British pound against the Swiss franc) provided two excellent examples of continuation patterns Figure 4.20). The first pattern was a seven-month continuation rounding pattern that experienced a premature breakout in early October, a return above the ice line, and then the valid breakout in late October. Rounding patterns are notorious for not providing nice, clean breakouts. An eight-week pennant or descending triangle was completed in mid-December.

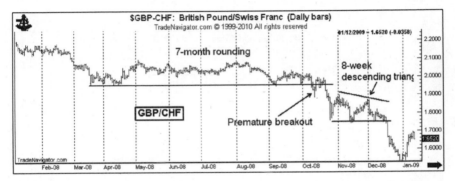

FIGURE 4.20   A Seven-Month Rounding Top Followed by an Eight-Week Descending Triangle in the GBP/CHF.

A Triangle and Running Wedge in Sugar

The sugar market generated the overwhelming proportion of profits for the Factor Trading Plan in 2009. Figure 4.21 displays a 14-month symmetrical

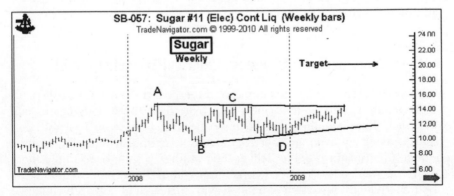

FIGURE 4.21   Weekly Chart Symmetrical Triangle in Sugar.

triangle on the weekly chart at the precise point of completion on May 1. This pattern launched the largest price thrust in sugar in 28 years. Figure 4.22 displays the daily chart of the actively traded October 2009 contract. This chart had a simultaneous breakout on May 1 of a six-month ascending or running wedge.

Classical charting principles applied to the stock market treat the rising wedge as a bearish pattern. However, many substantial price advances in forex and commodities are launched by an upward thrust from a rising wedge. I have labeled this type of chart development as a running-wedge pattern.

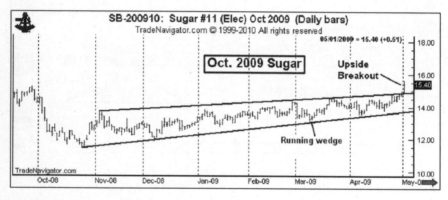

FIGURE 4.22   A Six-Month Running Wedge in October Sugar.

An H&S Bottom in Apple Computer

The only stock chart contained in this book, Figure 4.23 shows that Apple Computer completed a magnificent H&S bottom on the daily chart on March 23. Notice that the market retested the ice line on March 30, but the retest did not violate the Last Day Rule.

A Major Continuation H&S and Symmetrical Triangle in Gold

This market is an excellent example of three patterns. Figure 4.24 displays an 18-month inverted continuation H&S pattern on the weekly chart. As a side note, the minimum target of this pattern at 1340 or so has not been reached as of this writing. There is no rule that stipulates any target must be met. Chart patterns fail to deliver their implied price moves all the time.

There was quite a point of contention within the technical community about this pattern. A well-known Elliott Wave research firm, for which I have

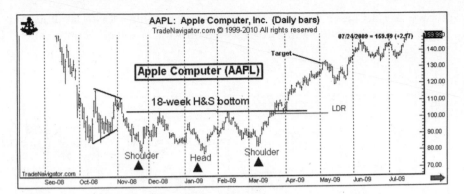

FIGURE 4.23   A Perfect H&S Bottom in Apple Computer.

FIGURE 4.24   Weekly H&S Bottom in Gold.

great respect, stated that labeling the pattern as an inverted continuation H&S patterns was a joke. Yet Edwards and Magee in the "bible" of classical chart principles, *Technical Analysis of Stock Trends*, stated:

> *Occasionally prices will go through a series of fluctuations which con-struct a sort of inverted Head-and-Shoulders picture which in turn leads to continuation of the previous trend. . . . One of these patterns which develop in a rising market will take the form of a Head-and-Shoulders Bottom.*

Figure 4.25 shows that the right shoulder of the weekly H&S pattern took the form of a massive six-month symmetrical triangle on the daily graph. Also note that the brief pause following the early September completion of the triangle formed a five-week H&S failure pattern. These types of small patterns are very useful in pyramiding a position. This small pattern also allowed me to move the protective stop from the initial Last Day Rule of the six-month triangle to the Last Day Rule of the five-week continuation pattern.

FIGURE 4.25 A Large Symmetrical Triangle and Small H&S Failure on the Daily Gold Graph.

A Series of Bullish Patterns in Copper

Figure 4.26 shows a wonderful series of continuation formations during the bull market in copper from March through the end of December 2009. Notice that the Last Day Rule of each pattern was never challenged, although the stair-stepping nature of the advance was difficult on the nerves. As a general rule, demand-driven bull markets contain a lot of backing and filling,

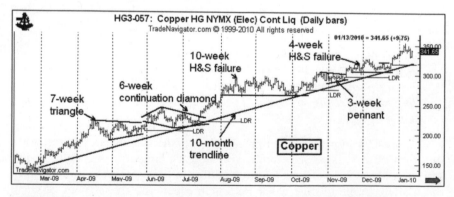

FIGURE 4.26 A Bull Market in Copper Loaded with Continuation Patterns.

whereas bull moves driven by severe supply shortages are much sharper. Most bear markets are also quite sharp, retracing in half the time the ground that was gained during the preceding bull trend.

A Failed Ascending Triangle in the USD/CAD Crossrate

Right-angled triangles have the strong tendency to break out through the horizontal boundary. In fact, a breakout of the horizontal ice line can almost be expected. Yet, on occasion, a right-angled triangle can break out of the diagonal boundary, usually grudgingly, as shown on the weekly chart in Figure 4.27.

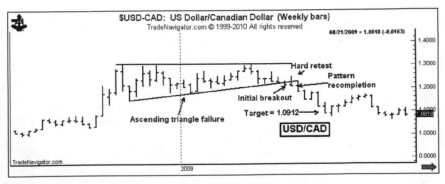

FIGURE 4.27   Weekly Chart Ascending Triangle in USD/CAD.

The seven-month ascending triangle in the USD/CAD had a bullish bias. As shown on the daily chart in Figure 4.28, the lower boundary of

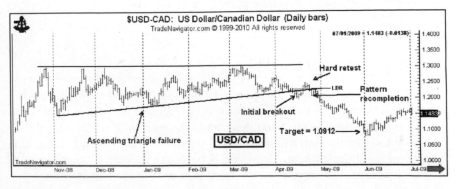

FIGURE 4.28   A Tricky Breakout on the Daily USD/CAD Chart.

the ascending triangle was called into question in mid April. However, even at that time, my thinking was that the lower boundary was just being redefined with a lower slope and that an upside breakout was just being delayed. Nevertheless, I went with a short sale on April 14 and was quickly stopped out above the April 13 Last Day Rule.

The downward thrust on April 29 and 30 confirmed the failure of the ascending triangle and called for a minimum move to 1.09, a target reached in early June. This market is a good example of how patterns initially biased in one direction can provide a good signal for a move in the opposite direction.

A 12-Week Rectangle in the Dow Jones Transport Index

A 12-week rectangle was completed in late July. Note that the Last Day Rule from July 23 was never challenged (see Figure 4.29).

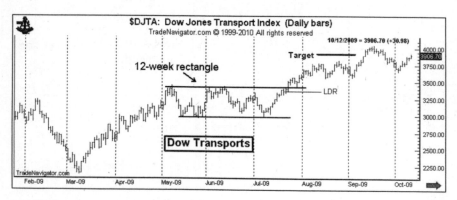

FIGURE 4.29   Continuation Rectangle in the Dow Transports.

A Rare Horn in Brent Sea Oil

A horn bottom occurs with a sequence of a major low and two higher lows intervened by two higher highs, as showed in Figure 4.30. The pattern takes the shape of a Viking horn. A requirement of the pattern is that overlap exists between the two upward thrusts within the pattern. Edwards and Magee did not cover the horn pattern. However, Schabacker identified the horn as a classical pattern. I often refer to the horn bottom as a sloping bottom.

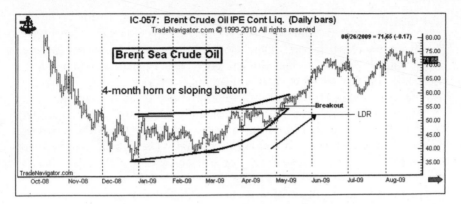

FIGURE 4.30   Sloping Bottom in Brent Sea Crude Oil.

The buy signal was triggered in early May when the April high was penetrated. Note that the Last Day Rule was never violated.

An H&S Bottom Launches the 2009 Bull Market in the S&Ps

I was emotionally committed to the bear case in stocks coming off the March 2009 low. While I saw the massive H&S bottom as shown in Figure 4.31, I did not believe it. I dabbled on the long side of stocks from time to time during the 2009 advance, but I was unwilling to accept the full implications of the major H&S bottom. The target of this H&S bottom at 1,252 was nearly met in April 2010.

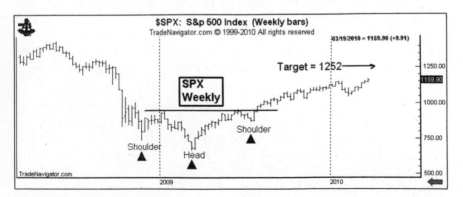

FIGURE 4.31   H&S Bottom in S&Ps.

Summary

The preceding charts represent textbook examples of classical charting principles. These patterns comprise a category of chart pattern that I call the "Best Dressed List"—those chart formations (or series of chart formations making up a large trend) that best exemplify price chart construction.

At the end of each year my net profitability is, in large part, dependent on correctly identifying and trading a major portion of those chart patterns that in hindsight become members of the Best Dressed List. In fact, my largest profits over the years have come from market situations similar to and including those shown.

In reality, these types of grand chart formations are more obvious after the fact than they are in real time. In my dreams, I imagine a trading year in which all of my trades are limited to these types of market situations. But dreams are dreams, and real life is real life. And in real life, many of the patterns I trade do not turn out the way these charts did. Some authors may produce material on classical chart patterns implying that these were the only situations they traded. But I am first and foremost a trader, not an author, and I need to admit that when I catch these ideal chart patterns it makes up for a lot of the losses I ring up along the way.

Points to Remember

- It is important for a trader to have a clear understanding what constitutes an ideal trade.
- Excellent chart trades do not come around every day but can take weeks and months to develop.
- Developing the patience to wait, wait, and wait some more for a market to declare itself is a goal, not a destination. As a trader, I seek improvement, not perfection.
- While chartists often attempt to jump the gun on a pattern (including me), markets usually make it abundantly clear when it is time to climb aboard.

How the Factor Trading Plan Works

It is time to get into the nuts and bolts of the Factor Trading Plan. Figure 5.1 shows the four main elements of the plan, including trade identification, trade entry, trade risk management, and trade order management. This chapter will tackle each element individually and in detail.

Trade Identification

I knew I wanted to be a trader before I knew I would become a chartist. Trading was the "what" of my career equation. Being a chart trader was the "how." When I entered the commodity business, my goal was to make money as a trader. In reality, I did not have a clue what that meant.

Chart trading made an enormous amount of sense to me at the point in my career when I began finding my way. Chart trading offered me a unique combination of benefits not available with the other approaches I had attempted or considered, including:

- A means to understand market trend
- An indication of market direction
- A mechanism for timing
- A means to determine risk
- A realistic target for taking profits

However, I quickly discovered that there was a huge difference between seeing chart patterns and actually trading them. Thankfully, the book *Technical Analysis of Stock Trends* by Robert Edwards and John Magee offered some suggestions to the practical challenges of being a chart trader. Yet, one of my major challenges wasn't addressed in the book; namely, when I began keeping charts, I saw patterns everywhere I looked. I needed to better define for myself exactly what I was looking for in a pattern in order to take a trade. Were all classical chart patterns created equal? Were some patterns a better fit to my personality, risk tolerance, and level of capitalization?

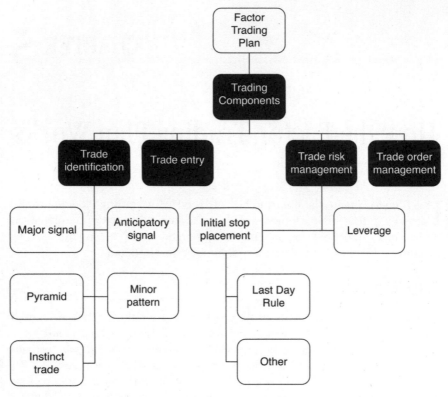

FIGURE 5.1   The Necessary Elements of a Trading Plan.

The Practical Problem of the Time Duration of Chart Patterns

With the benefit of hindsight, I now realize that the dilemma I was struggling with could be defined as *time framing*. There are two realities of classical charting principles that all serious chartists must confront.

First, it is patently easy to see chart patterns in hindsight. Promotional materials from various trading advisory services are replete with charts showing how they would have traded a certain market in hindsight. But I trade the markets in real time, and patterns clearly visible in hindsight might have not been so clear in real time. Chart structure constantly evolves. A pattern that eventually provides a profitable trend might be comprised of numerous smaller patterns, many of them failing to deliver an implied move. Further, a big move might be ushered in with several false starts.

A second and related reality is that many patterns seemingly clear at the moment of a trade fail to deliver and become swept up into a much bigger chart structure.

The Story of the "Big" Soybean Move

During my first year at the Chicago Board of Trade (CBOT), a trader in the soybean pit befriended me. This man lived in a mansion in Evanston, drove a luxury German car, and showed every indication of success (which, in fact, he had achieved). He told me one afternoon about how bullish he was in soybeans, at the time trading around $5.40. He said he had a giant position. So I watched the market for a few days. Prices crept up to about $5.60. I jumped in with a contract, only to have prices return to $5.40 the following week. Suffering from this losing trade, and seeking words of encouragement, I sought out my pit trader friend and asked him what he thought. His statement floored me. "I made a small fortune. Wasn't that a great move?"

As it turned out, my friend was a scalper who seldom held a position for more than 10 minutes. He normally did not take positions home with him overnight. To him, a two- or three-cent move was his goal. When he initially spoke to me, he had an instinct that soybeans could rally 10 cents within a day or two, and he was willing to hold a position overnight to realize that gain. But he did not explain this to me until after the fact.

So, in the end, I learned a very good lesson. Being a "bull" or "bear" means nothing without a time frame or price horizon attached to the words.

Because the structure of a chart becomes redefined over a period of time (especially in broad periods of consolidation), it is crucial for a trader to understand the time frame that determines candidate trades. If a trader tells me he is bullish on a certain market, I ask him if he is long, at what price, what is his target, what is his time frame, and at what price does he admit he is wrong. The concept of being bullish or bearish means nothing.

GBP/USD as an Example of Time Framing

Four charts of the British pound/U.S. dollar (GBP/USD) illustrate the importance and complications of time frame considerations.

Figure 5.2 is a weekly chart of GBP/USD from January 2009 through March 2010. The dominant stages of price behavior shown on this chart are the run-up in prices during the first half of 2009, the formation of the double top from late May 2009 through February 2010, and the bear trend that developed from the double top. Two secondary patterns can also be seen, a 19-week H&S top that was completed in late September 2009, but failed, and a 17-week continuation triangle that broke out in early February 2010 to launch the completion of the double top.

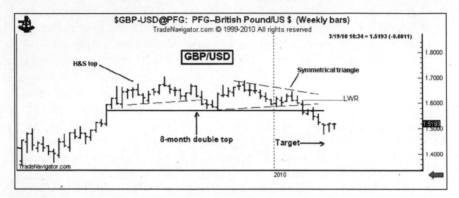

FIGURE 5.2   Double Top on the Weekly Chart of GBP/USD, June 2009–March 2010.

Figure 5.3 displays the daily price bars of GBP/USD for an 11-month period of time from April 2009 through March 2010. It is the daily bar chart companion version of the weekly chart shown in Figure 5.2.

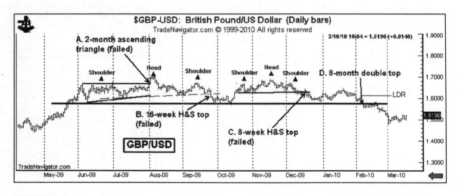

FIGURE 5.3   Double Top on the Daily Chart of GBP/USD, June 2009–March 2010.

This daily graph identifies classical chart patterns of eight weeks or more in duration to demonstrate how a broader period of consolidation is comprised of numerous small patterns—that at the time seemed to be important indicators of expected market behavior. The chronology of this chart was as follows:

A two-month ascending triangle (Pattern A) was completed in late July. This pattern failed to propel prices for more than three days. The brief rally out of the top of the triangle led to what became the head of a 16-week

H&S top (Pattern B). This H&S top broke out in late September and also quickly failed.

The advance from the early October low led to an eight-week complex H&S top (Pattern C). While the completion of this pattern experienced some initial downward momentum, prices stabilized at the December low and then chopped sideways to higher for the next four weeks. In the process, I was stopped out of the shorts I established based on the eight-week H&S top.

All of these patterns combined to constitute the broad eight-month double top completed in early February with a target of 1.440 to 1.470.

From my perspective, all four of these patterns (A through D) were worth trading—in fact, I traded them all. Had any of the first three patterns worked, they could have been considered as textbook examples of classical daily chart patterns.

Figure 5.4 examines the period September 2009 through March 2010, or the last seven months of the period covered in Figure 5.3, attempting to identify shorter-term patterns. In fact, seven patterns (labeled A through G) could have represented signals for the shorter-term classical chart trader. Figure 5.4 further demonstrates how smaller patterns become part of bigger patterns that become part of even bigger patterns and so on.

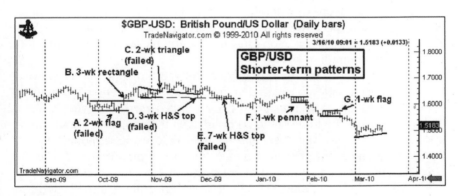

FIGURE 5.4 Daily Chart of GBP/USD, October 2009–March 2010.

Finally, Figure 5.5 is the daily GBP/USD chart from January through March 2010, the final three months of the original 15-month period of time from Figure 5.2. Here, again, it is possible to see even shorter-term patterns that made up part the chart landscape of this forex pair. A very short-term chart trader might have considered taking trades based on these mini-patterns.

In the example of the GBP/USD it would have been possible to base a trading perspective on the quarterly, monthly, weekly or daily charts or to

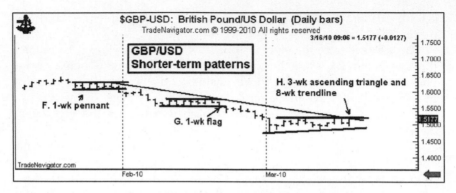

FIGURE 5.5   Daily Chart of GBP/USD, January 2010–March 2010.

drill down on the time frame to four-hour charts, two-hour charts, 60-minute charts, and so on.

I have used the example of the GBP/USD to make two points. First, a trading signal in one time frame might mean nothing in another time frame. Second, chart patterns of shorter duration often fail, only to become redefined as part of a larger chart formation.

Charts are a record of where prices have been, but trading is an operation that needs to be done in real time with an eye on the future. To be a successful chart trader, a person must have a firm fix on the time frame that will generate the trading signals.

Let me touch on one more point dealing with time framing. I believe it is important for a trader to use similar time frames to both enter and manage a trade. What sense does it make to enter a trade based on a weekly chart, and then manage the trade using an hourly chart? Or to enter a trade using a daily chart pattern, but then manage the trade using a monthly chart? I personally understand the importance of keeping time frames consistent because when I fall into the trap of not doing so it usually costs me money.

From my understanding, the Elliott Wave Principle is also sensitive to the issue of time frame by attempting to identify cycles or waves of differing degrees. By the way, this is the totality of my knowledge of the Elliott Wave Principle.

I have discussed this idea of time framing as a necessary precursor to introducing the signals sought and traded by the Factor Trading Plan.

The formula for the Factor Trading Plan in its most digested form is very simple:

- Identify clearly defined weekly chart patterns (with corresponding or supporting patterns on daily charts), seeking trades in what may become the best 10 examples each year of classical charting principles as defined in *Technical Analysis of Stock Trends*.

- Once a possible weekly chart pattern has been identified, attempt to establish an anticipatory position at a stage in the pattern when the final completion could be imminent.
- Increase the leverage of a trade at that point when the pattern in question becomes complete by way of a breakout.
- Within the context of significant trends launched from weekly chart patterns as cited above, seek at least one opportunity to extend or pyramid the leverage in the trade using continuation patterns of shorter duration.
- Identify the best two or three daily chart patterns in each monitored market each year.
- Enter trades in the daily patterns when the boundary lines of the patterns are violated by a breakout.
- Seek a very selective number of additional trades that history has shown to have a high probability of success over a short time frame (two or three days).
- Use a logical spot to place protective stop orders, risking no more than four-fifths of 1 percent of assets on each trade.
- Allow for trades that show immediate profits every opportunity to grow into bigger profits.

Sounds simple, right? Of course, the demons are in the details. You will hopefully be exposed to these demons as my five-month trading diary unfolds.

Four Categories of Trades

The Factor Trading Plan has evolved over the years to identify and trade seven different types of trades fitting into four different categories.

MAJOR PATTERNS Weekly chart patterns at least 10 to 12 weeks in duration with corresponding daily chart patterns of the same or slightly different configuration. The major patterns include three types of trades:

1. *Anticipatory or exploratory position*—an attempt to pre-position at or near the final high or low of the pattern
2. *Pattern completion position*—the point at which the pattern boundary is violated
3. *Pyramid position*—using a continuation pattern of much shorter duration than the launching pattern (perhaps as short in length as a three- or four-week flag or pennant)

MINOR PATTERNS   Minor patterns include two different types of trades:

1. Continuation patterns—daily chart patterns of at least four to eight weeks in duration
2. Reversal patterns—daily charts patterns of at least eight to ten weeks in duration

Minor patterns do not need confirmation by weekly charts.

INSTINCT TRADES   Instinct trades are market situations that do not fit the major or minor pattern categories, but for which I have a very strong instinct. These are usually very short-term trades from which I exit quickly with a small loss if wrong, or cover for a profit within a day or so if correct.

Over the years of my trading, I have developed a sixth sense on when a market is vulnerable to a sudden advance or decline of two to three days. I try not to overdo these types of trades for fear of becoming too short term in my overall market analysis.

MISCELLANEOUS TRADES   Miscellaneous trades are largely driven by short-term momentum within the framework of an existing trend.

As previously stated, chart formations are always more readily apparent with the benefit of 20/20 hindsight. But in real time, it is more difficult to both identify and trade the types of chart formations specified by my trading approach.

There are many times when a particular pattern fails, only to become part of a more extensive chart construction. Other times a chart pattern may completely fail and propel a trend in the opposite direction.

Yet other times I am correct in identifying a chart formation, but the initial breakout is premature. Finally, there are times when I have become too short term in my orientation and what I believe is a signal does not stand up to scrutiny in hindsight. Chart trading is an imperfect science.

It is tough to be perfect when trading imperfect markets. It is impossible to be right on every interpretation and then be right on every entry. The result is that many trades become throwaways. Even when I am dead-on in interpreting a chart formation, it may require more than one attempt to get successfully positioned.

Table 5.1 is the idealized construct of the Factor Trading Plan over the course of a typical year.

Summarizing Table 5.1, to accomplish the goals of the trading operations annually, an anticipated 235 trading events will occur, or approximately 20 per month, or eight trading events per market per year. At an average of one contract per trading event per $100,000 of capital, a total of 235 contracts per $100,000 of capital will be traded each year (or 2,350 contracts per $1 million).

TABLE 5.1   Trading Events by Category and Type of Trading Signal

Trade Signal	Annual Goal (Number of Successful Trades)	Number of Attempts to Reach the Annual Goal
Major patterns— breakout (weekly charts)	10	30 patterns with an average of 1.5 entry attempts each to catch the 10 that will be successful (45 trading events)
Major patterns— anticipatory (daily charts)	10	1.5 attempts in 20 weekly chart pattern situations that offer the opportunity for an anticipatory position (30 trading events); not all major patterns will offer this opportunity
Major patterns— pyramiding (daily charts)	10 (or one pyramiding opportunity in each of the successful trends)	Two pyramid attempts in 15 developing trends (30 trading events—includes pyramids on trends that end up failing); not all major signals produce trends where pyramid opportunities even develop
Minor patterns (continuation or reversal)	20 (or one clearly defined daily pattern that works in each of 20 markets monitored for this opportunity)	With false or premature signals, need to take three patterns in 20 markets monitored (60 trading events)
Instinct trades	20	40 trades to gain 20 winners
Miscellaneous	Trading situations that made absolutely no sense whatsoever with the benefit of hindsight	30 trading events, of which five may be profitable through luck

Built into the volume of 235 trading events represented by Table 5.1 is the expectation that 75 trades (or 32 percent) will be profitable over the course of a typical year (whatever typical is). Yet, over a shorter period of time and number of trading events, it is possible that only 15 or 20 percent of trades may be profitable.

Bottom Liners Defined

I use a concept I refer to as *bottom line trades,* or *bottom liners.* Imagine for a minute that I would stack into a pile the profit-and-loss (P&L) statements for every trade I have ever made. The stack over 30 years would be quite high (my guess is 20 to 30 reams of paper). Next, I know what my total net bottom line has been as a trader through the years.

Now imagine if I would remove P&L statements one by one starting with the largest single profit, the next largest profit and so on, in descending order. The point at which the cumulative total of the removed P&L statements match my net performance is termed the *net bottom line* trades. As a historical average, about 10 percent of trades represent my net bottom line. Based on the framework of annual trading presented in Table 5.1, about 20 trades (or less than two per month) will establish my bottom line during any given year. The other 215 trades each year will wash each other out—these trades will be throwaways.

When I conduct monthly, quarterly, and annual analyses of my trading, some of the more important metrics I look at are:

- Proportion of trades falling into each category—and the win/loss ratio within each
- The proportion of total trades that are profitable
- A measure of the net bottom liners
- Average profit per profitable trade and average loss per unprofitable trade

I have laid out the key elements of the Factor Trading Plan. But a plan is just a plan until it is implemented. Next, I will explore matters dealing with tactical implementation.

Trade Entry

Trade entry is such a vital component that Chapter 6 is entirely devoted to the topic. I am briefly mentioning the component here for the sake of flow only. Examples of actual trade entry will be found in Chapter 6.

I enter nearly all trades using stop orders, meaning that I buy strength and sell weakness. More precisely, once a chart pattern meeting my specifications becomes clearly identified, I place orders to take a position in the direction of the pattern completion—in other words, to go with a breakout.

I have developed a number of trading rules and guidelines over the years based on my experience of how chart patterns are supposed to behave. These rules are not a magic potion, but represent "best practices" to impose discipline on myself. Without such discipline I would likely evolve into a loose cannon and degenerate into knee-jerk emotional market maneuvering. I find the markets compelling. It would be extremely easy for me to lose the forest from the trees if I do not closely monitor my trading. Losing the forest from the trees—becoming too focused on shorter-term patterns and lacking patience to wait for really big patterns to develop—is my single biggest challenge as a trader.

Trade Risk Management

Trade risk management deals with how I manage a trading event once I have entered the trade. There are several elements to managing a trade.

Leverage

Leverage deals with how many contracts I enter per $100,000 unit of capital. Keep in mind that I limit my risk per trade to eight-tenths of 1 percent and often as little as one-half of 1 percent of assets. The leverage is determined by the price of entry and the price of the initial protective stop. For example, assume I enter a trade in T-bonds and my initial risk is more than a full point (let's say my short entry is at 121-00 and the initial protective stop is at 122-08). This represents a risk per contract of $1,250. If I traded one contract per $100,000, the risk would equal 1.25 percent of capital, in excess of my risk management guidelines. My main option would be to trade one contract per $200,000 (for a risk of six-tenths of 1 percent). An alternative would be to use a money management stop point representing about $700 per contract and trade one contract per $100,000 unit of capital.

Trade risk management deals with the percentage of assets I am willing to risk in any given trade, how I determine leverage (the number of contracts per specified unit of capital), and where I place an initial stop-loss protective order. These determinations guide the maximum risk taken on any given trade.

Setting the Initial Protective Stop Price

My preference is to use the Last Day Rule to determine the protective stop placement. See Chapter 3 for an explanation and examples of the Last Day Rule. There are instances when I select an initial stop that is different than the Last Day Rule. Fully explaining these instances is beyond the scope of this book.

Moving the Protective Stop and Exiting a Trade

Once a position has been established and the initial protective stop has been set, there are a number of techniques used by the Factor Trading Plan to exit a trade.

In nearly all cases, trade profits are taken if a market reaches the target implied by the pattern that launched the trade. Stops are also advanced in the direction of the position using several methods, including the Retest Failure Rule, the Trailing Stop Rule, and the Intervening Pattern Rule. Explanations and examples of these methods to move protective stops are found in Chapter 3.

Trade Order Management

Whereas trade risk management deals with the determination of the risks and leverage taken on any trade or combination of trades, trade order management deals with the actual physical process of entering and exiting trades.

My job as a trader is really nothing more than that of a glorified order placer. At its irreducible level, trading is basically the process of entering orders. I have no control over what the markets do. The real challenge of trading is to identify the controllable factors and build into the trading process means to control what can be controlled. The markets will do what the markets will do whether I buy, sell, hold, or do nothing. At the end of the day, the only control I have is over the orders I enter.

I will divide this section into trade order management on positions being considered for a new entry and trade order management on existing positions.

Entering New Orders

I review the weekly charts for about 30 different markets once each week—usually late Friday afternoon or early Saturday morning. This review gives me a good idea of any new developments taking place in the markets and if there are any new potential trades on the horizon.

The types of weekly chart patterns I want to trade take a very long time to develop. In fact, there are only about two to three significant weekly chart patterns that qualify an individual market for a trade in any given calendar year. Finding more than three weekly chart patterns in a specific market even during a strongly trending year would signify that I might be reading more into the charts than I should.

By early Saturday afternoon, I have a pretty good idea if an entry trade will set up in the coming week in any markets. Usually, I see weekly chart patterns develop many weeks, and sometimes months, before an actual pattern is completed. This is a problem because once I see a pattern developing, I become anxious to become involved. This is where patience comes into play.

I print off weekly charts (and accompanying daily charts) that might offer a trading opportunity for the coming week. In addition to the many wonderful online charting packages available (I use three different web-based programs), I maintain printed hard-copy charts of the markets I am either in or looking to enter. Part of this exercise is because I was weaned on paper charts. I find that actually drawing in price bars by hand each day puts me in better connection with the markets than scrolling through updated charts on the Internet.

Next, I turn my attention to the daily charts. I pay particular attention to the markets identified by my review of the weekly charts, although I look at the daily chart of the active contract of every market in which I would consider a trade.

While my bias is to focus on weekly charts, daily charts provide more trading opportunities than revealed by the weekly charts.

If a daily chart trading opportunity develops during the week, I will print out a hard copy of that chart. At about 2 PM Sunday, I gather the charts printed the previous day. It is at this time I determine the entry strategy, risk parameters, and leverage I will use for each market, assuming that a pattern breakout occurs. I launch the online trading platforms I use and begin placing entry orders and setting up trading alerts so that I will automatically be notified if any of my entry orders are executed.

I most commonly use good-until-canceled (GTC) open orders to enter and exit trades. Some markets are notorious for running stop orders during the nighttime hours. I carefully avoid entering GTC stops in the night sessions in such markets as the mini metal contracts, grains, softs, fiber, and livestock (which I seldom trade anyway). I use day orders in these markets, each day entering the orders when the normal daytime trading hours commence.

By the time the Sunday afternoon markets open, I have just about completed all of my order entry for new positions. Orders I do not place on Sunday afternoon (such as stops in thinly traded electronic markets) are placed early on Monday morning. I am normally awake and have checked Asian and European trading by about 3:30 AM mountain time. I am not a very good sleeper.

The exact time a trader does certain tasks and the process used are not important. I do certain things at certain times in certain ways because it works for me. The point is that a trader needs to develop a disciplined routine. The time of an action is less important than the action itself.

In addition to trading, I am a private pilot. Pilots go through a routine checklist during each phase of a flight—from preflight to postflight. A trader needs a similar routine.

In general, only a few new entry opportunities will develop during the trading week. It is a harsh truth that those trades I "discover" during the week (i.e., trades I had not seen coming the previous weekend) have probably been net losers over the years.

Different online trading platforms offer varying capabilities. My preference is to use trading platforms that offer the ability to place contingency orders. This means that if entry order using a stop is filled, then a protective stop-loss order will be placed automatically without my direct involvement. Without the ability to place contingency orders I would need to pay attention to the markets during the trading session. I will emphasize repeatedly during the course of this book that I want distance between myself and the markets during the trading day.

The more I follow the markets during the trading hours, the more apt I am to make an emotionally driven decision to override my trading plan. I know myself too well, and I know that my emotional reactions to intraday trading will be detrimental to my net bottom line over any period of time. Controlling my emotions is the biggest challenge that faces me as a trader. And this is a battle that never ends.

Existing Open Positions

Among all aspects of my trading, this is the one area that causes me the most aggravation and stress. How to handle a trade that immediately moves in the intended direction is the single most difficult aspect of trading, in my opinion. I lose sleep over this trading challenge. It is this component that I am most tempted to tweak at any given time based on trades that immediately preceded the moment.

It is easy for me to enter a trade, easy to take quick losses on trades that never work, easy to take pyramid trades, and easy to take profits at targets, but enormously difficult to deal with profitable trades that are somewhere between the entry point and the target.

At its most basic level, managing an open trade boils down to a balance between protecting a profit and allowing a trend the opportunity to run its course as implied by a completed chart configuration.

The process of entering orders on exiting positions is similar to that of the order flow for new trade entries. For every position held, two orders are in place in the market—a "limit" order for taking profits at the target and a stop order for exiting the trade if it turns against me. These two orders are commonly known as OCOs—one cancels the other. Within minutes of entering a new trade, I place both of these exit orders.

Each afternoon, I review the daily charts for each market in which I carry a position and make a determination whether any order should be modified. Most modifications occur during the late afternoons between the end of the day session when the closing prices are established and the beginning of the evening session, which represents the start of the next day's trading schedule.

Chapter 6 provides numerous specific examples of the tactics used in trade management by examining actual case studies.

Best Trading Practices

Best practices are those things that would contribute positively to a net bottom line over an extended period of time if followed habitually. Worded in the opposite way, not doing the best practices will likely reduce profitability. Maintaining and reviewing a list of best practices can keep a trader grounded in a right mind-set. Best practices vary from trader to trader. My best practices would include the following items dealing with order management:

- Review weekly charts only on Saturday when the markets are closed.
- Scroll through every market that I consider trading. Use the weekly rollover continuation charts as well as the weekly chart of the most actively traded contract month in the case of futures markets.
- Look at daily charts only once each day—during nontrading hours.
- Place entry orders only once each day and do *not* second-guess the original order once the trading session begins.
- Avoid intraday charts. Avoid watching markets during the trading day.
- Do not pay attention to any other trader or analyst. Base my trades on my own approach.

Points to Remember

- A trader must have an organized method to resolve what constitutes a trading signal. Time phasing is a hurdle all traders must clear in order to be consistently successful.
- A trader must have a framework that defines an overall trading plan, including how to enter trades and how to determine the risks involved. Most professional money managers risk no more than 1 percent on each trading event.
- A strategy for exiting trades must be part of a trading plan.
- A trading plan must address the issue of risk management, namely, what proportion of capital will be risked on any given trading event.
- A trading routine, especially analysis and order entry, should be developed and followed.

Three Case Studies Using the Factor Trading Plan

This chapter presents case studies of actual markets traded in 2009 by the Factor Trading Plan to illustrate the rules, guidelines, and principles introduced in earlier chapters of the book.

This chapter will use completed charts to answer such questions as:

- What does a trading signal looks like?
- How is a signal generated within the trading plan?
- How do I determine the placement for initial protective stops?
- How do I determine the number of contracts (i.e., the leverage for the trade)?
- What guidelines do I use to advance stops in the direction of a profitable trend?
- What provision is made for pyramiding a trade, and how does it work?
- How do I take profits?

The three case studies in this chapter include a particularly memorable and significant technical event producing two trades in the Dow Jones Industrial Average (DJIA) contract, a full year of trades in gold, and finally, a full year of trades in sugar.

These case studies were selected because they were markets in which I was active in 2009 and a variety of trading situations were presented. Gold and sugar were not typical markets in 2009. In fact, gold produced one of the best trades of the year and sugar was my single most profitable market for the year. I could have presented a case study in a market like the euro currency and U.S. dollar cross rate (EUR/USD) but chose not to. For the purpose of full disclosure, please know that there were some markets that completely frustrated me in 2009.

A Remarkable Technical Event in the Dow Jones

The DJIA produced a short trade followed by a long trade that will be featured in future textbooks on classical charting principles. A short trade is one in which a trader bets on a price decline. A long trade is one in which a trade bets that prices will climb. In forex and commodities, the sequence in which a trader buys and sells does not matter. A short position is established when a trader sells first, hoping to profit when a buy is made at a lower price. The opposite is true for a long position.

Short Trade: July 6, 2009

Once I identify a pattern that qualifies as a candidate trade, I place an entry order on my trading platform. Figure 6.1 shows the September 2009 contract of the Mini Dow Jones. On July 2, I identified a possible H&S top. I immediately placed an order to short the market if the neckline and right shoulder low were penetrated. My sell stop was at 8182. I became short on July 6.

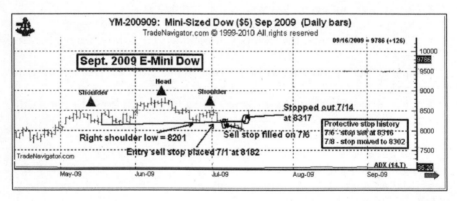

FIGURE 6.1   An H&S Top in the Dow Jones Industrial Average.

The primary method used to establish the initial protective stop is the Last Day Rule. This rule is based on the assumption that the breakout day is sacred and that the high of a downside breakout day or the low of an upside breakout day will be the demarcation point between the trading range of the pattern and the start of a sustained trend. As a very general rule, I risk a short trade to above the high of the day during which the breakout occurred (or to below the low of the upside breakout day). When very little of the bar of the breakout day is above the boundary line, I may elect to revert to the day prior to the breakout day to determine the Last Day Rule.

When the September Mini Dow broke out on July 6, only 30 points existed above the neckline of the H&S top. So, I elected to use the previous day's high and selected a stop of 8316, representing a potential loss of $670 per contract.

I shorted a single September Mini Dow contract per $100,000 of capital based on my normal risk tolerance of approximately six-tenths to eight-tenths of 1 percent.

I use the targeting methods detailed by Edwards and Magee in *Technical Analysis of Stock Trends*—a market breaking out of a chart formation will trade a distance equal to the height of the pattern itself. The high of the head within the H&S was 8828. The low of the right shoulder was 8194. The difference of 634 Dow points projected down from 8194 yielded a target for the trade of 7560. When I was filled on my short, I immediately entered an open order to cover the short at 7561.

My short position closed against me the very day I entered it. This is never a good sign. My historical bottom line would be greatly improved if I immediately had exited every trade that ever closed at a loss. Yet, the following day, July 7, the market dropped throughout the day and closed decisively below the neckline of the H&S top. This gave me a renewed cause for optimism. It also gave me an ability to move my protective stop to 8302, just above the July 7 high, a revised Last Day Rule. The market stopped me out on July 14 to officially end the trade, called the original H&S interpretation into doubt, and set the stage for a long position.

I should have known that the H&S top was suspect—the pattern was being discussed frequently on CNBC. Patterns being acknowledged as conventional wisdom normally do not work out as planned.

Long Trade: July 15, 2009

A pattern that I have found to be quite tradable in commodity futures and forex markets is the H&S failure. I consider this to be a pattern unto itself. The H&S failure pattern starts with a recognizable H&S formation. Whether the H&S is completed with a minimum of follow through (as in the case of the Dow) or the right shoulder begins to form but does not break the neckline, the signal is generated when the market climbs above the peak of the right shoulder of the H&S top (or declines below the right shoulder low of a H&S bottom).

After being stopped out of my short September Dow on July 14, I immediately placed a buy stop above the right shoulder high. As seen in Figure 6.2, it was filled the very next day, July 15, at 8568.

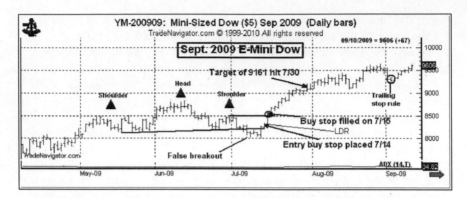

FIGURE 6.2   Textbook H&S Failure on the September DJIA Chart.

The Last Day Rule was based on the low of July 14 at 8327. I set my protective stop at 8319. The risk from 8568 to 8319 was $1,245 per contract, far greater than my desired risk of about $700 per capital unit of $100,000. So, I was faced with one of two decisions: to use a money management stop rather than the Last Day Rule or to restrict leverage to one contract per $200,000. I chose the latter option. By risking a position of one-half of a contract per $100,000 to 8319, my risk level was about six-tenths of 1 percent ($1,245 divided by 2).

The objective of an H&S top failure is determined by projecting the height of the H&S upward from the high of the right shoulder. In this case, I projected the height of the original H&S of 634 points upward from the July 1 right shoulder high of 8527, producing a target of 9161. This target was met on July 30. In the case of the long trade in the Dow, the profit was $3,100+ per contract, or $1,550 per $100,000 unit of capital.

There is an overpowering temptation to remain involved with a market that just provided a nice profit. The emotion of greed almost demands an immediate re-entry into the trade lest money be left on the table. When facing this emotion I need to remind myself that there will be new opportunities next week, next month, and next year. Discipline demands that once I exit a trade I need to go shopping in a different market. Incidentally, rather than taking profits at the target I could have elected to use the Trailing Stop Rule, which was triggered on September 2.

A Year Trading Gold

In 2009, the Factor Trading Plan entered seven trades in gold. Even though I traded the individual futures contracts, for ease I will trace the trading history on the weekly and daily continuation charts. Figure 6.3 displays an overview of my year of trading gold.

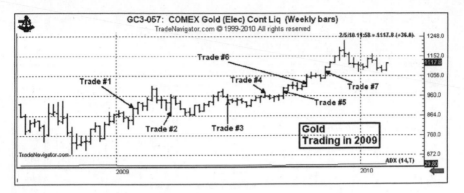

FIGURE 6.3   Gold 2009 Trades.

On January 23, I entered a long gold trade as the market broke out of an H&S bottom and trend line dating back to July 2008. See Figure 6.4. I bought a mini contract (a total of 33 ounces) of April gold at 884.2 per $100,000 of capital. My initial stop was just under the Last Day Rule at 853.8 with a risk on the trade of about 1 percent of assets.

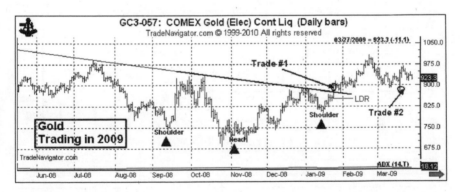

FIGURE 6.4   Gold Trade #1—H&S Completed in January.

I made mistakes on this trade. My interpretation was very flawed. A legitimate H&S pattern occurs when the head and both shoulders are singularly part of a process by which "strong hands" are distributing or accumulating a position. In hindsight, the right shoulder in January was probably disconnected with the left shoulder of September 2008. I think I was probably just looking for an excuse to be long gold. An H&S configuration that comprises just a portion of a more extensive trading range should always be treated as suspect. I tend to go in streaks with my interpretations. For a while, I see H&S on most charts I study, then for another period of time I see wedges everywhere I look, then it might be triangles, then channels.

I exited the trade on February 25 at 958.2 using the Trailing Stop Rule. Figures 6.5 and 6.6 display the three-step process of the rule.

FIGURE 6.5   Gold Trade #1—Trailing Stop Rule in Gold.

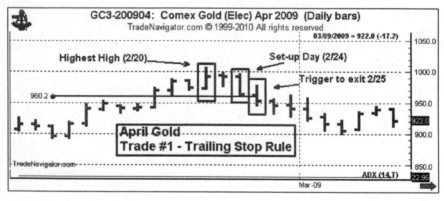

FIGURE 6.6   Gold Trade #1—Trailing Stop Rule Demonstrated.

A Government Report Causes Volatility and a Quick Loss

Several times per year a market will spin me faster than I know what is happening. This was just such a case, as shown by the out-of-line movement in Figure 6.7.

On March 18, I was stopped into a short position at 888.7 when the market sliced through the neckline of an H&S top early in the session in response to a government report.

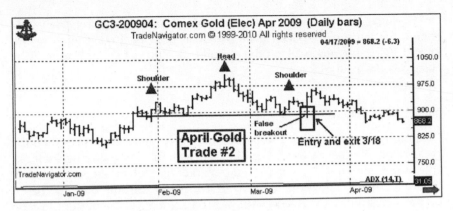

FIGURE 6.7   Trade #2—An Out-of-Line Movement in Gold.

The Last Day Rule at the time of the fill was at 916.3, but I used a money management stop of 900.7 in order to extend my leverage to two mini contracts per $100,000. I was risking about eight-tenths of 1 percent on the trade. I was literally stopped out within minutes. Back in the "good old days" of pit trading, I remember at times getting back a fill on my protective stop before getting the fill on the entry order. Talk about adding insult to injury!

Trading a Short Position on a Small Pattern

Keeping with my obsession over H&S patterns, I shorted one contract of August mini gold on June 12 at 942.4 (see Figure 6.8). This was way too small a pattern for me to be trading and was a violation of my basic guidelines.

FIGURE 6.8   Trade #3—A Small H&S Pattern in Gold.

Knowing that this was not a good trade, I jammed my protective stop, exiting the trade with a very small profit on June 24. I considered myself lucky for cheating my rules on the required duration of an acceptable daily chart reversal pattern.

Another H&S Pattern Fails

Continuing the H&S theme I went long mini gold on August 4 based on the completion of a seven-week H&S bottom with an upslanting neckline, as shown in Figure 6.9. On August 6, the market had a hard intraday retest of the H&S pattern. I adjusted my stop to just below the August 6 low based on the Retest Rule. I was stopped out for a six-tenths of 1 percent loss on August 7.

FIGURE 6.9   Trade #4—Another Failed H&S in Gold.

I hope these case studies are communicating a message I want to send clearly—that trade entry signals are relatively unimportant to my overall success. What I trade—indeed, what I call an entry signal—is secondary to money and risk management. Trade selection is highly overrated.

Spotting the Big Move

In early August, it was becoming apparent that something big was just around the corner in gold. The weekly chart displayed a massive inverted continuation H&S pattern, as shown in Figure 6.10. This rare pattern was discussed briefly by Edwards and Magee in *Technical Analysis of Stock Trends* and earlier by Schabacker in *Technical Analysis and Stock Market Profits: The Real Bible of Technical Analysis*.

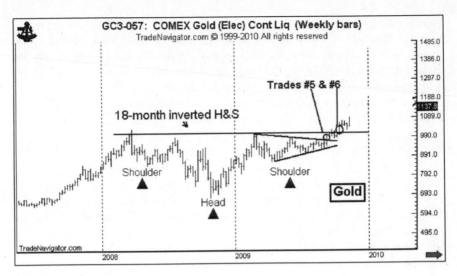

FIGURE 6.10 Trades #5 and #6—H&S Pattern on Weekly Gold Chart.

Further, the right shoulder of the H&S was taking the form of a six-month symmetrical triangle. The triangle had six significant contact points (labeled A-F in Figure 6.11). I get very excited when I see markets set up in such a magnificent way.

FIGURE 6.11 Trades #5 and #6—A Massive Symmetrical Triangle Serving as the Right Shoulder on the Gold Chart.

The advance on September 2 penetrated the upper boundary of the triangle and then rose above the last defining high within the pattern (point E). I went long December gold at 978. The objective of 1094 was determined by extending the distance from B to C upwards from E. Calculating the A to B distance would have also been acceptable. While I took profits at the target on November 4, the Trailing Stop Rule would have kept me in the trade until December 7. I could have gained another $45 per ounce—there is always another case of coulda, woulda, shoulda!

It is important to note that the lows of the breakout day of September 2 and the upthrust day of September 3 were never challenged. This is often the case with a substantial and valid breakout. Immediately following the breakout, the market drifted sideways for a month. In the process, the market appeared to be forming a small H&S top. I even advanced the protective stop on a portion of my long position to below the neckline of this small pattern (see Figure 6.12). On October 5, the market advanced through the existing right shoulder high of this small H&S pattern, providing a pyramid signal at 1014 with a target of 1050 (met quickly on October 8). I chose not to take profits at the target. Again, note that the Last Day Rule, the low of October 5, was also never challenged.

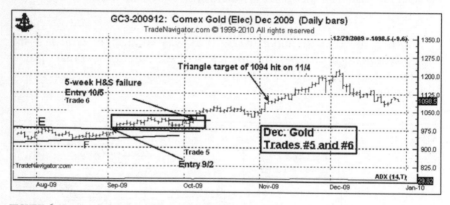

FIGURE 6.12   Trade #6—A Small H&S Failure in Gold.

The Gold Market Throws a Curve Ball

Seldom does a trade go from entry to the target without difficulty and challenge. The best laid plans of mice and men! Such was the case with the pyramid position established at the breakout of the four-week H&S failure on October 5 (trade #6). I chose not to take profits on this trade at 1050. Then, the decline on October 26 completed a small double top and placed the run for the glory into question. The October 26 decline was also a setup day for my Trailing Stop Rule. October 27 was the trigger day for the Trailing Stop Rule, but I did not jam my stop until the next day, when I was stopped out near the low of the bull market correction, as seen in Figure 6.13.

FIGURE 6.13   Trade #7—Fake-Out in Gold.

This situation created one of the most difficult challenges facing a trader—what to do when stopped out of a successful trade prior to the attainment of a much larger target. Unfortunately, there are no easy answers to this challenge, but there are some lessons.

Within days of completing the three-week double top, the market returned to its dominant bull trend. This raised the real possibility that the small top was a bear trap. It also established the possibility that the market was creating a fishhook buy signal. This is not a Magee and Edwards pattern, but something I have observed in my years trading chart patterns. A fishhook signal occurs when a pattern quickly fails followed by an immediate trend back into the failed pattern. The dynamic behind a fishhook buy signal is that weak longs get stopped out.

Markets almost always force sold-out bulls to chase a trend. The first real sign of a fishhook buy signal was on November 2 when the entire trading range was above the lower boundary of the three-week double top and the market closed near the high. I could have reentered at this point, but I stubbornly waited for a new high on November 3.

Fishhooks most often signal halfway moves that can be projected using swing targeting (see Figure 6.14).

The advance from the October 2 low to the October 14 high was approximately $85. Projecting this amount upward from the October 29 low of 1027 yielded a target of 1112, met on November 12.

Lessons from Trading Gold in 2009

I hate being jerked around in the markets. I hate buying at the top end of a trading range and selling at the bottom end. I hate false breakouts. I

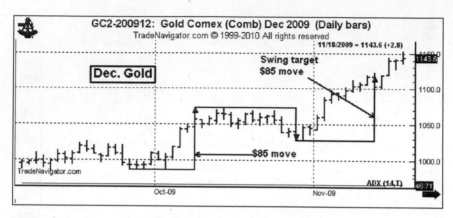

FIGURE 6.14   A Swing Target in Gold.

dread being right on the direction of a market but losing money by getting whiplashed in the process. This can happen if I get stopped out of a long on weakness, reenter on strength, get stopped back out on weakness, and so on. It is possible to lose $50 per ounce in a $20 trading range in gold and end up correct on the subsequent direction.

A choppy market does damage financially. Choppy markets can impose emotional and confidence consequences on a trader that are far worse. I can't remember all the times I have missed really big moves because I was gun shy from a period of choppiness that preceded the big moves.

The biggest temptation after a premature stop-out is to get right back in before receiving another solid signal. Getting into this cycle throws discipline and patience right out the window. I got lucky on trade #7 in gold. Had this trade slapped me around, my head would have really been screwed on wrong.

The second lesson is that smaller reversal patterns, such as the little double top, are not likely to provide a serious threat to a trend that began with a strong thrust out of a substantial pattern (the triangle in the case of gold), especially when the market has a great distance to go to reach the implied target.

Table 6.1 summarizes the gold trading signals in 2009.

The target of the 1320 from the inverted 18-month H&S on the weekly chart has not been met as of this writing in January 2010. This fact has imposed a bullish bias on my view of gold.

I waste a lot of ammunition by taking trading decisions within broader trading ranges—by not waiting for the decisive breakout. This was the case for the first four gold trades in 2009. It was not until the trades #5 and #6 that the market was really breaking out of a major pattern. Trade #5 was really the only trade worthy of the Best Dressed List.

TABLE 6.1   Record of Gold Trading Signals in 2009

Signal #	Pattern	L or S (contract month)	Entry Date/Price	Exit Date/Price	Resulting Move per oz.
1	Six-month H&S bottom	L (Apr.)	1/23 at 884.2	2/25 at 958.2	74
2	Six-week H&S top	S (Apr.)	3/18 at 888.7	3/18 at 916.4	(28)
3	Four-week H&S top	S (Aug.)	6/12 at 942.4	6/24 at 938.7	4
4	Seven-week H&S bottom	L (Dec.)	8/4 at 967.2	8/7 at 955.4	(12)
5	Six-month symmetrical triangle	L (Dec.)	9/2 at 978	11/4 at 1094	116
6	Four-week H&S failure	L (Dec.)	10/5 at 1014.4	10/28 at 1028.6	13
7	Six-month symmetrical triangle, failure of three-week double top, new highs	L (Dec.)	11/3 at 1076.2	11/12 at 1112	35
Total					202

Exiting a Trade

There are six general conditions I use to exit a trade once it has been established: two with the trade at a loss and four with the trade at a profit.

At a Loss

1. The chart pattern breakout I use to enter the trade is either a failure or a premature breakout. The market reverses and penetrates my Last Day Rule stop (or money management stop if used instead of the Last Day Rule for risk management reasons. (See Figure 6.7 for an example.)
2. The breakout fails to provide immediate thrust in the direction of the trade. Within days (per perhaps a week or so) the market experiences a hard retest of the pattern, penetrating the boundary line used to enter the trade. If a hard retest occurs, I may elect to adjust my protective stop in relationship to the hard retest. (See Figure 6.8 for an example.)

At a Profit

1. At the target. I normally take profits at the target indicated by the chart pattern used to initially establish a trade. (See Figures 6.11 and 6.14 for examples.)
2. Successful trades often develop smaller chart patterns during the course of a trend. Depending on the nature and duration of these continuation patterns, I may even pyramid a trend. I will also use the Last Day Rule of a continuation pattern to advance the protective stop on the initial position in the direction of a successful trend.
3. Prior to the attainment of a target, a market may form a pattern with implications counter to the position. In other words, an intervening pattern indicates that a reversal of trend is possible. I may elect to advance my protective stop in relationship to this intervening pattern. (See Figure 6.13 for an example.)
4. At any time during the course of a trend, I may choose to elect the Trailing Stop Rule. (See Figure 6.5 for an example.)

A Year Trading Sugar

Sugar was the market of my single most concentrated focus in 2009. My opinion of sugar in 2009 highlights the fact that as a chartist I am not a detached market observer. My biases often dictate my chart analysis.

Sugar was also my single most profitable market in 2009. As part of full disclosure, I want to emphasize that my trading experience in sugar in 2009 is not typical of my experience in most markets in most years. I only wish this could be the case. In fact, sugar provided nearly 40 percent of the net signal profits in 2009.

Yet the market completely frustrated my bullish bias during the first four months of the year as I lost money on trade after trade. Just because I am ready for a market to make a move does not mean that the market is ready to do so—or that it will ever be. A market could care less if I am bullish or bearish. In fact, if I am a bull, once I do my buying, my only influence is as a bear because I become a source of selling.

Starting the Year a Bull

I was a sugar bull on the first day of January in 2009. Figure 6.15 displays the weekly pattern I thought was dominant at the time, a possible nine-month continuation symmetrical triangle. In early 2009, the market was at the lower boundary of this triangle, so I was interested in establishing an anticipatory long position.

FIGURE 6.15   Sugar Weekly Chart in Early 2009.

Little did I understand how frustrating that process would become. Figure 6.16 shows a daily continuation chart listing all 11 of the Factor trading signals in 2009. My obsession with sugar resulted in far too many trades. An obsession with a market leading to overtrading has happened to me before, and it will happen again.

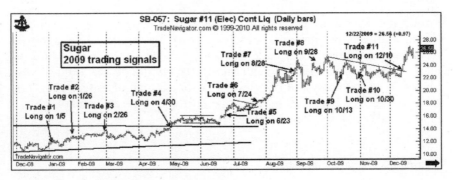

FIGURE 6.16   Trading Sugar 2009: 11 Trades.

Three Losing Trades Started the Year

Figure 6.17 shows the first three trades of 2009 in sugar. All three trades were losers despite the fact I was a major bull and the market was rising. Losing money trading the long side of a rising market challenges one's durability and sanity as a trader.

The advance on January 5 completed a two-month symmetrical triangle. I chose to use the last full day within the pattern, December 30, to determine the Last Day Rule. I was stopped out on January 14 for a 67 tick loss.

FIGURE 6.17   Trades #1–3—Early Frustration in Sugar Trading.

Buying New Highs

Bound and determined to be aboard a bull market, I kept buying new highs. Normally, this is not my style. I prefer to wait for recognizable patterns. I went long on January 26 (trade #2) and pyramided the trade when the market made yet another new high on February 26 (trade #3). The nosedive on March 2 took me out of both trades, costing a total of 94 ticks. The stop on trade #2 had been moved from the Last Day Rule of January 23 to a Retest Rule below the low of February 19.

Waiting for a Substantial Pattern

After being burned by buying new highs, I decided to wait for a recognizable pattern. And I got one in spades in late April.

For decades I have been part of an e-mail network of a dozen or so fellow chart traders. We share ideas and chart analyses. Following is the e-mail I sent the group on April 30:

April 30, 2009

A sweet trading opportunity

The longer-term charts indicate that sugar could be the trade for 2009. Several technical observations are worthy of note.

The weekly chart displays a textbook perfect symmetrical triangle dating back to March 2008. This 14-month triangle would be completed by a move above 14.72 in the nearby July contract.

This weekly chart must be viewed in the historical context of a possible base dating back to 1981. A decisive close above the 2006 high at 19.75 would establish a point and figure objective in the 60s.

The July contract today penetrated the upper ice line of a nine-week rectangle. It is not uncommon for a massive move to begin with the completion of a relatively small chart pattern such as this. Daily charts need to be combined with weekly charts, monthly charts, and even quarterly charts to develop a mosaic on market opportunities.

An e-mail update one day later, on May 1, 2009:

Today, the distant March 2010 contract strongly moved above the upper boundary of a six-month running wedge. This pattern is likely to serve as the slingshot for the bull move in sugar. This chart formation represents a very low-risk opportunity for a relatively large position.

So during a two-day period all the contracts of Sugar experienced a decisive break out (the July, October, March and continuation charts). The daily continuation and individual contract months provided slightly different pictures. The July contract completed a two-month rectangle, while the October contract completed a seven-month running wedge (see Figures 6.18 and 6.19). October sugar met its initial and most conservative target on June 24.

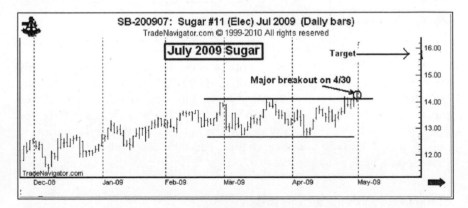

FIGURE 6.18   Trade #4—A Rectangle in July Sugar.

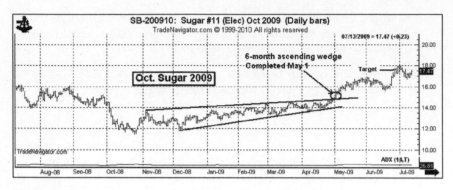

FIGURE 6.19   Trade #4—A Running Wedge in October Sugar.

The weekly chart triangle is shown in Figure 6.20. It is always a good sign when the weekly and daily charts complete major patterns at about the same time.

FIGURE 6.20   Symmetrical Triangle Launches Bull Move in Sugar.

Sugar was off to the races. Importantly, because sugar was in the early stages of a bull trend, the risk was small. The Last Day Rule risk in the July contract was 31 points, and 38 points in the October contract. This allowed me to assume larger leverage than is normal. The weekly chart gave me extra courage. If there was any doubt, the large-range upside breakout on May 1 was a Friday, a Weekend Rule. Markets that complete a weekly pattern on a Friday seldom fail.

The Market Pauses to Catch Its Breath

After its initial surge in May, the market drifted sideways for about five weeks, as displayed in Figure 6.21. Then, on June 23, the October contract generated a five-week "fishhook" buy signal (trade #5), allowing me to pyramid my position, again with relatively low risk to the Last Day Rule. The target was reached on July 30.

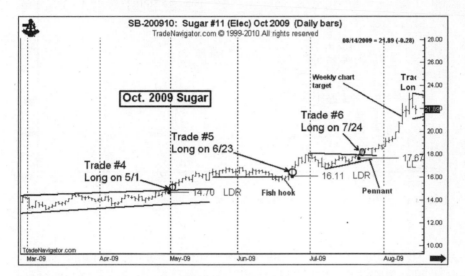

FIGURE 6.21 Trades #5 and #6—Two Continuation Patterns during the Bull Run.

Trade #6 is a classic pennant pattern. On July 24 the market made a new high for the bull trend and penetrated a three-week pennant, another opportunity to increase leverage. Once again, the Last Day Rule was never challenged. I had a tiger by the tail.

The weekly chart target of 21.22 was reached by the October contract on August 10. I exited my position. I cannot really articulate why I sometimes use daily chart targets, sometimes weekly chart targets, sometimes swing targets and sometimes the Trailing Stop Rule. There is no formula for this decision. It is a matter of making a decision, stepping up to the line and living with the consequences.

Entering a Choppy Period

By mid-August I had exited all the positions accumulated since May 1. I was looking for an excuse to get back into the market. I was becoming concerned that sugar was headed for 60 cents without me aboard. The market did not make me wait long.

But as trading would have it, I entered a four-month period of trading frustration. It is not uncommon for markets that have had a good run to enter a period of choppiness and signal failure, as witnessed in Figure 6.22.

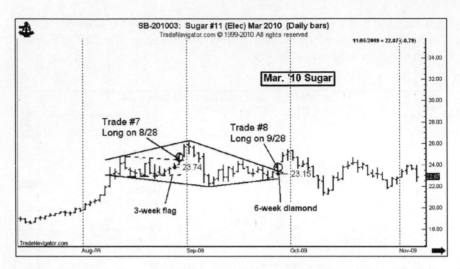

FIGURE 6.22   Trades #7 and #8—The Sugar Market Begins a Large Consolidation.

The market completed a three-week flag on August 28 for trade #7 (see dashed boundary). My thinking at the time was that the flag was a half-mast pattern and that the market was headed straight to 30 cents. Prices spurted for two days and then rolled over, stopping me out on September 4 at the Last Day Rule. I was again out of sugar and felt as though a good friend had died.

On September 28, the market completed what I interpreted to be a six-week continuation diamond formation. I returned the long side (trade #8). The Last Day Rule stop was hit on October 7. I was once again flat.

Focused on Being Long Sugar

At this point, I became obsessed with being long sugar. Overattention to a market most often leads to foolish trades. Foolish trades lead to losses. Both trades #9 and #10 were established without the benefit of completed chart formations as shown in Figure 6.23. These trades were driven by the fear of missing a move. Fear and greed are two emotions that will cost a trader money.

Both trades were established on days sugar rallied, on October 13 and October 30. Buying strength or selling weakness within a trading range is not a very good idea. Trade #9 was stopped out at the Last Day Rule on November 27. Trade #10 was stopped out earlier, at its Last Day Rule on November 10. Not only did I invent a reason for these trades, I also got stubborn with my money management, as highlighted by trade #9.

FIGURE 6.23   Trades #9 and #10—Sugar Trades without Clear Patterns.

The Market Finishes the Year Strong

The sugar market finished the year well, getting back on track on December 11. The advance on this day penetrated the upper boundary of a 15-week channel and completed a four-week H&S bottom, triggering trade #11 (see Figure 6.24).

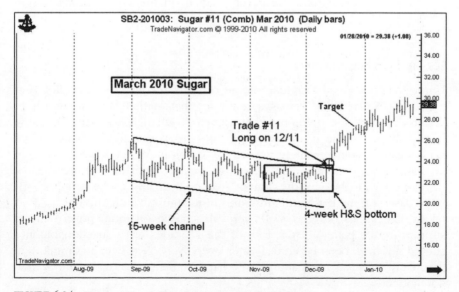

FIGURE 6.24   Trade #11—A Significant Buy Signal in Sugar.

TABLE 6.2   Sugar Signals and Trades in 2009

Signal # and (Position)	Pattern	Entry Date	Exit Date	Resulting Move in Points
1 (Long May)	Two-mo triangle	1/5	1/14	(67)
2 (Long May)	New high	1/26	3/2	(59)
3 (Long May)	New high	2/26	3/2	(35)
4 (Long Oct)	Seven-mo running wedge	5/1	6/24	+222
5 (Long Oct)	Five-wk fishhook	6/23	7/30	+206
6 (Long Oct)	Three-wk pennant	7/24	8/10	+309
7 (Long Mar)	3-wk flag	8/28	9/4	(98)
8 (Long Mar)	Six-wk continuation pyramid	9/28	10/7	(92)
9 (Long Mar)	Momentum	10/13	11/27	(76)
10 (Long Mar)	Momentum	10/30	11/10	(59)
11 (Long Mar)	15-wk channel	12/11	12/28	+365
11 trades, 7 losers, 4 winners				

As I have pointed out already in this book, smaller patterns often simultaneously launch larger patterns. Once again, the breakout was on a Friday, a significant fact. The target was reached on December 28, although the Trailing Stop Rule was not activated until January 11.

Table 6.2 summarizes the trading signals in the sugar market during 2009.

Lessons from Sugar in 2009

Unfortunately, I need to relearn some of the same lessons year after year after year. Sugar in 2009 was a reminder that market behavior tends to greatly lag a strong opinion I may develop. Often, I see something big taking shape on the charts well before a trend develops. Markets have no obligation to immediately reward my opinion. My tendency is to force an interpretation of the daily charts to comply with an opinion I have developed with the weekly charts. Two of the early trades (#2 and #3) were based on market momentum absent recognizable chart patterns. Two of the late trades (#9 and #10) were also based on momentum without support from a pattern. Thus, four of the 11 trades were questionable and should not have been entered. I enter every New Year with a commitment to greatly increase my patience. Perhaps some year I will achieve that commitment.

Points to Remember

- Some of the best trades are moves in the opposite direction of a trader's initial expectations (such as the case in the Dow Jones).
- A trading plan must go through losing periods in any given market to find the gems. Persistence pays off.
- Taking trades that anticipate a move can often be frustrating. Attempting to get positioned within a trading range can result in becoming gun shy when the real move occurs.
- Markets most often provide signals when the real moves begin. Waiting for substantial patterns to become complete is where the profits are to be found.

Characteristics of a Successful Trader

Figure 7.1 is the roadmap for Chapter 7, providing a graphic presentation of the content. In addition to the mechanical and procedural aspects of a comprehensive trading plan, there are also intangible components that are indispensable to consistently successful trading operations. I consider these components to be intangible because they do not have direct daily connection to the physical process of trading. While other professional traders might formulate a different list or add to mine, I consider the intangibles to include:

- Intimate knowledge of trading signals
- Discipline and patience to execute trade signals consistently and correctly
- An information feedback loop to analyze trading results and determine needed course corrections
- A leap of faith—the confidence to emotionally and psychologically go "all in" on a trading plan

I have found that correctly developing these intangible attributes and components is the largest single challenge I face. It is a process that is never ending. It is in this area where successful trading must overcome the pull of human emotion. Once a trader has developed sound money management principles for a trading plan, the war is then fought on the playing field of the intangibles. Yet very few authors on speculative market operations have adequately addressed this subject area.

Intimate Knowledge of Trading Signals

I cannot imagine what it would be like to look at a chart and wonder if there was a trade setting up. What an awful experience that would be! I

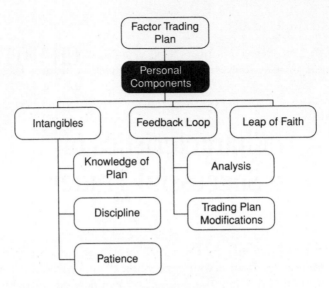

FIGURE 7.1   Characteristics of a Successful Trader.

have traded my approach long enough that I need only a brief, five-second glance at a chart to know if there is a trade pending for me.

In another 10 seconds with the same chart, I have a specific idea of what would need to happen to trigger a trading signal, what position size I would be likely to assume, and how much risk I would take if I enter.

My experience is that other professional traders—both those who use discretionary approaches and those who use systematic approaches—have the same intimate knowledge of their trading plans. They know what a signal is for them. They know if they are following their rules correctly because they know exactly what their rules are.

The longer I need to examine a chart, the less likely the market in question is offering a trading opportunity. For me, signals are patently obvious. Whether they will be profitable is another matter.

I recommend that novice traders spend a year or two paper-trading before they commit their first real dollar to risk. It takes this long to come to an understanding of what a trading signal is, how a market triggers a signal, and what type of risk management should be used.

Trading plans evolve over time—sometimes in subtle ways, other times in a more significant fashion. What might be a major change in my trading plan in my mind could appear insignificant to someone not intimately acquainted with my plan. But the point is this—traders need to understand why they make the trades they make, both entry and exit trades.

Discipline and Patience

Discipline and patience are opposite sides of the same coin. It is impossible to have trading discipline and patience if a trader does not know exactly what does or does not constitute a trading signal. Knowing what constitutes a proper trading signal precedes the practices of discipline and patience.

Whether a trade is profitable is *not* the measure of whether a trade should have been made. I cannot allow myself to be stressed out whether a certain trade was profitable or not. Profit cannot be the direct focus of my attention because I have no control over the outcome of any given trade. Order entry is the only thing I can control.

I know exactly what a trade is or is not for me. My challenge is to maintain the patience to wait for my pitch and the discipline to swing when my pitch is offered. Swinging at pitches outside of my sweet spot is the single biggest source of trouble for me. Of course, swinging at a pitch in my sweet spot is no guarantee that I will get a hit. Inevitably, trades in which patience and discipline were not key ingredients in the decision-making process have a far greater propensity to be losers.

Analysis of Self and of the Trading Plan

I am constantly studying and analyzing my trading performance for two major reasons: to determine if my trading plan is in sync with the markets and to determine if I am in sync with my trading plan. The two concepts are very different, and either can represent a real problem.

A major distinction must again be made between trading correctly and trading profitably. It is possible to trade correctly and not be profitable, just as it is possible to make money during a period when the trading plan is poorly implemented.

There have been times (weeks or months) when I have traded very poorly, yet made money. There have also been times when I have executed my trading plan flawlessly and lost money. My goal is correct trading with the belief that by trading correctly over a large number of weeks, months, and trading events, I will experience net profitability with a manageable amount of asset volatility. I analyze my trading monthly, quarterly, and annually.

The first question I ask is whether my overall trading plan was in sync with the markets. I have no interest in exploring whether modified rules would have produced more profits. I am not a big fan of this type of optimization. Optimization is a fool's game. Tweaking trading rules based on the period of time just completed could come back to haunt a trader in the next period of time.

I have been a private pilot since the 1980s and have owned several aircraft over the years. Airplanes have an instrument called the vertical speed indicator. This instrument measures the rate of climb or descent the plane has already experienced, and thus is a trailing indicator.

Flying according to the vertical speed indicator would result in an airplane always being behind the curve. When I think of optimization, I often think of the vertical speed indicator on an airplane. The past is the past. What was optimum in one quarter may not be optimum during the next quarter.

Yet I am interested if the markets reveal any change of behavior that could have permanence. No approach to trading can be built and then left alone perpetually. All successful trading approaches are the result of constant evolution based on changing trading conditions.

Over the years, my trading plan has evolved to address certain aspects of market behavior. For example, chart patterns are less reliable today than they were 20 or 30 years ago. Pattern breakouts—even when valid—tend to be sloppier than in distant years. The price objectives of patterns are far less reliable today than when I started trading the charts.

So I have made modifications to my trading approach based on general trends dealing with market behavior. But I have no interest in modifying my approach to optimize last month's or last quarter's results.

The second and far more important question I ask is whether my actual trading was in sync with my trading plan. Or, as is always the case to some degree, whether I cheated the trading plan. Traders who use a purely mechanical system can answer this question very easily. But I am a discretionary trader who adds complex layers of judgment to my trading decisions. I have developed measures—or rather a set of questions—to gauge whether my actual trading was out of sync with my overall strategy. These nine questions include:

1. How many trades did I make during the period? If I make more than 16 to 18 trades in a month, I know that I am reading too much into the charts and accepting patterns that are too short in duration. If I trade fewer than 10 to 12 times in a month, I know that I am becoming gun shy and need to adopt a less defensive posture.
2. How did the total number of trades distribute over the categories of trade types?
3. Will all of the trades made, whether profitable or not, stand the test of historical scrutiny? Will the trades, both the entries and exits, stand out on a chart a year from now as logical and reasonable?
4. Was each pattern I traded one of the four or five best examples of classical charting principles in the markets traded during the previous 12 months? Or did I accept a lesser chart pattern?

5. Did I enter any orders intrasession, or were the vast majority of my trading decisions made and orders entered during nontrading hours (late afternoon)?
6. Was I too quick to move protective stop orders with the goal of protecting open profits? I have found that trading decisions should be ruled by market behavior, not by equity fluctuations.
7. What percentage of my trades was profitable? What proportion were "bottom liners?"
8. What was my average risk per trade? If the average risk was outside of the band of six-tenths of 1 percent on the low end and 1 percent on the high end, what would have been my trade result if the leverage of all trades had been normalized at four-fifths of 1 percent?
9. Are there any broad money or trade management rule rules that I need to watch in the future for possible modification?

Every successful trader I know has developed criteria for appraising trading performance. My own criteria cannot be and should not be the criteria used by other traders. The point I am making is that every successful trader must have mechanisms in place for accountability and improvement.

I am a classical chartist. I have defined my trading signals in fairly precise terms (length and nature of specific pattern in question). I can easily look back in hindsight and identify the actions I should have taken. The major question for me is how closely my real-time trading was to what the markets offered. I can never perfectly make this subjective appraisal, but I have developed some metrics for analyzing my trading on this basis.

I also study my trading on a quarterly and annual basis in terms of how well I implemented my trading risk management and trade management components. I conduct some statistical analysis on these factors.

There is one more aspect to the self-appraisal of trading that is worthy of a special note. Making foolish mistakes can become a self-perpetuating cycle. One foolish trading mistake can produce the next mistake, and on and on it can go. A trader needs to learn the practice of self-forgiveness for stupid market maneuvers. This is especially true for discretionary traders as opposed to systematic traders because a discretionary trading plan has more room for emotional decision making. A time may come when a discretionary trader feels like he is being pulled into a cycle of poor judgment calls. When this happens (not if it happens), a trader needs to take a hiatus from the markets. Remember, there will be trades next month and next quarter and next year.

It Takes a Leap of Faith

The final component is the most difficult for novice traders, as well as for professional traders. This component deals with the confidence to take a leap of faith and become committed to predetermined trading operations.

I have heard many traders describe trading in the language of war, expressing various trading concepts in combative terms. My own experience is that trading is much more analogous to professional sports. Professional athletes speak openly and honestly about their need to make a commitment to their endeavors. How often have you heard an announcer make a statement such as, "The athlete was in his or her zone," "the athlete was playing with confidence, or "the athlete was too timid on that pitch (that jump, that race, etc.)"?

Perhaps you are a trader who has carefully thought through all of the trading components and contingencies for a trading plan, but have a sense of self-doubt or lack of confidence that prevents you from making a full commitment to your trading operations. Just as cancer and heart disease are the two major killers in America (together accounting for half of all deaths), doubt and second-guessing are the two major killers of a sound trading plan.

This last component, the leap of faith, is perhaps the component that is the biggest ongoing struggle for novice and professional traders alike. I would be lying if I suggested that I have it all together in this area. The leap of faith has been defined by other traders as the upstream swim against human nature. And indeed it is!

Every experienced trader knows when he or she commits a trading sin. I know instinctively when I swing at a pitch outside of my strike zone. Yet the ability to control one's emotions is the final hurdle a trader must clear.

Traders must daily endure the human emotions of fear, second-guessing, greed, false hopes, self-doubt, etc. I must focus and keep myself in a frame of mind where implementing my game plan is all that really matters the result—of the last trade or brief series of trades is irrelevant. It is easy to trust a trading plan when the last 10 trades have been profitable. But being committed to a trading plan when the past 10 trades were losses is a horse of an entirely different color.

When I have been whipped around over a series of trades, every fiber of my being wants to bypass the next signal. When I have had a series of trades turn from a profit to a loss, I have an overwhelming urge to subsequently find an excuse for taking the first small profit the markets offer up.

The emotional drive of fear and greed attempt to constantly move me away from my "best practices." If you struggle with this aspect of your trading, you are not alone.

Points to Remember

The Factor Trading Plan consists of three major components, each with important subcomponents:

Preliminary Components
- A personality and temperament consistent with speculative markets
- Adequate capitalization
- Overall risk management philosophy and principles

Trading Components
- A method to identify candidate trades
- Guidelines and rules for entering trades
- A framework for managing the risk in each trade
- Procedures for determining how to take losses or profits

Personal and Character Components
- The intangibles of intimacy with the trading plan, discipline and patience
- An information feedback process for analyzing results and making course corrections
- The leap of faith

A Five-Month Trading Diary: Let the Journey Begin

Part III is a day-by-day, week-by-week, trade-by trade, emotion-by-emotion, victory-by-victory, and loss-by-loss account of my trading from December 2009 through April 2010. The time frame and dates are arbitrary and chosen to represent a typical trading period. I begin the trading period without having any idea whether I will be profitable.

Chapters 8 through 12 are the "month chapters"; each represents a different month of trading. I comment on trades in the order they are entered, on the fly, in real time. And when I trade a specific market more than once, I compare the entries and exits.

I attempt to explain why I enter trades, how I manage trades, and what I think about trades after the fact. I skip describing some trades if the comments and lessons for the trades are redundant. However, a record of all signals is shown in Appendix A.

I think by journaling. I have maintained a journal of my trading endeavors since 1981. Writing helps my mind become engaged in the trading process. I will add journal entries, as they are interesting, revealing, or educational. My journal entries may deal with trading techniques, possible trades, challenges with my trading plan, the uphill climb against my emotions, or other interesting tidbits. I analyze my trading at the end of each month and quarter and I will include excerpts from each analysis.

My major challenge as a trader is to translate the components of the Factor Trading Plan into real-time trading operations. I believe that every professional trader knows exactly what it is that he must do to maximize success. Doing it becomes the hurdle.

The criterion for a valid trading signal (as differentiated from a profitable trade) is whether each entry and exit, when plotted on a graph, can withstand scrutiny after the fact. Recognizing chart configurations on completed charts after the fact is a lot different than trading charts in real time.

Bringing these two time dimensions—clearly seeing the patterns after the fact and responding in the present—into sync is the challenge. I cannot allow myself to read too much into any given chart at any given time. I need to allow charts time to fully mature.

My measure of success, or lack of the same, will be due in large part to whether my trading rules and guidelines are in sync with the markets. No trading approach is perfect, and markets and trading approaches get out of sync. What counts is whether I execute my trading rules and guidelines correctly.

For each trade, I will cite the following items:

- The market being traded
- The category of trade (from Chapter 5)
  - Major pattern (breakout signal)
  - Major pattern (anticipatory signal or early entry)
  - Major pattern (pyramid signal, a continuation pattern in an ongoing move)
  - Minor reversal or continuation signal—patterns on daily charts without confirmation from weekly graphs
  - Instinct trade
  - Miscellaneous trade (driven largely by short-term momentum or other factors). These trades largely respond to what chart pattern might develop as opposed to chart patterns that have already been completed.
- The pattern identified
- The exit rule used (from Chapters 3 and 5)
  - Last Day Rule (or Last Hour Rule)
  - Retest Failure Rule
  - Trailing Stop Rule
  - Target
  - Intervening pattern—one that resets the Last Day Rule or indicates a reversal of trend
  - Other

I will also include a chart or two of each completed trade with notations as appropriate.

Do I have any expectations as I begin this process? Well, yes! Remember, I am a conservative trader—the leverage I use today is one-third the leverage I used during most of my trading career. I am far more risk averse than I was in decades past. The exact leverage I use on any given trade will depend on the degree of confidence I have with a specific signal and on the risk inherent in how the breakout occurs.

Remember, the Factor Trading Plan is not designed to turn $10,000 into a million. My goal is a consistent double-digit annual rate of return with limited capital volatility. During tough periods, I scale my leverage back even further. I increase my leverage (or "gearing," as some foreign traders call it) when the markets start to click. I am sure that experienced Las Vegas gamblers would tell me I do it the wrong way around—that I should leverage up through a string of bad trades and leverage down during a profitable period.

The trading leverage used by the Factor Trading Plan is very conservative. Many readers may be shocked at the limited leverage I employ. As a trader, I think in terms of units of $100,000. I refer to each unit of $100,000 throughout the journal as a *trading unit*. Leverage, or number of contracts, is expressed in relationship to the $100,000 trading unit.

For example, I may state that I bought or sold one-half of a contract per trading unit. This would equate to one contract for each $200,000. In the forex markets, the reference will be to the leverage taken in the trade. If I state that I shorted 35,000 GBP/USD per trading unit, this means that I went short 35,000 pounds per $100,000 of trading capital.

I will be in hog heaven if I achieve a rate of return of 10 to 15 percent during the next five months. If the markets do not cooperate, or if I poorly implement my game plan, then keeping my capital intact may be the best I can expect.

A significant concern as I start this real-time trading diary experience is that I trade best when I remain detached from the markets. I have the tendency to overread the charts if I am too close to intraday price behavior.

Writing this book may force me into much closer contact with the markets than I would prefer. I wonder how this could affect my ability to exercise my craft, but it will give me an opportunity to share my emotional journey as well as my trading experiences.

With a plan in place and my worries laid bare, let the games begin!

CHAPTER 8

Month One

December 2009

I entered December 2009 quite frustrated by my trading performance during the previous two months. October and especially November were beastly months for me. There are just certain times during a year when I cannot buy a good trade.

Consider this awful fact: Of a series of 27 trades during October and November, 24 were liquidated at a loss and only three at a profit. (However, I did carry a number of profitable open trades into December.) Being profitable on only 9 percent of trading events is well beyond a statistical aberration. Yet, being wrong on 90 percent of my closed trades resulted in a trading loss of only a few percent of my capital. Over the history of my trading, I have been profitable in approximately one-third of trading events.

If you are unacquainted with futures trading, you may be shocked that I expect to be right only one-third of the time. After all, shouldn't a trade have at least a 50/50 chance of making money? Remember, I use relatively tight protective stops. I generally enter trades that offer $3 for every $1 risk. With a $3 to $1 risk/reward ratio, the 50/50 probability does not apply.

Additionally, over any smaller series of trading events, I could be profitable in as few as 10 to 20 percent of trades. A statistical formula dealing with a random distribution of sequential profits or losses for a trading approach with a 33/66 percent long-term win/loss ratio can determine the odds of encountering an extended losing or winning streak. The probability data can be plotted on a bell curve or distribution table.

Being wrong on 91 percent of trades over a series of 27 trading events reaches the outer extreme of a bell curve distribution. The standard deviation of this occurrence is quite extraordinary. But it is explainable. The reason is that the distribution of profitable and unprofitable commodity and forex trades in a data set is not random in the way coin tosses or dice rolls are random. Dice and coins do not have emotions. Traders do!

My recent losing streak included some self-defeating trading practices, which skewed the statistical probability of randomized results. Getting spooked by markets can lead to defensive trading practices that can prolong a trading drawdown. So, how exactly does this work?

The hardest trades to emotionally execute for a discretionary trader—trades for which every cell in a trader's body screams to avoid—are often the best trades. In contrast, trades that are emotionally easy to execute are often trades consistent with the conventional wisdom of the market-place. Conventional wisdom is usually wrong. During a losing streak, a discretionary trader (as opposed to a systematic trader) can revert, at least subconsciously, to those trades that seem safe. Nearly every losing trade during the recent string developed an immediate profit. From time to time over the years, I have toyed with the idea of grabbing a quick $500 to $1,000 per contract profit and walking away from trades.

The analysis of my trading in October and November (not shown in this book) revealed too many trading events. I had become too short term in my market analysis and was overreaching for trades that I should not have taken.

Excessive market activity on my part is normally linked to three types of trading events:

1. Too many major pattern anticipatory signals in an attempt to pre-position for a major breakout that may never occur. Weekly chart patterns can take a long time to come to fruition. I tend to exercise an itchy trigger finger to get involved when I see a weekly pattern developing.
2. Too many minor pattern signals—accepting patterns of lesser quality. The question I should always ask when looking at a minor pattern is: "Is the daily pattern I am considering one of the best two or three minor daily chart patterns in this market in the past year?" If the answer is no, then I should skip the trade. As a reminder, a minor signal in my approach is a chart configuration visible only on the daily graph without confirmation of any sort from weekly chart developments. As a general rule, a minor signal should be a minimum of four to eight weeks in duration for a continuation chart pattern and eight to 10 weeks in duration for a reversal chart pattern.
3. Lesser standards on major pattern pyramid signals within an ongoing major trend. I become too eager to pyramid a profitable trade.

These three types of trading events can synergistically lead to a temporary lack of confidence in my trading plan.

My attitude coming into December was that I needed to be choosier about the patterns I would trade. Instead of identifying 18 to 20 or so trades monthly, I needed to reduce the number of new trading events to around 13 to 15.

There is one other consideration I was taking into account. December is often a tough month for trading. Large traders are reluctant to press their advantage on positions as they face the holiday period. Volume begins to dry up in mid-December. Holiday markets are notorious for running stops on both sides of the market in thin trading conditions. This is an important fact because I normally enter and exit trades using stop orders.

This was the backdrop for the beginning of this book. I was thinking to myself: "Oh great, I am starting the trading diary right in the middle of my worst trading spell in quite some time. And I am starting the diary in a month that has given me fits over the years. Wonderful!"

Trading Record

During December, I entered 13 new trading events in 12 different markets. Two trades were carried as open positions into January.

EUR/USD: The First Trade of the Diary Period

Signal Type: **Major Completion Signal**

Throughout November and December I had watched the euro/U.S. dollar (EUR/USD) with an interest toward the short side. In fact, I had been whipped around in two attempts to get short, one in early November and then again in mid-November. Figure 8.1 shows that the market had developed a trend line from the March 2009 low. Normally, I do not trade trend-line violations. Trend lines fall into a category of chart development I called *diagonal patterns.* Yet, the more a market tests a trend line, the more valid—and tradable—an eventual violation becomes, especially if a recognizable pattern occurs prior to the trend-line violation.

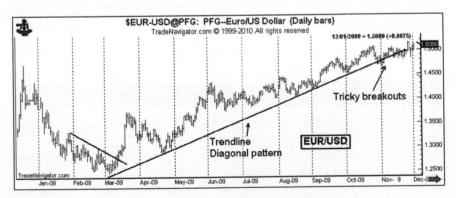

FIGURE 8.1 **A Major Trend Line with False Breakouts in EUR/USD.**

Finally, a tradable top began to form. The advance on November 25 and 26 into new highs quickly failed and had the earmarks of a bull trap. The market broke hard on November 27 and then retested the bear-trap highs. Now I had four chart developments that supported a trade, as seen in Figure 8.2:

1. A bull-trap.
2. The potential for a decisive penetration of the dominant trend line.
3. A trading channel from July to provide a price target. A market completing a channel can be reasonably expected to move the width of the channel in the opposite direction.
4. A secondary and lower channel from the November low.

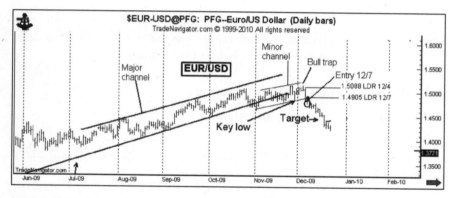

FIGURE 8.2   A Bear Market Begins in EUR/USD.

The major signal breakout came on December 7 with the penetration of the November 27 low. This marked the first trade made for the diary. The high of December 7 became the Last Day Rule, but I chose to risk the trade to above the December 4 high. My position was short 35,000 EUR/USD per trading unit of $100,000 for a risk of about 1 percent of assets. I could have taken twice the leverage if I had chosen to use the actual Last Day Rule stop from December 7.

The target was reached at 1.4446 on December 17.

Looking Back

In hindsight, I realize that this was just the first leg down in a massive bear trend. I leave money on the table by taking profits at targets. I am not out to pick tops and bottoms. In a sense, I play my game between the 30-yard lines, not from goal line to goal line.

GBP/USD: An H&S Top Stutters, Then Is Completed

Signal Types: **Two Minor Reversal Signals**

By late November, I was considering the possibility that the GBP/USD was forming a massive double top dating back to mid-May 2009. I often refer to a double top as an *M* top. The October low was the midpoint low. There was a real potential for a Best Dressed List trade in the GBP. The decline on December 9 completed a seven-week H&S top pattern. I thought the pattern could launch the move to complete the double top.

I shorted 50,000 GBP/USD per trading unit on December 9, using that day's high as the Last Day Rule. Unfortunately, this protective stop was hit on December 16 near the high of the day (see Figure 8.3).

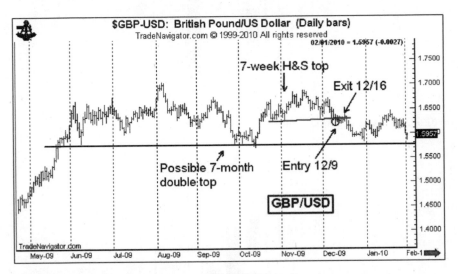

FIGURE 8.3 A Potential Double Top in GBP/USD.

The December 16 high proved to be the high of the rally. The market immediately turned lower without me. Such is life! It happens! Sometimes the market gives me another opportunity to get back in; sometimes it doesn't. In this case, it did, and there is a lesson in it.

I know just enough about candlestick charts to be dangerous. While I believe knowledge of weekly candlesticks could help my trading, I am a high/low/close bar chartist and have not taken the time to adequately delve into the study of candlestick patterns.

There is one candlestick pattern I do follow, the hikkake, thanks to a good friend and fellow chart trader, Dan Chesler (an independent market strategist based in south Florida; Chesler Analytics, www.chesler.us). Dan alerts me to hikkake patterns in markets he knows I am trading. I have no interest in a hikkake in any market I am not trading or looking to trade.

The hikkake is a failed inside-bar pattern. The inside bar is a candlestick formation that occurs when a day's candle range is inside the range of the previous day. In the case of a hikkake sell signal, the inside day is followed by one to two days of advances above the high of the inside day, followed by a decline back below the low of the inside day. See Figures 8.4 and 8.5 for examples of the bear and bull hikkake patterns.

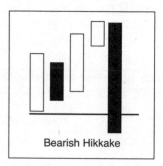

Bearish Hikkake

FIGURE 8.4   **A Bear Hikkake Pattern.**

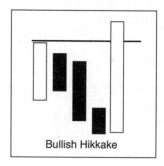

Bullish Hikkake

FIGURE 8.5   **A Bull Hikkake Pattern.**

I am most interested when a hikkake occurs consistent with my overall viewpoint and trading strategy in a particular market. So, as I was getting stopped out of GBP on December 16, I knew that a hikkake sell signal was possible.

The decline on December 17 sprung the hikkake and recompleted the H&S pattern, confirming each other. I reentered the short side of the market

(40,000 GBP per trading unit), using the December 17 high as the new Last Day Rule (see Figure 8.6).

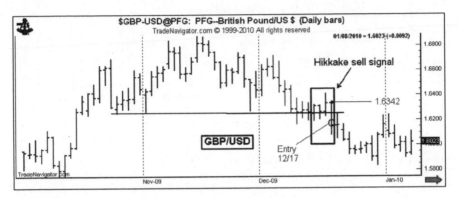

FIGURE 8.6   A Bear Hikkake in GBP/USD Confirms the H&S Top.

This stop-out and reentry brings up an interesting point. Was it painful to resell the market 160 points lower than where I covered shorts just one trading day earlier? In some ways, the answer is "yes"; in other ways; the answer is "no"—"yes" in that it is never fun to lose a 160-point opportunity profit in a market, "no" in that the Last Day Rule has been my most dependable chart-based money management technique over the years.

In hindsight, we can see that the hikkake did its thing. But what if the market had not completed the hikkake, but instead traded strongly higher? I would have felt like a fool if I had overridden the Last Day Rule and yielded instead to the possibility of a hikkake. Remember, the hikkake is not foolproof. A study of any chart can yield multiple examples of hikkake patterns that failed.

There is another dimension to this discussion. I viewed the two trades in GBP/USD as separate trades, each subject to its own rules and guidelines, yet part of a continuous campaign to be short GBP/USD. From the standpoint of my trading rules and guidelines, it was irrelevant that the two trades were only a day apart.

The target of the second GBP trade was 1.5668. I covered the short position on December 30, without a good reason other than emotional nervousness (see Figure 8.7).

In the end, my Trailing Stop Rule would have been triggered on December 31, the Last Day Rule on January 14. It is an exception when I end up for the better by overruling my trading guidelines and rules as happened with this trade.

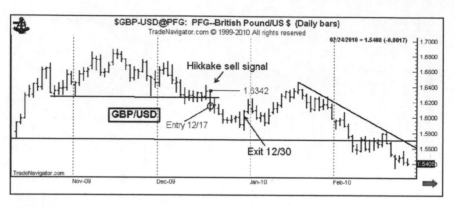

FIGURE 8.7   Taking a Small Profit in the GBP/USD.

Trading Spot Forex Markets

I started out my career trading foreign currency markets through futures contracts at the International Monetary Market (IMM; part of the Chicago Mercantile Exchange). By the mid-1980s, I began trading the spot interbank or dealer market rather than futures contracts. I prefer the spot market for many of the reasons identified in the table on the pros and cons of each trading vehicle shown below. Though it is not within the scope of this book to provide educational background on currency trading, there are pros and cons to both markets (see following list). Understanding them can shed light on the trades described in this chapter.

The IMM quotes and trades currency pairs in a consistent manner. All the major pairs at the IMM are expressed as the price of the foreign currency in U.S. dollars. For example, at the present time the pound is at $1.5985, the Swiss franc at $0.9681, the yen at $0.010906 (slightly more than a penny), the euro at $1.4356, and the Canadian dollar at $0.9625. In each case, the symbol would be expressed as the foreign currency unit divided by USD—GBP/USD, EUR/USD, CHF (Swiss)/USD, CAD/USD, JPY/USD.

Quoting and trading currency pairs in the spot market can be more complicated. In some cases, the pairs are traded similar to the IMM, such as the GBP/USD and EUR/USD. However, in other cases, the spot market trades the inverse (or reciprocal) expression of the IMM price.

For example, in the spot market, the Canadian dollar is expressed as the number of Canadian dollars per USD, or USD/CAD. USD/CAD is the reciprocal of CAD/USD. Saying that the CAD is worth $0.9625

Trading Spot Forex Markets (*Continued*)

TABLE 8.1   Dealer Spot vs. IMM Futures

Item	Dealer/Interbank Spot	IMM Futures
Variety of forex pairs	Advantage spot; major and minor currency units in all combinations	Only major currency units, mostly in combination with the USD
Funds protected	Only by faith and credit of individual dealer	By the IMM's clearing firm
Quotes and trading	Each dealer and trading platform can have slightly different bids and offers	Standardized, a single market
Size of trading units	Flexible	Standardized
Volume, liquidity, hours of trading	Advantage spot	
Regulatory oversight	Commodity Futures Trading Commission (CFTC)/National Futures Association (NFA) has become involved	NFA/CFTC
Margin requirements (or leverage)	Approximately equivalent	Approximately equivalent
Trade settlement	Several days for interest and roll charges to catch up to trade	Same day

(symbol is CAD/USD) is the same thing as saying there are 1.0390 CADs per USD (symbol is USD/CAD).

The formula for conversion from USD/CAD to CAD/USD and back is simple (1 divided by 0.9625 equals 1.0390; or 1 divided by 1.0390 equals 0.9625). As the price of USD/CAD goes up, the price of CAD/USD goes down by the reciprocal value. If I thought the USD was going to gain in value on the CAD, I could either go long the spot USD/CAD or go short CAD/USD at the IMM.

Futures traders interested in trading the spot forex market should be aware of one important thing. Not all spot forex dealers and brokers are equal. There is one huge difference, and futures traders know the difference by the words *skid* and *slippage*. Skid occurs when a stop order is filled at a worse price.

(*Continued*)

Trading Spot Forex Markets (*Continued*)

There are some forex brokers who nearly always fill stops on the nose with little or no slippage. Huge skid can occur with other forex brokers. I believe that the brokers and dealers who impose skid on traders are ripping them off. The forex markets are the most liquid markets in the world. There should never be much skid. Skid occurs as a profit center for the forex brokers in question. Forex dealers who rip off their speculative clients know who they are. I know who you are. I am not naming names, although I could. You are abusing small speculators. Shame on you! Stop it! You are already imposing huge bid/offer spreads on speculative clients—learn to be satisfied earning the bid/offer spread!

March Sugar: A Four-Month Channel Is Resolved

Signal Type: **Major Breakout Signal**

Next up was my best trade of the month, and one of my better trades in all of 2009—in fact, a member of 2009's Best Dressed List.

I had been frustrated from August through early December, expecting another thrust higher in sugar based on the monthly chart. In fact, I experienced four losing trades during this time period as I attempted to get pre-positioned for a run to the stars.

The market finally completed a three-month-plus major signal breakout of a continuation channel on December 11. If you look at Figure 8.8 carefully, you will see that the final four weeks of this channel developed an H&S bottom pattern.

FIGURE 8.8   Sugar Breaks Out of a Four-Month Channel and One-Month H&S Bottom.

As usual with valid breakouts, the Last Day Rule was never threatened. I took a position of one contract per trading unit of $100,000 for a risk of about eight-tenths of 1 percent (0.8 percent). I should have had more guts to assume more leverage—and I knew it at the time.

I got bumped out of half my position (one-half contract per trading unit) on December 22 based on the Trailing Stop Rule, and covered the remainder of the position on December 28 at the pattern target of 2736.

Looking Back

I took a couple more shots at this market during January 2010 before the market eventually topped. In 2009, sugar was my single most profitable market. It is not unusual for a market that causes me fits for a year or two to become highly profitable at some point, just as it not unusual for a market that is highly profitable one year to become a source of trading losses the next. It is important for chart traders to remember that we do not trade markets—we trade chart patterns. The labeling on the chart is unimportant.

March Cotton: A Pattern to Trade Too Small to Trade

***Signal Type:* Miscellaneous Trade**

This next trade was a great example of allowing my emotions to dictate decisions when I am missing a big trend. Cotton was in a strong trend, and every day I saw it going higher.

I used the excuse of a three-week pennant to go long on December 14. I moved my stop in relationship to the retest on December 18 and was stopped out on December 22 with the Retest Failure Rule (see Figure 8.9).

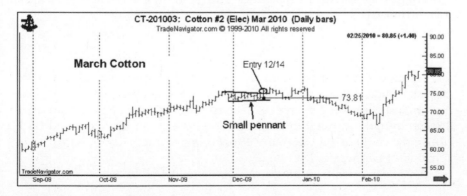

FIGURE 8.9 An Emotional Trade in Cotton.

The results are seldom good when I find an excuse to get aboard a market I have missed from an earlier trading signal.

March Soybean Oil: A Case of Getting Whipped in Both Directions

Signal Types: **Major Breakout Signal and Instinct Trade**

The gap up on November 16 completed a triangle bottom in March Soybean Oil. I should have gone long on November 16, or on November 24 or November 27 when the triangle was retested. I just did not step up to the plate. Had the market gone straight up, I would have kicked myself for missing a great trade. But, finally, I went long at the December 15 retest of this triangle, believing that the market would not close the November 16 gap (see Figure 8.10).

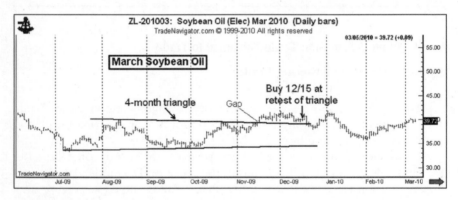

FIGURE 8.10   A Breakout of a Symmetrical Triangle in Soybean Oil Lacks Follow-Through.

As shown in Figure 8.11, on December 17 I was stopped out when the market completed a four-week H&S top pattern. I also went short. This short was an instinct trade. A four-week pattern is not enough of a chart structure for me to trade. I exited the short position when the market closed back above the neckline on December 28. Zero for two in soybean oil trades in a matter of two weeks.

My leverage on both trades was seven-tenths of a contract per trading unit.

FIGURE 8.11 A Small H&S Top Reverses the Bottom in Soybean Oil.

AUD/USD: Selling the Breakout and Then Selling the Retest of an H&S Top

Signal Type: **Two Major Breakout Signals**

The 10-week H&S top in the AUD/USD was a possible candidate for the Best Dressed List. The only problem I had with the trade was that the right shoulder low consisted of a one-day spike. Yet I go by the general rule that "function should follow form."

I shorted the market on December 16, actually leading the breakout by a day. My leverage was 45,000 AUD per trading unit. I exited the market on December 28 for a small profit based on the Trailing Stop Rule. See Figure 8.12.

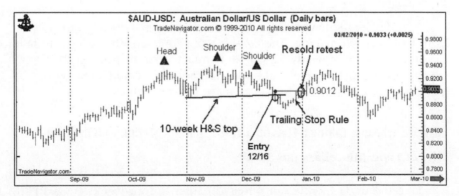

FIGURE 8.12 A Failed H&S Top in AUD/USD.

Then I reestablished my short at the retest on December 31, only to be stopped out on January 4 using the original Last Day Rule.

March DAX: Riding a Winner into a Loser

Signal Type: **Major Breakout Signal**

On December 16 the March Deutscher Aktien Index (DAX) completed a textbook ascending triangle. The market faltered for the next two days but did not violate the Last Day Rule at 5810. Then, on December 21, it appeared as if the DAX would take a run for the roses. My leverage was one-half contract per trading unit.

As shown in Figure 8.13, the breakout proved to be an end-around. I was stopped out at the Last Day Rule on January 21. The Trailing Stop Rule would have let me out of the trade on January 15, but I got stubborn.

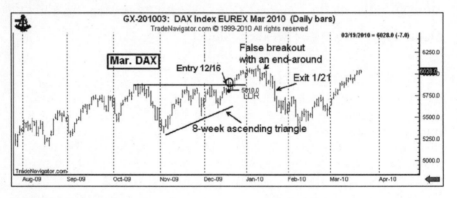

FIGURE 8.13   An Ascending Triangle in DAX with an End-Around Move.

A trade like the DAX creates agony and makes me question my trading plan and decision making. The DAX is a big contract; I had an open trade profit in the trade of nearly $2,800 per contract. Then the market did a slow and agonizing turn. I gave it all back, and more. Watching a market day by day do a round trip is not fun. I call these *popcorn* trades.

March Soybeans: Taking a Loss on a Trade, but Not Staying with the Idea

Signal Type: **Miscellaneous Trade**

Like the trade in soybean oil cited earlier, a four-week reversal H&S top is not a pitch I should swing at. I went short on December 17, the day before the actual breakout. The market declined for three days, then reversed. I got stopped out on December 28 using the Last Day Rule (see Figure 8.14).

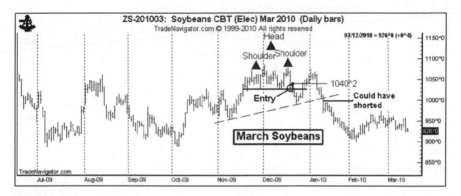

FIGURE 8.14 A Small H&S Top in Soybeans Turns into a Larger H&S Formation.

I want to use the soybean chart to make one more point about the H&S formation. It would have been tempting to have redrawn a larger H&S with the left shoulder in October and the right shoulder in early January. And, in fact, this pattern would have produced a profit without ever challenging the breakout entry. Yet I did not call this larger pattern an H&S top for two reasons, even though a profitable surge was the outcome.

First, an H&S reversal needs to reverse something. This larger pattern was just part of a broad trading range. Second, I prefer to have a more horizontal neckline and more symmetry between the height and duration of the left and right shoulders. Nevertheless, I counted this sharp decline as a missed trade.

March Mini Nasdaq: An Ascending Triangle Produces a Profitable Trade

Signal Type: **Minor Continuation Signal**

The advance on December 21 completed a three-week-plus continuation ascending triangle, putting me long one mini contract per trading unit. It was also possible to interpret this pattern as a six-week continuation inverted H&S pattern, but the left shoulder was poorly formed (see Figure 8.15).

I chose the first interpretation because it had the lesser target. The uptrend in the stock market was long overdue a correction at the time, in my opinion, so I did not want to use the more aggressive objective. The market reached its lower target on December 28.

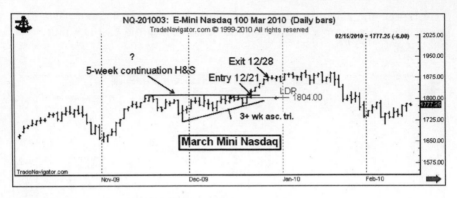

FIGURE 8.15   An Ascending Triangle in the Mini Nasdaq.

USD/CAD: A One-Day-Out-of-Line Movement

Signal Type: **Minor Reversal Signal**

I shorted the market on December 29, which proved to be a one-day-out-of-line movement. I was stopped out at the Last Day Rule on December 30 (see Figure 8.16).

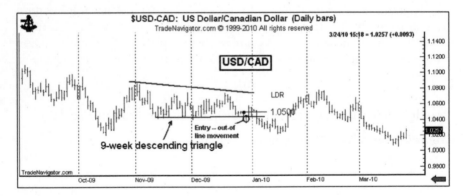

FIGURE 8.16   A Descending Triangle in USD/CAD Initially Stutters, Then Fails.

It is not a very good sign when a market closes against me the same day I put it on. My net bottom line over the years would have improved if I had exited all trades that closed against me.

Summary

There are losing trades, losing days, losing weeks, losing months, losing quarters, and, unfortunately, there can even be losing years. I have experience with all of these. December was a tough month when I consider open trade profits from the end of November that disappeared before being closed in December. But this book is covering the period from early December forward, so I will limit my specific comments to trades from this period.

Compared to the benchmarks of the Factor Trading Plan, the profile of trades opened in December is shown in Table 8.2.

TABLE 8.2   December 2009 Trading Signals by Category

Signal Category	December Entries (number and % of total)		Historic Benchmark	
Major patterns				
Completions	6	(46%)	4	(19%)
Anticipatory	0		2.5	(13%)
Pyramid	0		2.5	(13%)
Minor patterns	4	(31%)	5	(26%)
Instinct trades	1	(8%)	3	(17%)
Miscellaneous trades	2	(15%)	2.5	(13%)
Total	13	(100%)	19.5	(100%)

I do not get too concerned when the profile of trades for a single month is askew from the historical benchmark norms. I am more interested in quarterly and annual trends away from the norm.

Of the 13 trades that were opened during December, 11 were closed by the end of the year: five as profits and six as losses. This ratio exceeds the historical benchmark of only 30 to 35 percent of trades being profitable.

The fourth quarter was a tough trading environment for me. Many trades started out well, only to reverse direction and result in losses. Other times, I was too quick to advance a protective stop, only to be stopped out and have a market then go in its expected direction. It was not a great quarter for commodity trading advisors (CTAs) in general. Figure 8.17 is a graph showing the widely followed Lyxor Short-Term CTA Index.

The index was down (6.2 percent) in the fourth quarter. But from my point of view, misery does *not* like company. I must compare my performance to my own approach and not to others. It is easy after the fact to identify modifications to one's trading plan that would have done well in retrospect.

FIGURE 8.17 Lyxor Short-Term CTA Index.

Source: Lyxor Asset Management (www.lyxorhedgeindices.com/index.php).

When analyzing a concluded trading period, I draw a distinction between three aspects of the trading equation:

1. What type of markets did we have (trending or choppy)?
2. How well did my trading plan and its rules synch with what the markets offered?
3. How well did I execute the plan?

The type of markets experienced is an uncontrollable variable. There is nothing I can do to change market behavior. However, I do have some general control over my trading plan, although it is impossible to alter trading rules to optimize the results of any given trade or series of trades. I have even greater control over the degree to which I correctly execute my trading plan—or, stated in the negative, the degree to which I violate my own rules.

It is entirely conceivable that I could be more pleased with my trading during an unprofitable period in which I faithfully implement a predetermined game plan than with my trading during a profitable period in which I mismanage some trades and do not fully exploit other signals.

Trades established in December, when closed, produced a profit of 1.5 percent. Some of these profits were closed in January. On a Value Added Monthly Index (VAMI) marked-to-the market basis, my trading performance for December was up .04 percent.

A complete trade-by-trade record for this book can be found in Appendix A.

CHAPTER 9

Month Two

January 2010

I am really glad the fourth quarter of 2009 is now history. I can start a new year. I traded only proprietary capital during the first nine months of 2009. My proprietary account was profitable in 2009 due primarily to trades in Sugar and Gold. I discontinued implementing the full Factor Trading Plan for proprietary capital to make ready for trading a commodity pool account, of which I would be a major stakeholder. The pool took a long time to get going but was finally functioning in October 2009, just in time for a drawdown. The fourth quarter served up an ample portion of humble pie. I have never developed a taste for humble pie and seriously doubt I ever will. The taste is bitter.

Drawdowns are a way of life for a trader. Periods of capital drawdown bring about tremendous introspection. When trading is going well, it is easy to think trading will never get bad again. When trading goes sour, it is difficult to remember the profitable times.

I have experienced significant drawdowns during each of the 17 years I traded proprietary funds as my full-time occupation. (I quit trading for a few years to pursue some non-profit endeavors). Table 9.1 is a rank order of my worst drawdowns through the years.

My point is that trading is not an easy endeavor or everyone would be doing it. Trading is tough work. All of the drawdowns listed were from years when I was much more risk tolerant and traded significantly greater leverage. The current Factor Trading Plan is a carbon copy of previous years in terms of entry signals and exit strategies, but leverage that has been reduced by two-thirds. Cutting leverage by this magnitude reduces the risk of large drawdowns, but it also minimizes upside potential. I have lived through drawdowns before, and I will live through them again in the future.

TABLE 9.1   Factor LLC's Worst Drawdowns

Period	Peak-to-Valley Drawdown, Month Ending*	Duration in Months from Peak to Valley
Dec. 1981–Mar. 1982	(33.7%)	4
Apr. 1986–July 1986	(32.2%)	4
Sept. 1987–Apr. 1988	(27.2%)	8
July 1982	(26.3%)	1
Mar. 1985–June 1985	(21.1%)	4
Mar. 2008–May 2008	(19.7%)	3
Jan. 2007–Mar. 2007	(19.5%)	3
Dec. 1983–Feb. 1984	(18.2%)	3
July 1988–Dec. 1988	(15.4%)	6
July. 1984–Oct. 1984	(12.9%)	2
Aug. 1985	(11.8%)	1
Apr. 1989	(11.6%)	1

*The data above represent actual proprietary trading performance. The leverage currently being employed by the Factor Trading Plan is one-third of that used prior to October 2009. The Author's Note at the end of this book contains the disclosure statements related to the past performance of Factor LLC.

Identifying Trading Opportunities

I like to start the new calendar year by identifying trades I believe offer tremendous opportunity for profits in the upcoming months. For 2010, I chose six: short British pound/U.S. dollar (GBP/USD), short Standard & Poor's (S&Ps), short T-bonds, long gold, and long sugar. We may see how right I am by the end of the book.

GBP/USD: Still Building a Major Double Top

The dominant pattern in this market remains the seven-month double top on the weekly graph (see Figure 9.1). A decisive close below 1.5600 would complete this formation and establish an objective of 1.440, with a further possibility of reaching the 2009 low at 1.3500. I feel certain that this will be a Best Dressed move in 2010—the question is whether my trading rules will be in sync with the decline.

S&P 500: A Breakout of the Channel Is Coming Soon

The U.S. stock market has experienced a near-historic bull run from the March 2009 low. There are some signs that the market rally is getting short

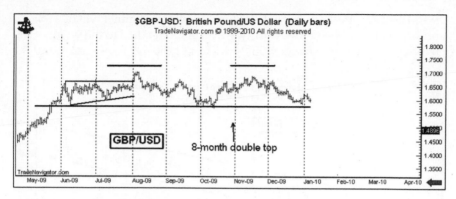

FIGURE 9.1   Possible Eight-Month Double Top in GBP/USD.

of breath. As shown in Figure 9.2, the market exhibits a six-month channel. Prices have been unable to test the upper range of this channel, a sign that momentum is being lost.

FIGURE 9.2   Six-Month Channel and Three-Month Wedge in S&Ps.

Most recently, the market is coiling into a two-month rising wedge, a bearish pattern. The rising wedge is characteristic of a countertrend rally. The targets for this market, pending a downside breakout, are 1030, then 980.

30-Year T-Bonds: A Bear Market in the Making in Every Time Frame

How do you spell *sovereign default?* The longer-term charts in the U.S. T-bond market look like a catastrophe waiting to happen. Three charts are presented. First, in Figure 9.3A, the quarterly chart dating back to the early

1980s displays a trading channel. At some point, this channel will be violated and prices should then move downward an amount equal to the width of the channel. The probable target would be a test of the 1994 lows at around 80.

FIGURE 9.3A   Multidecade Channel in T-Bonds.

Figure 9.3B is a weekly continuation chart of the bonds. This chart displays a 29-month H&S pattern. As this pattern unfolds, prices move closer and closer to the lower boundary of the dominant quarterly chart channel. At this time, the right shoulder appears to lack symmetry with the left shoulder. The right shoulder would be of equal length to the left shoulder in March or April 2010. I anticipate a top in late March.

FIGURE 9.3B   Two-Year H&S Top on the Weekly T-Bond Chart.

Finally, Figure 9.3C shows that the right shoulder of the weekly H&S top could itself be a possible complex H&S pattern on the daily chart. All that is needed is a right shoulder rally not to exceed 121 followed by the penetration of the neckline.

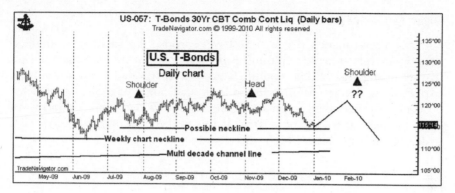

FIGURE 9.3C   Possible Six-Month H&S Top on the Daily T-Bond Chart.

This market is set up for cascading chart events. The H&S on the daily chart could launch the H&S on the weekly chart, which could launch the completion of the channel on the quarterly chart. T-bonds, in my opinion, offer the best opportunity to make $25,000 to $30,000 per contract during the next two years. But timing is everything. If a trader is right on direction, but wrong on timing, then the trader is wrong period.

Gold: The Bull Market Has Room to Go

A version of Figure 9.4 is displayed in figure 6.10 in chapter six. The advance in October 2009 completed an inverted H&S bottom pattern on the weekly and monthly gold charts. This pattern has an unmet objective of 1350.

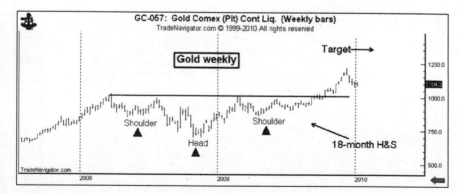

FIGURE 9.4   Inverted Continuation H&S Bottom Pattern in Gold.

Sugar: Quarterly Chart Indicates 60 Cents

Sugar is a wild market that can and will surprise the smartest of traders. This boom-to-bust market epitomizes the term *popcorn rally*. While the bull market in sugar as of this writing (January 5, 2010) could end when least expected, the longest-term charts indicate that Sugar has the potential for 60 cents. The monthly graph in Figure 9.5 shows the entire period from 1981 through 2009 as a base area. If this is the case, sugar could easily make new all-time record high prices.

FIGURE 9.5   28-Year Base on the Monthly Sugar Chart.

Dow Jones Industrials: A Multigenerational Top in the Making?

This is my "pie-in-the-sky" chart. While quarterly and annual charts are not practical for tactical trading decisions, they do make good fun in creating crazy price predictions. Figure 9.6 is a semilog quarterly chart of the Dow

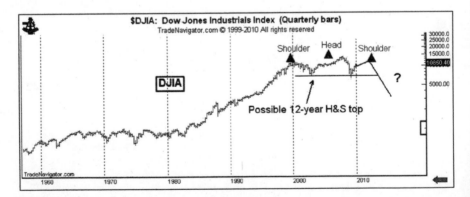

FIGURE 9.6   A Possible 12-Year Top in the DJIA.

going back decades. I can't help but notice the possible H&S top. If this interpretation is correct, the market is presently in the right shoulder rally. Symmetry would be achieved by a rally in the Dow Jones Industrial Average (DJIA) to around 11,750 with a right shoulder high sometime in 2013, plus or minus a year. At Dow 11,500, I would not want to own a single stock. This chart is being presented just for fun—for now.

Amending the Plan

After some serious soul searching over fourth quarter 2009 trading activity and performance, I am making a strategic tweak in the Factor Trading Plan. The change deals with the number of trading events I will enter each month.

My goal is to raise the bar on the criteria a chart pattern must meet in order to be considered for a trading signal, thereby imposing upon myself the need for increased discipline and patience.

I have previously discussed in this book a weakness I realize in my own trading—the tendency to jump the gun on patterns rather than allowing charts to become fully mature before assuming a trade. Table 9.2 presents the profile of the amended Factor Trading Plan.

TABLE 9.2 Amended Factor Trading Plan

Signal Category	Preexisting Benchmarks	Amended Benchmarks
Major patterns		
Completions	4.0	4.0 (29%)
Anticipatory	2.5	1.5 (11%)
Pyramid	2.5	1.5 (11%)
Minor patterns	5.0	4.0 (28%)
Instinct trades	3.0	2.0 (14%)
Miscellaneous trades	2.5	1.0 (7%)
Total	19.5	14.0 (100%)

As mentioned, I have absolutely no control over whether a particular trade or series of trades will produce a profit. Trade profitability is not a controllable factor. I have control only over my order flow and risk parameters. There is no way I can will myself to be more profitable. I can control only those elements that are controllable. The modifications I am making to my trading plan deal with the frequency and criteria of signals.

There is one other factor of my trading in recent months that I need to address besides signal criteria. My average risk per trade since October has been one-half of 1 percent of trading capital. This is lower than I would like and lower than what is called for by the risk management framework of my trading plan.

I could increase my risk per trading event in one of two ways: (1) I could widen my initial protective stop and maintain my leverage, or (2) I could increase my leverage or gearing (number of contracts per unit of capital) and maintain the existing methods to determine the initial protective stop.

I have always been satisfied with the Last Day Rule as a risk management tool. So the solution, in my opinion, is to increase leverage or number of contracts per unit of capital. However, I will not do this until I can put together a month or two of solid performance. I want to increase leverage with the market's money, not with my own. I am a believer in pressing an advantage with profits, not with base capital.

It was with this amended plan that I began trading in January.

Trading Record

July Sugar: A Running Wedge Quickly Falters

Signal Style: **Major Breakout Signal**

I had successfully traded the bull market in sugar since April 2009 (although I had losing trades along the way). I believed sugar had a long way to go. In fact, in the back of my mind, I thought sugar could challenge its all-time highs in the 60-cent range. Thus, I was monitoring sugar for buying opportunities.

On January 4, July sugar advanced to complete a two-week-pluls running wedge pattern. This advance also confirmed the four-month rectangle that had been developing since early September. I bought one contract per trading unit, risking six-tenths of 1 percent.

The small running wedge had formed at the upper ice line of the rectangle. Often, these smaller patterns propel prices out of larger patterns. However, as shown in Figure 9.7, the advance quickly stalled, and on January 11 the decline triggered the Last Day Rule stop.

March Corn: Jumping the Gun on a Pattern

Signal Type: **Minor Continuation Signal**

This trade is a wonderful example of playing breakouts too tightly. Breakouts should be decisive in order to be valid. Drawing tight pattern boundary lines is an invitation to get sucked into a false or premature

FIGURE 9.7   Running Wedge Confirms a Rectangle in Sugar.

breakout. I committed this trading sin in this corn trade. My risk on the trade was six-tenths of 1 percent.

Where a boundary line is drawn can make the difference between no trade and a losing trade. Figure 9.8 shows that I had the boundary line drawn with a slight downward angle to define the 10-week triangle in corn. I went long on a marginal breakout of the triangle only to be stopped out within a couple of hours. My entry buy stop was only one penny above the October and November highs. I needed to make the market do a better job of proving itself.

FIGURE 9.8   One-Day Fake-Out in Corn.

Figure 9.9 shows the boundary line drawn horizontally. A breakout needs to be decisive, even if it means that a larger risk per contract must be taken from the point of entry. No breakout took place with a horizontal boundary.

FIGURE 9.9   A Slightly Different Look at the Same Corn Chart.

Looking Back

In hindsight, I allowed my bias in favor of a bull market in corn to dictate my trade. I was too eager to be long corn. As a trader, I need to constantly remind myself that I cannot afford the luxury of being bullish or bearish. Bullishness and bearishness represent an emotional commitment. I need to limit myself to positions. Opinions don't matter. Positions speak for themselves.

I committed another trading sin in this trade. As a general rule, pattern breakouts in markets such as the grains, softs, and livestock should not be trusted if they occur during the nighttime electronic session. I discussed this subject in Chapter 5 in the section on trade order management. The marginal breakout in corn was driven a price spike in the overnight electronic market. Even though my entry buy stop was too tight to the market, it would not have been filled had I entered it only in the day session hours.

USD/JPY: A Rising Wedge Wears Me Out

Signal Type: **Minor Reversal Signal**

For several years I had been monitoring the yen, believing that the U.S. dollar was destined for a huge bear move. This bias originates from the massive descending triangle on the monthly graph, confirmed in October 2008 (see Figure 9.10). This pattern, if valid, has an eventual target of 60 to 65 yen per U.S. dollar. Thus, I have been predisposed toward sell signals in the currency pair. This predisposition was based on a sound technical overview, not on a love affair with the yen.

FIGURE 9.10   12-Year Descending Triangle in USD/JPY.

The decline on January 12, as shown in Figure 9.11, completed a five-week reversal rising wedge on the daily chart. I established a position of short $30,000 per trading unit. I was stopped out of the position on February 3 based on the Trailing Stop Rule.

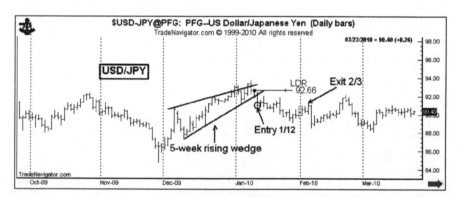

FIGURE 9.11   Five-Week Rising Wedge in USD/JPY.

March Mini Nasdaq: Short-Term Pattern Leads to Immediate Loss

***Signal Style:* Miscellaneous Trade**

I had a successful long trade the March Mini Nasdaq in December. Yet my bias was that stocks were grossly overvalued and that a bear market was just a matter of time. Forcing my bias, on January 12, I established a short position (one contract per trading unit) based on an interpretation of a two-week broadening top (see Figure 9.12). My trading plan does not allow for trading minor reversal patterns less than 8 to 10 weeks in duration. I was stopped out of the position the next day based on the Last Day Rule.

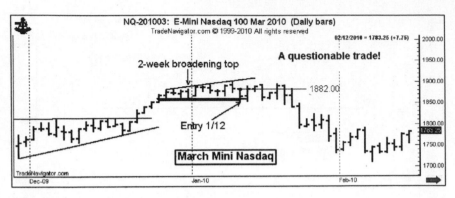

FIGURE 9.12   Small Two-Week Broadening Pattern in Nasdaq.

Looking Back

This was an example of a signal that did not really make sense at the time of the trade, much less in retrospect. I felt at the time that the stock market needed to go down. It is possible to allow a bias to dictate the analysis of a chart. There is a fine line between identifying legitimate patterns in alignment with a bias and making up patterns to support a bias.

The Importance of Pattern Interpretation

At this point in the book, you are probably asking yourself such questions as:

- When does a pattern become a pattern?
- Isn't pattern identification purely subjective?
- What happens if chartists see the same chart differently?

In my opinion, these questions just do not matter. Trade identification is the least important of all trading components. The trading process itself and risk management are much more crucial components to overall success in trading operations. No two successful traders select trades in exactly the same way. There is a wide range of methods used by professional traders to identify what is and is not a trading signal in their trading operations. So I am not terribly concerned if some of my interpretations are not right on. My trading success, in the long run, does not depend on my ability to read the charts perfectly.

March T-Bonds: A Retest of a Double Top Ignores the Ice Line

Signal Types: **Major Breakout Signal, Retest**

On December 12, the T-bond market completed a four-month double top. I missed the signal and shorted the retest on January 13, stopping myself out on January 15 using the Retest Failure Rule (see Figure 9.13).

FIGURE 9.13   T-Bonds Unsuccessfully Retest a Four-Month Double Top.

As a general rule, it is not the most profitable practice to buy or sell pattern retests several weeks after the fact. The most profitable trades are those that breakout and never look back.

March Corn: A Classic Breakaway Gap

Signal Type: **Major Breakout Signal**

The vast majority of price gaps are pattern gaps—gaps that occur within a trading range that are covered or filled in a matter of days or weeks. But, traders should always consider gaps through major boundary lines to be potential breakaway gaps. Legitimate breakaway gaps do not get filled, at least not until a meaningful trend has been completed. Importantly, the gap completion of a pattern is a significant development from a classical charting perspective. Patterns that are completed with unfilled gaps often far exceed the implied price objectives.

On January 13, the corn market experienced a very large gap (8 cents) to complete a 12-week triangle. I did not have an entry stop in place at the time because I did imagine this development. I shorted the market on January 14 when the market retested the ice line.

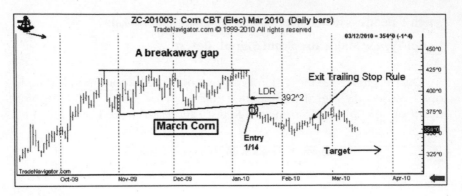

FIGURE 9.14   A Breakaway Gap Completes a Top in Corn.

In the case of such gaps, the Last Day Rule becomes the closing price preceding the gap, as shown in Figure 9.14.

I was stopped out of the trade on February 16 based on the Trailing Stop Rule.

Looking Back

I should have maintained the Last Day Rule Stop on the corn trade. Completions of large patterns are not soon violated. The Trailing Stop Rule does not allow an important pattern breakout to work itself out. (Corn eventually reached the downside target of the 12-week triangle.)

March Wheat: A Symmetrical H&S Pattern

Signal type: Major Breakout Signal

One day after corn broke out, the March wheat completed a classic 13-week H&S top (see Figure 9.15). The primary features of this top are that the right and left shoulders are very balanced or symmetrical in duration and in height. Similar to corn, I was too quick to jam my stops based on the Trailing Stop Rule. (The H&S target was reached and greatly exceeded in June 2010.)

The Trailing Stop Rule historically has been an excellent money management tool, but in the past year the rule has taken me out of trades too

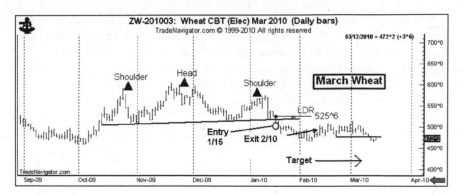

FIGURE 9.15   A Classic H&S Top Pattern in Chicago Wheat.

early. I am considering a modification of the rule to disengage it until a market has moved further toward its implied target. I may have more to say on this subject as the book continues.

EUR/JPY: A Small H&S Top Launches a Major Top

Signal Type: **Major Anticipatory Signal and Major Breakout Signal**

In recent months, I had monitored the ongoing development of a large rounding top on the weekly EUR/JPY chart, as shown in Figure 9.16. I had been hoping that the market would form a small pattern to allow an early entry.

FIGURE 9.16   Rounding Top on the Weekly EUR/JPY Chart.

Figure 9.17 shows that the decline on January 15 completed a small H&S top on the daily chart. I have stated that I should not take small patterns. This is true for stand-alone minor signals, but not for opportunities late in the development of weekly patterns. The Factor Trading Plan allows for the use of shorter patterns to establish an anticipatory position. My position was 30,000 euros per trading unit.

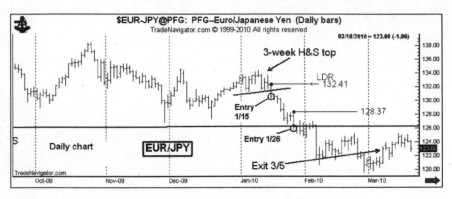

FIGURE 9.17 The Late Stages of the Rounding Top in EUR/JPY.

The target of this trade was a test of the neckline on the weekly chart. The target was reached on January 21. I took profits. In situations like this, I will occasionally stay with an anticipatory position to determine if a major breakout signal occurs. I elected not to wait in this case.

On January 26, the ice line of the 10-month rounding top or complex H&S gave way, and I once again shorted the market.

My leverage was light (20,000 euros per trading unit) because the Last Day Rule was more than 200 pips away from the entry. I exited the trade on March 5 based on the Trailing Stop Rule.

I hope you are picking up a pattern from my January trades in corn, wheat, EUR/JPY, and others; namely, I have gotten into the bad trading habit of jamming my protective stops too quickly. Bad trading practices can emerge subtly and with seemingly good reason (to protect profits in this case). I need to deal with this going forward.

Looking Back

Trading dilemmas never end. A trader never solves all the issues standing in the way of greater success. It seems as though when one dilemma is resolved, another dilemna takes its place.

March Mini S&Ps: Mismanaging a Short Position

Signal Types: **Two Major Breakout Signals**

I traded the March Mini S&Ps twice during the remainder of January.

I had been monitoring a possible three-month rising wedge. As is sometimes the case, the lower boundary of this wedge extended backward connected perfectly with an important low (the March 2009 low).

On January 19, I shorted the market when prices sliced through the lower intraday boundary. However, this first thrust out of the pattern was premature, and I was stopped out of the trade the same day (see Figure 9.18).

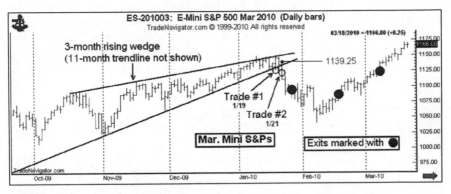

FIGURE 9.18   Three-Month Rising Wedge in S&Ps Produces Sell Signals.

The market confirmed a downside breakout on January 21, and I took a more leveraged than normal position (1.5 contracts per trading unit). My risk was 1.2 percent of capital, in excess of my trading guidelines. My thinking at the time was that this trade would start 2010 in grand fashion. In fact, I thought the trade had the potential to be a "seven percenter" (7 percent rate of return on equity). At last, the great bull market of 2009 was over—or so I thought.

I took a one-third profit on January 26 at the initial target of 1086. My next target was 1010 and I thought the market would reach it quickly. I was stopped out of the next one-third on February 16 based on the Trailing Stop Rule. It is embarrassing to admit that I rode the final one-third all the way back to the starting gate and was stopped out on March 5. This portion of the position represented a popcorn trade—a round tripper.

Looking Back

The January 19 trade in the S&Ps was a legitimate attempt to short the market, although untimely. The entry would have stood the test of historical scrutiny if the market had continued to fall following the January 19 breakout. The measure of a good trade (as opposed to a profitable trade) is if the chart supports it after the fact.

May Sugar: Correctly Managing a Pyramid Trade

Signal Type: Major Pyramid Signal

I was not quite done with the opinion that sugar was destined for 60 cents. On January 19, the May contract completed a small pennant. I went long. Small continuation patterns within a major trend can be very profitable to trade. I exited the trade on February 3 when the market closed below its dominant bull trend line. February 3 also fulfilled the Trailing Stop Rule (see Figure 9.19).

FIGURE 9.19　An Eight-Day Pennant in Sugar.

The Importance of Volume

Edwards and Magee make a very big deal about volume. In fact, they insist that certain volume characteristics are necessary to confirm the completion of a chart pattern.

There are a couple of reasons why I have basically ignored the subject of volume up to this point in the book.

The Importance of Volume (*Continued*)

First, volume figures are not even available in the forex markets. I trade more forex than anything else.

Second, I do not believe that volume is as important in commodity futures as it is in the stock market. Volume in stocks is always relative to the total number of shares outstanding. So volume in stocks is a significant measure relative to the total ownership base or float.

Futures contracts do not have a fixed number of shares or contracts outstanding against which the volume on any given day or week can be compared. Open interest (the number of contracts open representing an equal number of long and short holders) has no limitation. The open interest for each futures contract created (e.g., July 2011 corn) starts at zero and ends at zero when the contract expires.

Other commodity traders have studied the implications of volume and open interest. I have chosen to ignore these factors in my trading.

April and June Gold: Three Months of Chart Redefinition

Signal Types: **Instinct Trade, Minor Reversal Signal, Minor Continuation Signal, and Two Minor Reversal Signals, a Major Anticipatory Signal, and a Major Breakout Signal**

Looking Back

This entry was written in early April, with the hindsight of a series of five frustrating trades that began in January. I am breaking the mold on the month-by-month format in order to track gold through a series of trading signals. The gold market from January through early April was a great example of a concept I call *market redefinition*—a process where one pattern fails and becomes part of a larger pattern and so on, until finally the market declares itself.

Following a strong and profitable trend, a market will often enter a period where false signals become the rule. Gold had a brilliant move from late October through early December 2009. I featured this trend in one of the case studies in Chapter 6.

Beginning on January 20, 2010, I began a series of frustrating trades in gold that continue to this writing (April 2010). When will it ever end! I am now into what probably will be my fifth straight frustrating trade in gold, and the year is only a few months old.

Figure 9.20 shows my first gold trade of 2010. This was an instinct trade. The chart displayed a three-week H&S reversal pattern. I liked the compactness of the pattern, even though it was small. I legged out of the trade at three different prices, gaining about $1,000 per trading unit. I considered myself lucky! I typically exit instinct trades within two to five days after entry.

FIGURE 9.20   A Three-Week H&S Top in Gold.

The next trade, as displayed in Figure 9.21, was the minor reversal completion of a nine-week descending triangle on February 4. I really thought this was going to be a big winner. The market reversed the next day, and I was stopped out with the Retest Failure Rule on February 11. This pattern was large enough to be a major breakout trade, but a corresponding pattern was not visible on the weekly graph.

FIGURE 9.21   A Nine-Week Descending Triangle in Gold Fails.

Next, as shown in Figure 9.22, the advance on February 16 completed an 11-week falling wedge on the daily chart. This was a minor continuation signal. My position was one mini contract per trading unit of $100,000. I was risking a meager .4 percent. I did not have an entry stop order in place at the breakout, so I went long on February 18. Skittish about gold, I took quick profits on half my position the next day, February 19, and was stopped out of the other half on February 24 based on the Retest Failure Rule (see Figure 9.22).

FIGURE 9.22   An 11-Week Falling Wedge on the Daily Gold Chart.

The adage should be, "If at first you don't succeed, be ready to lose and lose again." I got back into the long side of gold (one mini contract per trading unit) on March 2 when the daily chart completed a nine-week inverted H&S pattern (see Figure 9.23). This minor reversal trade was short-lived. I was stopped out March 8 with the Retest Failure Rule.

FIGURE 9.23   An H&S Bottom Pattern in Gold.

On March 18, I entered into my journal a dilemma the gold market was presenting, as shown in Figure 9.24. Conflicting signals were being presented. The chart displayed a possible three-month H&S bottom dating back to mid-December, with a left shoulder low on December 22 and a right shoulder low on March 12.

FIGURE 9.24   The Gold Chart Is Set Up for a Buy or a Sell.

A bearish pattern was also emerging, in the form of a five-week H&S top. The patterns were interlocking in the sense that the head of the smaller H&S top pattern was the right shoulder high of the larger bottom pattern. Interlocking H&S patterns often produce powerful moves.

My practice is to go with whatever patterns become complete, and not to second-guess one pattern over the other. The minor H&S reversal top was completed on March 22. I went short (one mini contract per trading unit) with a risk of .1 percent of capital. I was stopped out on March 25 based on the Last Day Rule.

The best and largest patterns are commonly comprised of many smaller patterns, mostly failures. This is exactly what happened in 2009 when gold went up, went down, and went nowhere, only to provide a fantastic move in the fourth quarter. This is where we are right now in gold (April 2010). Many of these smaller patterns appear to be more significant at the time they develop than later when they become part of something much bigger. I have this reality built into the Factor Trading Plan by anticipating the need to trade 45 major breakout signals in order to catch 10 that really work.

At last I think I have a handle on the market. Figure 9.25 displays a 15-week inverted H&S bottom formation. On April 1, the advance sliced through a possible four-week channel serving as the right shoulder of a four-month inverted H&S bottom pattern. I established a long on April 1 of one mini contract per trading unit.

. The H&S bottom was completed on April 7. I added to my position using the Last Day Rule at 1133.1 as the basis for the stop on my entire position. This four-month H&S has a target of 1230, a test of the December high.

FIGURE 9.25 An H&S Bottom in Gold Resolves Previous Uncertainty.

The objective of 1350 remains from the October 2009 completion of the inverted weekly chart H&S (presented in the Case Study section). Time will tell if this will finally be the pattern that works, or if this pattern, too, will become part of something bigger. I will report on the outcome of this trade in Chapter 12.

GBP/JPY: A Small Triangle Established the Final High of a Larger Triangle

Signal Type: **Major Anticipatory Signal**

Figure 9.26 displays a textbook example of the type of signal for which I seek to become pre-positioned during the late stages of a major chart

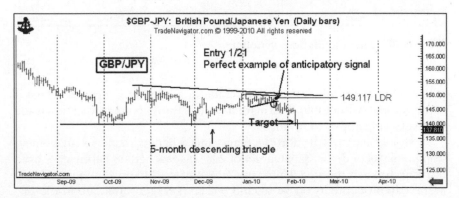

FIGURE 9.26 A Possible Descending Triangle Forms in GBP/JPY.

pattern. Dating back to late September, the GBP/JPY had formed a possible right-angled descending triangle.

On January 21, the market completed a three-week symmetrical triangle. As is often the case, a small daily chart pattern formed at the tail end of a major weekly chart pattern. The target of the trade was the lower boundary of the major descending triangle. I took profits at the target on February 4.

March Copper: A Small Horn and Trend-Line Violation Are Quickly Reversed

Signal Types: **Major Breakout Signal, Miscellaneous Trade**

The decline on January 27, as seen in Figure 9.27, completed a three-week horn or sloping top. While this was a relatively short pattern, the decline also sliced through a 10-month channel boundary. This qualified the signal for consideration to the 2010 Best Dressed List. The risk was substantial, so I traded only one contract per $400,000 of capital.

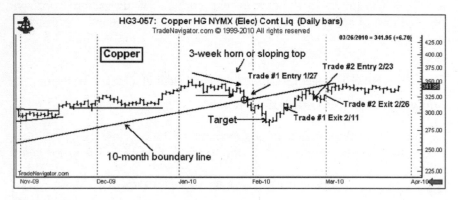

FIGURE 9.27   Three-Month Horn in Copper.

This was a terribly mismanaged trade in a number of respects. First, I had a strong instinct that this market would thrust hard to the downside with very little ability to bounce.

I should have used more leverage and a tighter money management stop point. Second, the initial target of 290 was reached on February 4. I did not ring the cash register! Third, the Trailing Stop Rule was triggered early in the day on February 11 at around 302.20. I waited until late in the day and covered at 311.60.

I have emphasized in this book that the profit or loss of a trade tells only a small part of the story. It is possible to execute a trade poorly and make money. Similarly, it is possible to execute a trade well and lose money. The copper trade was an example of the former. I made 12 cents on the first trade, but walked away in defeat.

This market situation is also an example of how one misstep can easily lead to the next misstep. Errors have a way of becoming compounded. It is easy for a trader to think that a particular market owes him or her something. Markets owe us nothing!

My mismanagement of the initial copper trade led to the next misstep in the market. After being stopped out, I watched the market continue to rally. On February 19, the market retested the boundary of the major trend line that had been clearly violated on January 28.

On February 22 and 23, the market turned back down. I sold the close on February 23 (trade #2). This was an emotional trade. I was still thinking that the copper market owed me money because I had left so much on the table from the earlier trade.

Sanity returned, and within a day or two I realized that the February 23 short was not the smartest trade. I have found that mistakes should be covered immediately. No questions asked! I exited the trade on February 26.

GBP/USD: Using a Candlestick Pattern to Make a Trade

Signal Type: **Minor Continuation Signal**

I was bearish on GBP/USD throughout January based on the potential double top on the weekly chart. I wanted to be short. On January 29, I shorted 30,000 British pounds per trading unit. I entered the trade based on the hikkake setup on January 27 and 28 (see Figure 9.28).

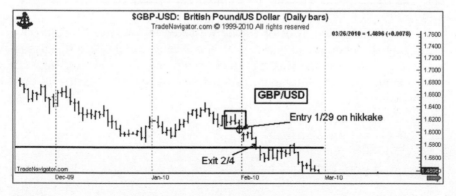

FIGURE 9.28   Another Hikkake Pattern in GBP/USD.

Hikkake patterns do not provide specific price targets. I took profits on February 4, believing that the ice line of the double top would provide support. I also knew that if the ice line gave way, I could immediately return to a short position.

Chapter 10 will pick back up the saga of the GBP/USD.

Summary

Financially, I had a pretty decent January, the best month in a while. I entered 16 trades in 11 different markets. When closed (not all in January), 10 of the trades were profitable, producing a profit of 6.3 percent. Actual performance in January, reported in compliance with marked-to-the-market Value Added Monthly Index (VAMI) guidelines, was a positive 6.8 percent.

Table 9.3 compares the 16 entry signals against the amended benchmark goals of the Factor Trading Plan.

TABLE 9.3   January Trading Signals by Category

Signal Category	Amended Benchmarks		January Trade Entries (# and % of total)	
Major patterns				
Completions	4.0	(29%)	8.0	(50%)
Anticipatory	1.5	(11%)	2.0	(19%)
Pyramid	1.5	(11%)	1.0	(0%)
Minor patterns	4.0	(28%)	3.0	(19%)
Instinct trades	2.0	(14%)	1.0	(6%)
Miscellaneous trades	1.0	(7%)	1.0	(6%)
Total	14.0	(100%)	16.0	(100%)

I felt I had made a lot of rookie mistakes in January. It could have been a much better month than it was. Specifically, I took some signals that were too short term and was too quick in moving my protective stops on trades launched from substantial patterns, such as was the case with corn and wheat.

Month Three

February 2010

I enter February after having a good month in January. Not a great month, but quite acceptable. I will take a 6 percent-plus month any time, But I should emphasize that my historical trading performance has been comprised more of quick bursts followed by long pauses than by annuity-type returns.

The distribution of the Factor Trading Plan's monthly returns dating back to 1981 is shown in Figure 10.1. The leverage I currently employ is about one-third of the leverage I traded prior to 2009, so the monthly returns have been adjusted on a pro forma basis. One would logically expect a distribution of a large number of monthly returns to resemble a traditional bell curve, higher in the middle with down-sloping tails on each end.

My guess is that most professional managers in the commodity and forex markets have their peak number of months in the 0 to plus 4 percent columns and do not have an extended tail into the 20 percent-plus zone. In contrast, the Factor Trading Plan has its peak in the 0 to minus 2 percent column, with almost 30 percent of the months represented. The important implication of my monthly performance distribution is the need for a long dragon tail to the right. I need the 8 percent-plus months to achieve long-term profitability. In fact, 12 percent of the trading months have produced a rate of return (ROR) of 8 percent-plus.

Sticking to the Plan in Choppy Markets

The optimum success of the Factor Trading Plan depends on three conditions:

1. That the majority of commodity and forex markets do *not* enter prolonged periods of choppiness. I define choppiness as either congestion

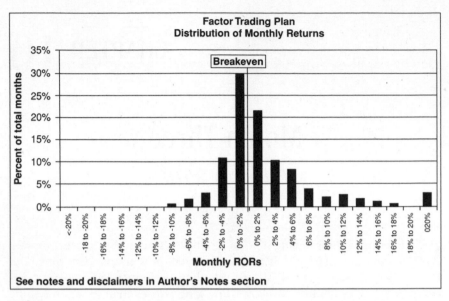

FIGURE 10.1 Factor Trading Plan Proprietary performance: Bell Curve of Monthly Results.

or an advancing or declining trend where the waves experience overlap with the previous waves.

2. That a certain proportion of trades (perhaps 25 to 30 percent) will experience pattern breakouts that will not reach an implied price target, but will at least have some immediate follow through.

3. That a certain proportion of trades (perhaps 15 percent) will trend uninterruptedly to an implied target.

The commodity and forex markets (with a few exceptions) have been in broad and choppy trading ranges for the past nine months. I hate buying high and selling low repeatedly within broad trading ranges. This is perhaps my worst fear as a trader. I dread getting whipped around in an area of congestion. I covered this matter in Chapter 9 in the section dealing with gold.

Whenever I enter a trade, I have the expectation that the market will trend and not return to its previous period of choppiness. So I have the constant tension of whether a market breaking out of a chart pattern will trend to a target or simply redefine an area of price congestion.

There is a fine line between allowing a market room to run and protecting profits. It is my desire to give a market every opportunity to reach a target. It is also my desire to avoid popcorn trades. Is there any easy way to

> ## The Roadblock to Successful Trading Is Not the Markets!
>
> Many novice traders falsely believe that the battle to profitability is with the markets. Or with other traders! I hate to be the bearer of bad news, but the battle to consistent profitability is won or lost in a trader's head and gut. The battle to profitability is with one's self. Successful trading is learning what to do and how to do it and then overcoming one's emotions to get "it" done (discovering the "it" is the challenge for traders, and the "it" is different for everyone).
>
> There is a very fine edge between consistent profitability and unprofitability. To be consistently profitable, I must overcome the markets' drive to throw me off my game plan. The markets challenge every fiber of a trader's intellectual, emotional, psychological, physical, and spiritual being. In the end, though, it is not a trader's battle with the markets that determines outcome. It is one's battle to overcome those human character traits that interfere with consistent patience and discipline.

balance these two scenarios? Unfortunately, I have not found the solution. But I keep working at it—34 years after starting my futures market career. Perhaps people a lot smarter than I have figured out a way to handle the dilemma.

Trading Record

During February, the Factor Trading Plan triggered 16 trading signals in 12 different markets. Three of these signals were covered as part of Chapter 8, two trades in gold (entry dates February 4 and February 18) and one trade in copper (entry date February 23).

GBP/USD: The Double Top Is Finally Completed

Signal Types: **Major Breakout Signal, Major Breakout Signal (Secondary Completion), and Major Pyramid Signal**

The nine-month double top was finally completed in British pound/U.S. dollar (GBP/USD) on February 4, as shown in Figure 10.2. There was little doubt in my mind that this signal would become a featured member of

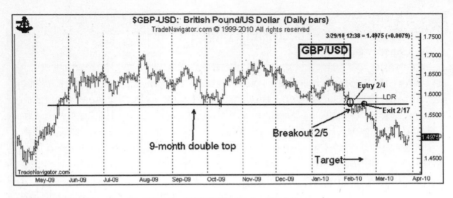

FIGURE 10.2 The Double Top in GBP/USD Picks Up Steam.

the 2010 Best Dressed List. It remained quite another matter if my trading guidelines and rules would fully exploit the move.

True double bottoms and tops are actually quite rare, according to Schabacher, Edwards, and Magee (the fathers of classical charting principles), although pundits in the financial press constantly refer to the pattern. The two major criteria of a double top (or bottom) are:

1. The peaks of the tops must be at least two months apart. In the case of the GBP/USD, the peaks were slightly more than three months apart. The two tops also must be at approximately the same height. Again, GBP/USD qualified.
2. The height between the peaks and the midpoint low must be at least 15 percent of the value of the commodity/forex pair or stock. In the case of the GBP/USD, the height was 11 percent—a little shy of the criteria. Yet I thought it was close enough to count.

I entered a short position on February 4, although the actual breakout date was February 5. I took a position of 30,000 short GBP per trading unit. The Last Day Rule for February 5 was 1.5776. I used a protective stop that was slightly higher, at 1.5806. My stop was hit on February 17, a trading day that once again knocked me out in the process of developing a bearish hikkake pattern.

Double tops are actually allowed to travel halfway back into a double top area. So, in a sense, my strict use of the ice line and Last Day Rule in the GBP/USD was wishful thinking.

I have discussed the concept of the ice line as an idealized hard-and-fast level that turns back all retest attempts. This is not true for the double top and bottom patterns.

Looking Back

At a minimum I should have used the February 4 high as my Last Day Rule. In fact, my trading rules specify that when very little of the trading range occurs within the pattern on the day of the breakout, I should revert to the previous day to determine the Last Day Rule.

The hikkake pattern plagued the GBP/USD throughout the decline from the November high. I use the word *plagued* because my trading rules do not adjust very well to the chart sequence contained in the hikkake pattern. The hikkake is just a very short-term version of my fishhook formation. Figure 10.3 displays the numerous hikkake patterns that occurred during the price drop in early 2010.

FIGURE 10.3   A Series of Hikkake Patterns in GBP/USD.

While the hikkake rally of February 17 stopped me out, the hikkake sell signal on February 18 allowed me to reestablish a short position of 40,000 British pounds per trading unit, albeit 220 pips lower than my stop-out one day earlier.

Finally, on March 24, the chart completed a three-week flag as shown in Figure 10.4. This represented a major pyramid signal. I increased my short position by 30,000 British pounds per trading unit with the Last Day Rule at 1.5049.

Continuation patterns within a major trend allow me to increase my leverage. These patterns also allow me to advance the protective stop on a core or initial position. I moved the protective stop of the short position entered on February 18 in relationship to the Last Day Rule of the short position entered on March 24. Thus, the protective stop on my entire short

GBP/USD position was set at 1.5061. This stop was hit on March 30, and I was once again flat in a market that I believe would eventually hit a much lower target.

Figure 10.4 displays the sequence of trading events in the GBP/USD during February and March again breaking the mold of the month-by-month format. Showing several months together helps show trades as part of a campaign.

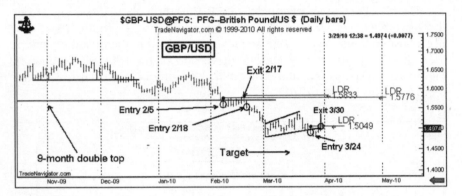

FIGURE 10.4 Completed Double Top and Three-Week Flag in GBP/USD.

This market has been frustrating for me as a trader. I have been a bear since early November and have very little to show for it relative to the size of the move we have experienced. There is always one market each year that gets into my head. This year, so far, it is the GBP.

This market alone should have been a five-percenter (return on trading capital). I was generally underleveraged in the market, and my patience was too short in giving the market the opportunity to bloom.

April Mini Crude Oil: The Problem in Trading Fan Lines

Signal Type: **Major Breakout Signal**

The fan principle was identified by Edwards and Magee as a classical charting structure. Figure 10.5 shows the fan principle in action on the crude oil weekly chart. By the way, note the H&S bottom formation at the March low.

The advance from the March low had not accelerated, but in fact had continued to violate a series of trend lines with decreasing angles of attack. This is the hallmark of the fan principle. This indicated that crude oil was losing momentum on a grand scale. In simple terms, crude oil prices were flirting with disaster.

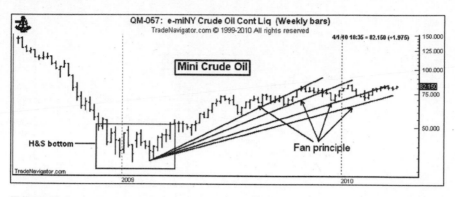

FIGURE 10.5   Fan Principle on the Weekly Crude Oil Chart.

The target of the fan principle assumes a complete retracement of the fan itself—in other words, crude oil would return to the March 2009 low. The fan principle is difficult to trade because it represents all the practical problems of trading diagonal chart boundaries.

Figure 10.6 showed one possible resolution to a pending price decline. Since October 2009, the daily continuation graph displayed a possible double top pattern with a breakout point of 69.50.

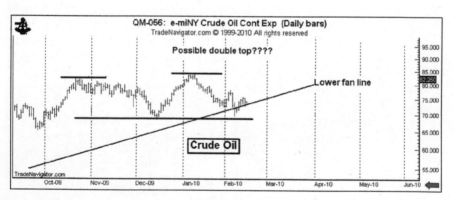

FIGURE 10.6   A Possible Double Top in Crude Oil.

Thus, my trading bias, based on the fan principle and the possibility of an double top, led me to look for shorting opportunities. As shown in Figure 10.7, the decline on February 5 penetrated the lower fan line, but prices immediately traded back above the fan boundary. On February 12, I took a shot at the short side, thinking that the retest of the fan line was failing and prices were ready to decline. I was stopped out on February 16 based on the Last Day Rule.

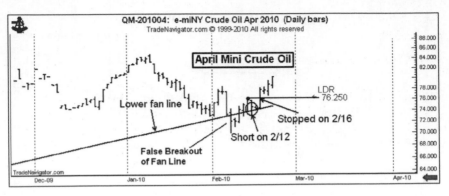

FIGURE 10.7   False Breakout of a Fan Line in Crude Oil.

The Similarities of Trading to Professional Athletics

Over the years, I have been amazed at how comments by world-class performers in all areas of human endeavor (from sports to business to the arts) are applicable to trading.

In 2009, I was watching the Wimbledon tennis match where Venus Williams slaughtered the world's number one seeded woman player at the time, Dinara Safina, by straight-set scores of 6-1 and 6-0. One of the announcers made a comment during the match that applies perfectly to the endeavor of commodity trading. The NBC announcer basically said, "It is hard enough for Safina to beat Williams when she is not even winning the fight with herself in this match."

Successful market speculation is an upstream swim against human nature. The human aspect of trading is far more important than trade identification, the subject that gets most of the attention of books, seminars, and web site trading services.

For a trader or any professional, the main battle takes place in the emotional, mental, and psychological realm.

A tennis professional knows what he or she must do to excel in a particular match (increase the speed of a second serve, or stay on the baseline more, or increase endurance for a long match). The challenge for professional traders and athletes is to prepare for and execute what needs to be done well. The battle is within.

June T-Bonds: Unsuccessful Attempt to Parlay Small Patterns into a Big Move

Signal Type: **Major Anticipatory Signal**

The quarterly, monthly, and weekly charts of the 30-year T-bond markets scream sovereign credit default. The longer-term charts of T-bonds are found in Chapter 9, Figures 9.3A–C. My long-term outlook led me to look for shorting opportunities in the T-bonds. At the time, I viewed any shorting opportunity as a major anticipatory signal. I had an interest in catching the right shoulder of the H&S top on the weekly chart.

Figure 10.8 displays two small technical developments that led me to short the T-bonds. The market formed a broadening top pattern in late January and early February. Broadening patterns are normally reversal in nature. The decline on February 17 completed a small flag. I shorted the market at the retest of the flag on February 18. I was stopped out on February 22. My leverage was 0.5 contracts per trading unit.

FIGURE 10.8 Attempting to Catch the Right Shoulder Top with Two Small Bear Patterns in T-Bonds.

Looking Back

This is one of many examples in the book showing that my interpretation of daily charts is influenced by my perspective of longer-term weekly and monthly chart patterns. Given the longer-term chart structure in T-bonds, I viewed these trades as very low-risk and high-reward opportunities. I would take trades like this every day of the week.

June 10-Year T-Notes: An Attempt to Extend the Leverage of My T-Bond Trade

***Signal Type:* Miscellaneous Trade**

At the same time the T-bonds were showing a tradable chart setup, the June 10-year T-notes formed a tiny three-week H&S top. I viewed this small pattern as a means to gain further leverage in a play toward higher interest rates (lower prices). I shorted the June T-notes on February 18 and was stopped out on February 23 based on the Last Day Rule. The pattern, as shown in Figure 10.9, was much too short.

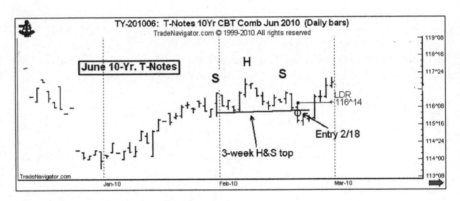

FIGURE 10.9   A Small H&S Top in T-Notes.

GBP/JPY: A Major Descending Triangle Is Completed

***Signal Type:* Major Breakout Signal**

For background and reference in this forex pair, see Figure 9.26 and the corresponding comments in Chapter 9.

The decline on February 23 penetrated the lower boundary of the five-month descending triangle in this market. Note in Figure 10.10 that the thrust down was launched from a 12-day flag in mid-February. This was a possible half-mast pattern. As such, this flag provided a target of 131.87. The target of the descending triangle was 128.10.

Following the sharp decline into the March 1 low, the market chopped higher. This lack of follow-through characterizes the choppiness of many forex pairs and commodity futures contracts at the time. Using the Trailing Stop Rule, my position was liquidated on March 12.

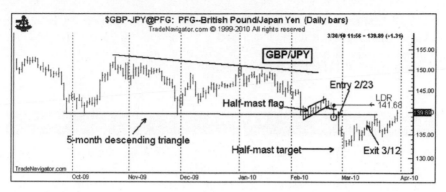

FIGURE 10.10 Five-Month Descending Triangle in GBP/JPY.

October Sugar: The Surprise Move Is Down

Signal Type: **Minor Reversal Signal**

It is difficult for me to turn on a dime. I know other traders who frequently use a "stop and reverse" strategy in their trading. This may be easy to do for mechanical systems traders, but for discretionary traders it is more of a challenge. At least it is for me.

I had been a sugar bull since early 2009. So it was with great reluctance (and extremely light leverage) that I established a minor signal short position in October sugar on February 23, based on an eight-week reversal rectangle as shown in Figure 10.11A.

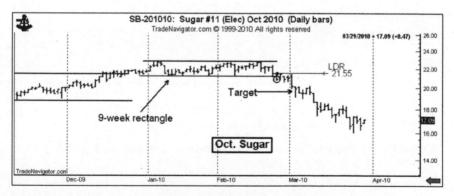

FIGURE 10.11A Rectangular Top in October Sugar.

The Last Day Rule from February 23 was almost nipped on February 24, but held fast. The market reached its minimum target on March 2. As bullish as I was on sugar for such a long time, it was ironic that *the* huge move would be the March 2010 price collapse.

Looking Back

There have been many times in my trading career when the really big move is in the opposite direction of my bias and expectation. Sugar was just such a case in 2010. I was looking for 60-cent sugar and the surprise move was down. Figure 10.11B shows the collapse in sugar. There were numerous small pyramid opportunities in this decline. I missed them all due to my predisposition toward higher prices.

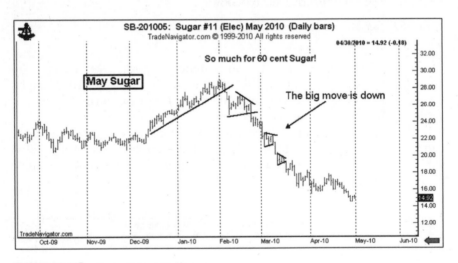

FIGURE 10.11B   Sugar Prices Collapse.

Soybean Oil—A Series of Long Trades

Signal Types: Instinct Trade, Two Minor Continuation Signals

I entered three soybean oil trades in February. As of February, the weekly soybean oil chart had displayed a possible 14-month ascending triangle, as shown by the weekly July contract chart in Figure 10.12. I entered February predisposed to be long soybean oil.

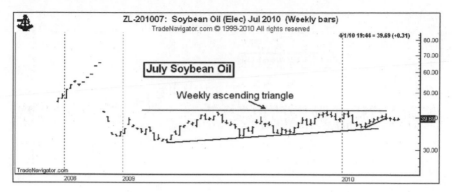

FIGURE 10.12   Weekly Soybean Oil Chart Displays Massive Triangle.

Soybean oil prices were driven unmercifully lower in January. As shown in Figure 10.13, the March contract had a series of lower highs for 19 straight days, taking prices into an area of support on the weekly graph. Often such relentless declines into an area of major support will result in "V"-type bottoms. I had an instinct that the market was ready for a strong one- to two-week rally, to be signaled by the first day with a higher high. I went long on February 2. As with most instinct trades, I look for quick profits. I exited the trade on February 10.

FIGURE 10.13   "V" Bottom in March Soybean Oil.

Then the market formed a small pennant in late February. I entered a long position (two contracts per trading unit) on February 25. This trade and the one to follow were minor continuation signals. The breakout on February 25 proved to be a one-day-out-of-line movement. The market reversed and stopped me out the same day (see Figure 10.14A).

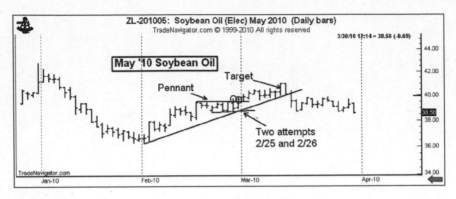

FIGURE 10.14A   Pennant in May Soybean Oil: First Breakout Fails.

How many times do I need to make the same mistake? The mistake I am referring to is entering stops for the grain markets in the overnight electronic session. The entry stop for the February 25 trade was triggered in the overnight session but would have never been triggered in the day session.

I reentered the trade on February 26—during the day session—when the pennant was once again completed. Figure 10.14B is an hourly chart showing that the day session breakout did not occur until February 26. I was looking only for a small profit. I took profits at the target of 4069 on March 10.

FIGURE 10.14B   Pennant in May Soybean Oil: Second Attempt Works.

June Mini S&Ps and June Mini Dow: Two Questionable Trades

Signal Types: **Minor Reversal Signal and Miscellaneous Trade**

My next two trades fell into the same category—trades driven more by my emotional commitment to the short side of the stock market than by sound charting principles. I think that any discretionary technical trader who says he or she is unbiased is a liar. Discretionary technical traders have a predisposition toward certain opinions and positions.

I viewed the decline from January 19 to February 5 as just the warm-up to a much larger bear trend. I also thought the rally to the February 22 high was simply a retest that took the form of a small H&S pattern. I had been stopped out of two-thirds of my short Standard & Poor's (S&P) position during the late February advance. I still held a one-third short position.

As shown in Figures 10.15 and 10.16, I interpreted the decline on February 25 as a breakout completion of small H&S top patterns in the June Mini S&P and June Mini Dow. The S&P pattern had better definition than the pattern in the Dow. I shorted both markets (one contract of each per trading unit).

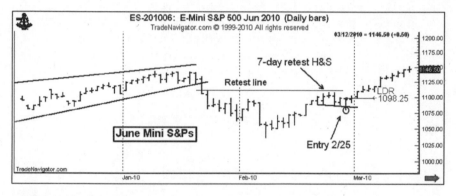

FIGURE 10.15 Small H&S Top in S&Ps Retests Larger Potential Top.

FIGURE 10.16 Dow Jones Tests Mid-January Breakdown.

Of course, the rally from the February 5 low proved to be much more than a retest, but rather another leg in a historic bull move. The head and shoulders breakout was a fishhook. I should have recognized it as a buying opportunity. I was stopped out of both positions at their respective Last Day Rules, the S&Ps on February 26 and the Dow on March 1. My combined loss for both positions was 1.3 percent of assets. On March 5, I was stopped out of the final one-third short position (from January 21) in the S&Ps.

EUR/GBP: Cashing In Quickly on a Channel Breakout

Signal Type: **Major Anticipatory Signal**

One of the advantages of the spot forex market is that I can take trades that are U.S. dollar neutral.

In mid–February, I noted that the euro/British pound (EUR/GBP) chart exhibited a possible 13-month inverted H&S bottom formation on the weekly chart, as shown in Figure 10.17. The chart indicated that the euro could trade at an 8 to 10 percent premium to the pound.

FIGURE 10.17   Possible 13-Month H&S Bottom Pattern in EUR/GBP.

The right shoulder of this pattern had taken the form of a four-month-plus channel pattern. Let me say a word about support and resistance lines, which I have completely ignored in the book until now. I do not trade support and resistance principles, and I think I am probably worse off for it. I know some excellent traders who pay much attention to support and resistance levels in their trading.

Figure 10.18 displays the channel on the daily chart, and also shows how a level of support, once broken, can become a level of resistance. Through November, December, and early January, the 0.8800 level provided support in this currency pair. The market penetrated the support on January 15. Then, in late January and through most of February, the previous level of support became a level of resistance.

FIGURE 10.18   Four-Month Channel in EUR/GBP.

Multiple confirmations of a trading signal can be very significant. The upside completion of the channel on February 25 also climbed back above the support/resistance line. The pattern target of the channel was 9002, quickly reached on March 1.

Summary

February was a nonevent. Sixteen signals were entered during the month in 11 different markets. Of the 16 trades entered, seven were closed at a profit and 10 at a loss (although not all in February)—a profit ratio of 43 percent. The distribution of trades by category was close to the amended benchmarks. The trades entered in February were closed at a gain of 0.9 percent. On a marked-to-the-market Value Added Monthly Index (VAMI) basis, February experienced an actual loss of 1.23 percent. The difference reflects the fact that the VAMI calculation marks all positions to the market at the end of a month whether the trades were carried in from previous months or not closed until later months. Table 10.1 shows the distribution of trades entered in February by signal category.

TABLE 10.1   February Trading Signals by Category

Signal Category	Amended Benchmarks		February Trade Entries (# and % of total)	
Major patterns				
Completions	4.0	(29%)	4.0	(25%)
Anticipatory	1.5	(11%)	2.0	(13%)
Pyramid	1.5	(11%)	0	(0%)
Minor patterns	4.0	(28%)	6.0	(38%)
Instinct trades	2.0	(14%)	1.0	(6%)
Miscellaneous trades	1.0	(7%)	3.0	(19%)
Total	14.0	(100%)	16.0	(100%)

February and several previous months lacked the "bottom liners" discussed in Chapter 5. About 10 percent of my trades historically have produced my net bottom line. These are the really profitable trades, each returning at least 2 percent return on capital. The remaining 90 percent of trades historically have been washes. Without the bottom liners my trading is reduced to just trades that wash each other out. Each month, the Factor Trading Plan needs a couple of really profitable trades, properly leveraged, to produce the desired results.

CHAPTER 11

Month Four
March 2010

The market is a great teacher! It also delivers chastisement in large doses. I have always known that there were flaws in the Factor Trading Plan; trading is a process of uncovering flaws and attempting to fix them . . . only to find more flaws. The Factor Trading Plan is no different than any other approach. Every consistently successful trader spends time diagnosing and applying fixes to flaws. Two steps forward, one step back! On and on it goes!

The interesting thing about the markets is that the flaws are never visible during the good months and good years. Good times provide cover for the deficiencies of a trading plan.

During tough times (i.e., drawdown periods), markets have a way of exploiting flaws in a trading plan. I know many traders who become very introspective during the drawdown periods as they attempt to figure out ways to improve their approach. The first step to improve an approach is to identify the flaws.

The challenge is to find the fundamental flaws, not just to make changes that would have optimized trading during the drawdown phase. Simulation and optimization of combinations of technical indicators is something anybody can perform with any number of trading and analysis platforms. I contend that this type of optimization produces very little lasting fruit. Trade identification, at the end of the day, is less important than risk management and the human element.

I am in a drawdown period at this point in my trading journal. Not severe, but definitely a hindrance. I don't like losing. I also don't like *not* winning. My trading plan has always emerged from prolonged periods of treading water with changes, sometimes subtle, sometimes more significant. Almost always the changes have dealt with trade and risk management, not with trade identification.

I am on the scent of some fundamental flaws in my trading approach, which will be discussed in more detail in the concluding chapters of this book.

Trading Record

I entered 16 trading events in 12 different markets during March. Three of these trades were discussed in previous chapters (two gold trades in Chapter 9 and a GBP/USD trade in Chapter 10). These trades discussed earlier will not be covered in Chapter 11.

USD/CAD: Remaining Persistent with a Pattern

***Signal Types:* Major Anticipatory Signal, Major Breakout Signal, Major Breakout Signal (Secondary Completion)**

I entered three trades in March in the U.S. dollar/Canadian dollar (USD/CAD). While each trade had its own specific rules and risk management strategy, I considered all three to be part of the same trading campaign.

Figure 11.1 displays what I saw as the dominant chart development in the forex pair, a five-month descending triangle. This pattern is a prime candidate for the 2010 Best Dressed List.

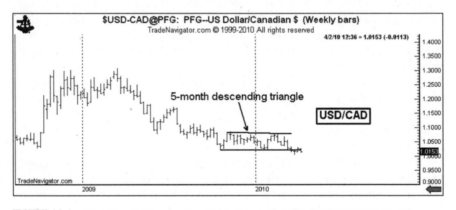

FIGURE 11.1 Five-Month Descending Triangle on the Weekly USD/CAD Graph.

Figure 11.2 shows the trades in this market on a daily chart. I shorted the market on March 3 based on what I perceived to be a triangle dating to the January low. This was a major anticipatory signal. I sold 50,000 USD/CAD per trading unit.

The decline on March 12 penetrated the lower boundary of the dominant five-month descending triangle. I shorted another 50,000 USD/CAD, increasing my total position to short 100,000 USD/CAD per trading unit. I used the Last Day Rule from March 11 to set a protective stop and subsequently lowered the stop on March 22 to 1.0256. On March 24, the market

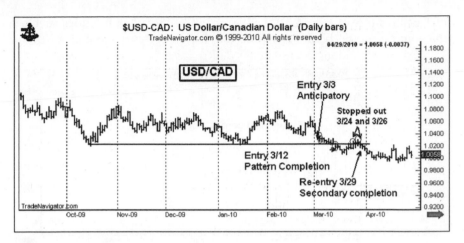

FIGURE 11.2 Descending Triangle on the Daily USD/CAD Chart.

rallied back into the descending triangle, stopping me out of half of my position. I moved the protective stop on my remaining position based on the Retest Failure Rule. I was stopped out on March 26.

I have a provision in my trading rules for reentering a position in markets that display a significant weekly chart pattern. The reentry guidelines dictate that one of two things must occur to reestablish a position:

1. The market must recomplete the pattern and penetrate the price extreme high or low established during the initial breakout. Under this criterion, the USD/CAD needed to trade below the March 19 low at 1.0062.
2. Under the second criterion, the market must recomplete the pattern on a closing price basis.

On March 29, the market closed back below the lower boundary of the dominant descending triangle. I reestablished a short position of 30,000 USD/CAD with a risk of one-half of 1 percent. The March 29 high at 1.0273 became the new Last Day Rule. (This position remained open on April 20 when the diary for this book closed.)

May Soybeans: Small Patterns Continue to Haunt Me

Signal Type: **Miscellaneous Trade**

On March 4, I shorted soybeans based on the completion of a three-week continuation H&S pattern. This trade fit into the miscellaneous category. I quickly exited the trade (on March 8), taking a loss of three-tenths of 1 percent (see Figure 11.3). (I am embarrassed to admit to trades such as this, but I want this book to provide full disclosure—warts and all.)

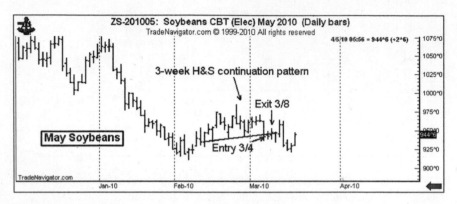

FIGURE 11.3   Three-Week H&S top in May Soybeans Quickly Fails.

May Mini Crude Oil: Rising Wedge Illustrates Difficulty with Diagonal Patterns

Signal Type: **Major Anticipatory Signal**

I have already discussed my overall bearish perspective for crude oil. The decline on March 12 completed a major pattern anticipatory sell signal in the way of a six-week rising wedge. This trade was made on a Friday, and I went home feeling like I had a real winner. On Monday, the market followed through. More confidence (see Figure 11.4)!

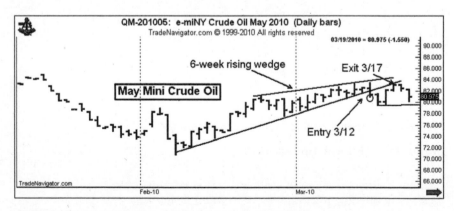

FIGURE 11.4   Six-Week Rising Wedge on Crude Oil Chart.

The textbook understanding of the rising wedge calls for a swift and un-interrupted price decline. Yet on March 16, the market reversed strongly to the upside. I jammed my stop because such a strong rally is uncharacteristic of the rising wedge pattern. I was stopped out on March 17.

AUD/CAD: A Triangle Causes Multiple Losses

***Signal Types:* Instinct Trade, Major Anticipatory Signal, Major Breakout Signal, Minor Breakout Signal**.

These were trades spanning two months, presented in this chapter to provide a context for repeated attempts to exploit a chart development.

The Australian dollar/Canadian dollar (AUD/CAD) is a textbook example of the comedy of errors that can occur when a symmetrical triangle works its way too far toward the apex. Because prices had traveled beyond two-thirds to three-fourths of the way to the apex, I should have ignored this pattern. Instead, I got whiplashed by a series of signals. This market spun me like a top.

As shown in Figure 11.5, the dominant pattern was a possible three-month symmetrical triangle. The upper boundary, when extended back in time, connected with the November high.

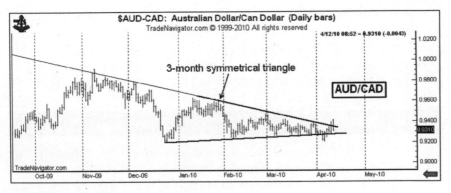

FIGURE 11.5   Sloppy Breakouts Occur with Three-Month Triangle in AUD/CAD.

Within the larger three-month triangle, a three-week triangle formed in mid-March (see Figure 11.6). I used this smaller three-week triangle to get a head start on the trade and shorted the breakout on March 19. This was an instinct trade. This thrust was short lived and the market quickly reversed, stopping me out for a day-trade loss of 0.007 percent.

The market then rallied, and on March 30 actually penetrated the upper boundary of the triangle. I viewed this as a possible bull trap. I shorted the

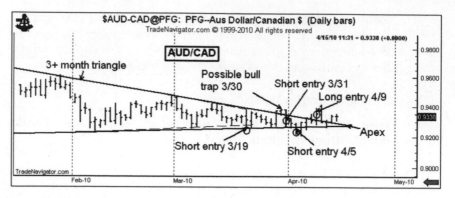

FIGURE 11.6   Daily Chart of AUD/CAD Displays Treacherous Trading Conditions.

market on March 31 when prices traded below the March 30 low. My hope was that I was getting short near the upper boundary. This was a major breakout anticipatory signal.

On April 5, the market surged through the lower boundary of the triangle, closing below the March low. This was a major completion signal. I added to the position and thought I had a great trade pending. However, the market reversed the next day and stopped me out of my entire short position on April 7.

Then, on April 9, the market rallied through the upper boundary of the triangle and penetrated the March 30 high. I thought that this was a classic "end-around" minor completion buy signal. I went long. The market reversed the very next day, April 12, and once again I was whiplashed by this forex pair. Four frustrating trades based on the same chart construction!

Looking Back

The major lesson to be learned is that triangles are not valid when prices work too far toward the apex. This does not mean that I should not attempt the first breakout, but that if the first breakout fails I need to cross the market off my pending trade list.

EUR/USD: A Classic H&S Failure Pattern

Signal Type: Minor Pattern Continuation

The EUR/USD experienced a substantial bear trend from the November high into the February low as shown in Figure 11.7.

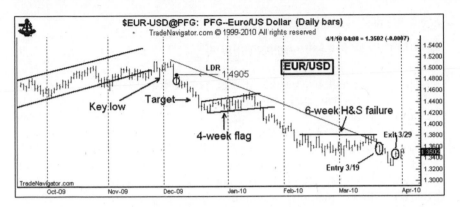

FIGURE 11.7   A Small H&S Bottom Failure Is Triggered in EUR/USD.

Figure 11.8 is a blow up of Figure 11.7. From February 5 to mid–March, the market appeared to forming a complex H&S bottom or rounding pattern. On March 12, the market nicked a 15-week trend line. I suspected a bull trap.

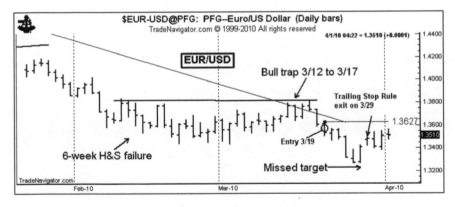

FIGURE 11.8   Bull Trap Precedes H&S Failure in EUR/USD.

I shorted the market on March 19 when the H&S failure was confirmed. I could have taken the short a day earlier on March 18. The target of the pattern was 1.3223. The market failed to reach its target and turned up on March 26, closing above the March 25 low. This was a setup for the Trailing Stop Rule. This rule was triggered on the open of March 29. I exited the short trade for a small profit.

June T-Bonds: Yet Another H&S Failure

Signal Type: **Major Anticipatory Signal**

As cited in previous chapters, I was looking for an opportunity to short this market at the late stage of the right shoulder of a possible 12-month H&S top (see Figure 9.3A-C in Chapter 9). I was interpreting the weekly chart from a bearish perspective.

Note in Figure 11.9, the daily June T-bond chart was forming a possible nine-week inverted H&S bottom formation. The market attempted to climb above the ice line on March 18, but could not hold the rally. Suspecting a H&S failure in the making, I entered a sell stop below the March 19 low and was stopped into a short position on March 24 at 117.02. My position was short one-half a contract per trading unit.

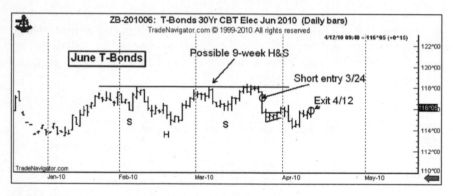

FIGURE 11.9   T-Bonds Turn Down at the Neckline.

I was stopped out of the trade on April 12 based on the Trailing Stop Rule.

May Wheat: A Sustained Decline in Wheat Continues to Frustrate Me

Signal Type: **Minor Continuation Signal**

The H&S top completed in mid-January had an unmet target of 426. After chopping sideways from early February through mid-March, the market thrust into new lows on March 25, as seen in Figure 11.10. I went short at 470.50 with a Last Day Rule of 478.25 and a target of 426. I established an underleveraged position of 0.5 contracts per trading unit. I was stopped out on April 7 based on the Last Day Rule.

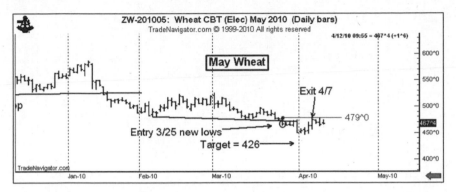

FIGURE 11.10 New Lows in Wheat.

Is There a Best Time of Day to Establish a Trade?

The answer to this question is "yes!" Intraday trading is very deceptive. A trader can be misled by price leaps and dives during the trading session. It is quite easy to believe a chart pattern is destined to be completed based on intraday action, only to be disappointed by the end of the day. Just as I cannot predict the next short-, intermediate-, or long-term price trend in a market, I especially cannot predict how a market will close based on its intraday price behavior.

The single most important price of the day is the closing price, posted midafternoon each day. This is the price at which position traders, as opposed to day traders, are willing to hold a position overnight. Even though I often enter and exit a position intraday, the closing price is the only one that really matters. Everything else is noise.

May Corn: A Stair-Stepping Decline

Signal Type: Minor Continuation Signal

The May corn trade mirrors the May wheat trade. The daily chart had a target of 344 from the three-month triangle completed on January 13. After drifting sideways through most of February and March, the market made a new low on March 25, as shown in Figure 11.11. This new low completed a descending triangle dating back to the early March high.

I established a short position. The pattern target from the three-month triangle was met on March 31. However, I elected to go with a swing target,

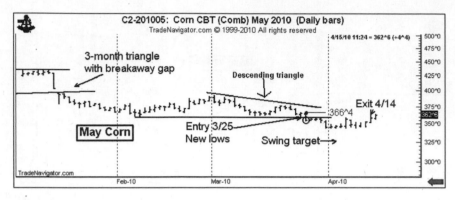

FIGURE 11.11   Corn Fails to Follow Through After New Lows.

assuming that the drop from the March 1 high would equal the January decline. This swing target was also in the area of the September 2009 low.

The market experienced a retest rally on April 7. I was stopped out of the trade on April 14 based on the Retest Failure Rule.

November Soybeans: A Bear Trap

Signal Type: **Minor Continuation Signal**

The decline (in the first 15 minutes of pit trading) on March 31 penetrated the lower boundary of an eight-week continuation symmetrical triangle. This breakout proved quickly to be a one-day-out-of-line movement. I recognized it as such and exited the trade quickly (see Figure 11.12).

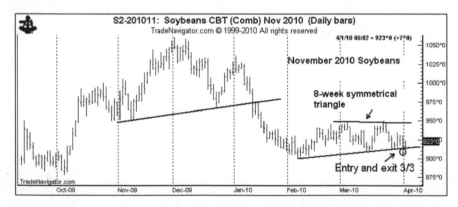

FIGURE 11.12   Symmetrical Triangle in November Soybeans.

This pattern highlights the fundamental problem with diagonal patterns, to which symmetrical triangles belong. It is possible for prices to penetrate a diagonal boundary line without clearing the previous high or low within the pattern. This is part of the reason I prefer to trade breakouts from horizontal boundary lines.

May Copper: An Easy Trade I Missed

Signal Type: **Missed Trade**

I keep a record of patterns that I miss. There are usually two such patterns per month. I usually miss them because I am biased in the other direction, not because I do not see them. Sometimes I miss a trade only to see it a day or two later. In late March, I had a bias toward the short side of copper. I thought the February to March rally was a test of the January high. I also saw a possible four-week descending triangle forming. Right-angle triangles are usually resolved by a breakout through the horizontal boundary.

As shown in Figure 11.13, a small nine-day symmetrical triangle formed at the end of the descending triangle. The advance on March 26 completed the symmetrical triangle and set up the violation of the descending triangle on March 29. I could have established a long position on either March 26 or March 29. This was a nice four-week continuation pattern.

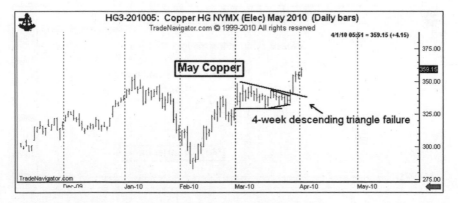

FIGURE 11.13 Triangle Propels Copper Prices Higher.

Looking Back

Missed trades bring forth a very important point. Patterns that are fully mature and ready to launch a trend more often than not provide an opportunity for breakout traders to go in either direction. In fact, a condition of a mature pattern is that logical breakout stops are self-evident on both sides of the pattern. To take this a step further, unless a market can be "bracketed" with breakout orders to go either long or short, then one might question the legitimacy of either order.

May Orange Juice: An "End-Around" Triangle Failure

***Signal Type:* Minor Continuation**

Finally, I will point out a trade I took for my proprietary account but not for the pool because of the extreme illiquidity of the market. The decisive breakout on March 1 completed an eight-week symmetrical triangle. This pattern should have propelled the market to at least 170. Note that prices moved to the apex of the triangle before breaking out. Symmetrical triangles that move three-quarters or more toward the apex cannot be trusted. As shown in Figure 11.14, this triangle did not even reach the January high before performing an end-around.

FIGURE 11.14   A Classic End-Around in Orange Juice.

Summary

March was the toughest month since November with a negative performance of 3.7 percent, marked-to-market Value Added Monthly Index (VAMI) method. Of the 16 trades entered in the month, only four, or 25 percent, were profitable, for a net loss (closed trade basis) of 2.5 percent. One trade (USD/CAD) remained open. None of the closed profits was in the "bottom liners" category.

Table 11.1 lists the category of entry signals for March.

TABLE 11.1 March Entry Signals by Category

Signal Category	Amended Benchmarks	March Trade Entries (# and % of total)
Major patterns		
Completions	4.0 (29%)	2.0 (12%)
Anticipatory	1.5 (11%)	4.0 (29%)
Pyramid	1.5 (11%)	1.0 (6%)
Minor patterns	4.0 (28%)	7.0 (41%)
Instinct trades	2.0 (14%)	1.0 (6%)
Miscellaneous trades	1.0 (7%)	1.0 (6%)
Total	14.0 (100%)	16.0 (100%)

CHAPTER 12

Month Five

April 2010

This is the final diary chapter in Part III of *Diary of a Professional Commodity Trader*. The performance during the first 18 weeks was not as stout as I would have liked, but that is part of trading. There are losing trades, losing weeks, losing months, and even losing years.

Of the top 20 professional trading firms during the past five years (based on my analysis of risk-adjusted performance), there were a total of 17 losing years among them, or 17 percent of the total combined years (20 trading firms times 5 years equals 100 years of trading). This means that nearly one in five years was a net loser for the group. Even though the average losing year was small (a few percentage points), a losing year is a losing year.

In the opening paragraphs of Part III of this book, I stated that, "I will be in hog heaven if I achieve an actual rate of return of 10 to 15 percent during the next five months." Entering April, my performance since December 7, 2009 (the start of the diary) was a gain of 5 percent-plus (closed trades only). This equated to 12 percent-plus annualized. With one month to go, my original goal was beyond reach unless early April offered some great surprises. But I was not shocked by the performance since December, since I had but a small handful of "bottom liners." These trades are an absolute necessity to reach profit my goals.

Some novice traders who fall behind their expectations adopt the attitude of "doubling up to catch up." I am not tempted to do this. There are ups and downs in the net asset value of all trading operations. Taking additional risk is the way to ruin, not recovery.

Had this book been written in any other five-month period of time, the results could have been drastically different—perhaps better, perhaps worse. There is no magic crystal ball in commodity and forex trading. The best a trader can do is to develop trading principles and guidelines that provide a slight edge—and then attempt to exploit this edge over time. This concept of "edge" cannot be overemphasized.

Most Las Vegas gaming facilities pay around 95 to 97 cents on the dollar in their slot machine operations. This means that the "house" has a very slight edge on any given pull of the slot machine arm. It is just as likely for a gambler to win as to lose in a single-pull slot machine event. The "house" is betting that the slight edge, employed over thousands and thousands of pulls, will produce a net profit. But for any given pull, the edge is almost meaningless.

Trading operates on the same principle. I have developed a method of selecting trades, entering trades, and managing trades—all within an overall risk management construct—that I believe provides me an edge. It is this edge that I attempt to exploit. Over any given trading event or small series of trading events, and during any given week or month, the edge may not provide a net profitable result.

It has been a tough 12- to 15-month period for the wider community of commodity and forex trading operations. Using some of the most widely followed Commodity Trading Advisor indices (Stark, MAR, Barclays, Lyxor) as proxies, trading operations have lost money net in the past year. In fact, according to the Barclays CTA Index, 2009 was the first losing year for commodity and forex trading operations in the past 10 years, and only the fourth losing year since 1980.

In light of the historical gains in the global stock markets in 2009, commodity and forex investments seem quite unattractive. Yet go back to the book's introduction and look at the chart in Figure I.4 to gain a historical perspective on commodities/forex as an asset class compared to the U.S. stock market.

As a trader who understands speculative endeavors, I would place my own personal assets with a solid commodity manager over a stock mutual fund manager any day of the week. On a risk-adjusted basis, my saddle will go on the commodity horse.

Relying on Classical Charting Principles

Chart patterns of any time duration (yearly, quarterly, monthly, weekly, daily, hourly) are comprised of numerous patterns of shorter duration that fail to generate the implied move. For example, a four-month weekly chart pattern will consist of numerous daily patterns that appeared to be legitimate at the time of their formation but failed to deliver. In turn, the daily formations are comprised of numerous hourly chart formations, some of which produced a move to their implied targets, many more of which failed.

Patterns that produce significant trends are easy to see after the fact. Similar patterns that fail and blend into longer patterns are much more difficult to isolate after the fact. Classical charting principles are fluid. Patterns are constantly evolving and becoming redefined.

Chart traders are faced with two options:

1. Develop an uncanny sense for when a chart formation will mature and become fruitful—and attempt to postpone trading activity until a pattern is ready to work, somehow eliminating or greatly reducing trading activity on the patterns that will fail. This challenge is primarily one of extraordinary patience.
2. Trade all clearly defined patterns, using sound money management, knowing that the vast majority of these patterns will fail and become components of a larger chart structure or become part of a chart that cannot be defined by classical charting principles.

Some technicians believe that they can use their technical techniques to continually get a handle on the markets. I think this is foolish thinking that serves better as promotional sound bites than as the basis for real-time trading operations.

I want to remind chartists that many price charts cannot be understood based on classical principles or other technical tools. Many substantial trends occur without being launched by chart patterns that are definable.

Obviously, the first option—that of trading only markets that are ready to trend immediately—would be the most profitable and least frustrating. The question is whether the option is realistic for all chart traders. For some traders with an extreme ability for patience, the first option may be partially achievable. For most chartists, the second option is probably the most realistic.

Trading Record

June Gold: Several Months of Confusion Are Resolved with an H&S Bottom

Signal Type: **Major Anticipatory Signal, Major Breakout Signal**

I last covered gold in Chapter 9, where I leapt ahead to track my gold trades covering several months. I discussed in that chapter the frustrations when a chart goes through a period of redefinition.

The advance in early October 2009 completed an 18-month inverted continuation H&S bottom pattern. See the weekly gold graph in Figure 12.1. There were several ways to draw the neckline on this chart. I always prefer to draw a horizontal boundary that best fits the highs or lows in question. This pattern has an unmet target of 1350. My bias is to trade a market in the direction of an unmet target on the weekly and monthly charts. But, remember, targets are *not* sacred. I have seen some chart traders become wiped out waiting for a target to be reached.

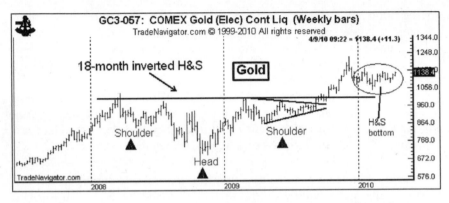

FIGURE 12.1   Another Look at the Inverted H&S on the Weekly Gold Graph.

Last month (March), the dominant pattern in gold was the possible four-month inverted H&S pattern on the daily June gold contract, as shown in Figure 12.2. This same chart was also featured as Figure 9.25 in Chapter 9. The advance on April 1 penetrated the upper boundary of a channel that constituted the right shoulder of this daily H&S formation. I went long one mini contract per trading unit at this breakout.

FIGURE 12.2   Four-Month H&S Bottom on the Daily Gold Chart.

The advance on April 7 completed the four-month H&S bottom. This pattern had an initial target of a retest of the December 2009 high at 1230. My thinking was that this H&S pattern could propel the market to the 1350 target initially set by the weekly H&S pattern completed as shown in Figure 12.1. I increased my leverage. I really thought I had a good trade on the books.

The market retested the neckline on April 13. Then, on April 16, gold prices cascaded, stopping me out of my position with the Last Day Rule. While as of this writing I am flat, I believe the H&S bottom will propel prices much higher.

EUR/GBP: A Questionable Buy

Signal Type: **Miscellaneous Trade**

This and the following trade in euro/Japanese yen (EUR/JPY) represent opposite sides of the same coin. Both trades deal with the concept of pattern retests and how signals are generated relative to such retests.

On April 5, the euro/British pound (EUR/GBP) declined to a price that had been serving alternatively as a support and resistance zone (Figure 12.3). I discussed this support and resistance line in Chapter 10; see Figure 10.18. As an instinct trade, I established a long position. I felt that the trade was extremely low risk, that I could use the low of April 5 as a protective stop based on the Retest Failure Rule. I was stopped out the next day.

FIGURE 12.3   Alternating Support and Resistance Line in EUR/GBP.

Looking Back

Trades such as this remind me of catching a falling knife. This was not a breakout trade. The market had been in a free fall prior to my purchase. In fact, in hindsight I can see that a bearish horn (or sloping) top was completed on the same day of my long entry. At a minimum, I should have waited for at least a one-day reversal before attempting a long-side trade.

EUR/JPY: Market Becomes Tricky around Important Ice Line

***Signal Type:* Major Breakout Signal—Recompletion**

Just as I bought the EUR/GBP at the retest of a support zone, I shorted the EUR/JPY relative to its line of support/resistance. As shown in Figure 12.4, the rally in early April retested a major rounding top on the weekly graph. I viewed this as a shorting opportunity.

FIGURE 12.4   Retest of Rounding Top on the Weekly EUR/JPY Chart.

The daily chart (Figure 12.5) shows that the retest actually climbed above the ice line of the weekly chart top for three days in early April. Then, on April 6, the market experienced a sharp decline below the ice line. This represented a sell signal because the original pattern was recompleted on a closing basis. I should have shorted the close on April 6, but I did not have an order in place.

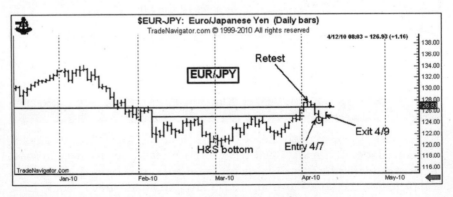

FIGURE 12.5   Retest of Top on the Daily EUR/JPY Graph.

I shorted the market on April 7. I was nervous with this trade from the onset. While the major weekly chart top was still the dominant classical chart structure, the daily chart had completed a seven-week H&S bottom on March 31. The market was caught between a boulder (the weekly chart top) and a hard place (the minor head and shoulders bottom). April 8 was a one-day reversal. I jammed my stop and exited the trade on April 9 for a loss of two-tenths of 1 percent.

Looking Back

This market had a massive overhead rounding top on the weekly chart and an underlying head and shoulders bottom on the daily chart. As a general rule I rely on the most recent pattern. There are times of conflict on a chart. During these times, it is often best to wait for a clear resolution.

November Soybeans: Textbook Ascending Triangle is Completed

Signal Type: **Minor Reversal Signal**

One good sign of a bear trap is when a market spikes through a boundary line, closes back above the boundary line the same day and then spends the entire next day above the boundary line, closing higher. This scenario is exactly what happened in November soybeans on March 31 and April 1. I could have fully justified a long purchase on the April 1 close.

The subsequent advance on April 15 completed a 10-week ascending triangle, as shown in Figure 12.6. I established a long position of 2,500 bushels per trading unit of $100,000.

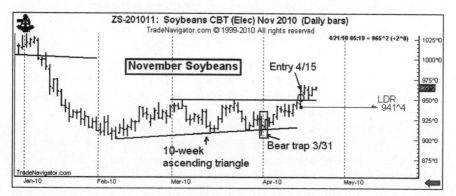

FIGURE 12.6 Symmetrical Triangle Completed in November Soybeans.

Figure 12.7 shows that as of the date of this writing the November soybean chart is building a 17-month ascending triangle on the weekly chart. This is the type of pattern that should lead to a magnificent trend and will be a chart to watch as 2010 progresses.

FIGURE 12.7   Massive Symmetrical Triangle Base Shown on the Weekly November Soybean Chart.

Outlook for the Future

Several markets stand out to me as "markets to watch" as time rolls forward. These are markets with extremely significant big-picture weekly chart structures under development. I have mentioned several of these markets throughout the book as part of trading events.

Dow Jones Industrials: A Historic Head and Shoulders in the Making?

Something truly amazing is taking place in this market—and if it comes to fruition, it will go down as one of history's most significant chart developments. The monthly and quarterly charts of the Dow Jones Industrial Average (DJIA) display a possible H&S top with a down-slanting neckline (see Figure 12.8). Down-sloping necklines are normally a sign of greater potential weakness than flat or up-slanting necklines.

It is often the case that a line drawn off the highs of the right and left shoulders will be parallel to the neckline. Figure 12.9 is a blow-up of the H&S top. The current rally from the March 2009 low has reached this parallel line. It is possible for the rally to penetrate the parallel line and extend to the height of the left shoulder (Dow 11,750).

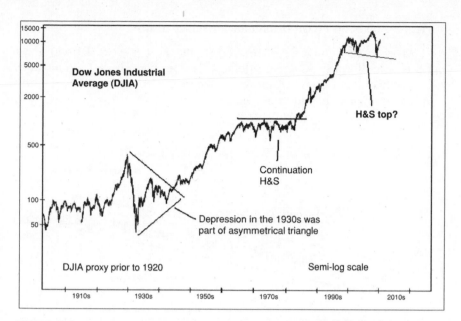

FIGURE 12.8   100-Year Dow Chart Shows Potential Top of Historic Magnitude.

FIGURE 12.9   14-Year Dow Monthly Graph Confirms Possible H&S Top.

There is a tendency toward symmetry in H&S patterns, although symmetry is not a requirement. The right shoulder could extend several more years to reach symmetry with the left shoulder in duration. However, the most powerful H&S patterns originate from abbreviated right shoulders.

30-Year T-Bonds: Sovereign Default for the United States?

As I have noted previously in this book, the U.S. 30-year T-bond chart predicts some form of sovereign default. The problem is that higher rates are conventional wisdom. As shown in Figure 12.10, the quarterly T-bond chart has formed a channel from the early 1980s low.

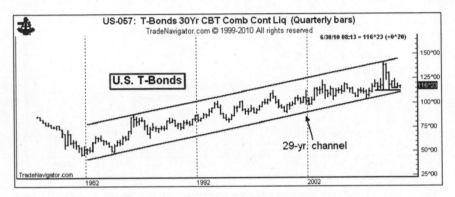

FIGURE 12.10   29-Year Channel on the Quarterly T-Bond Graph.

Figure 12.11 displays an H&S pattern on the weekly chart dating back to late 2007. Further, the right shoulder of this larger H&S pattern is an H&S formation itself. This smaller H&S pattern dating back to June 2009 appears to be quite mature. This means that the market needs to start down soon, or the entire weekly chart will be subject to redefinition.

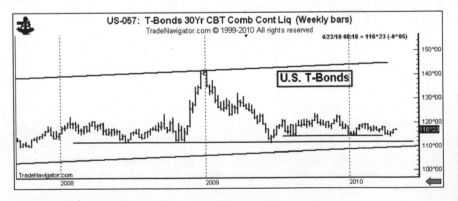

FIGURE 12.11   Weekly T-Bond Chart Displays Possible H&S Top.

In mid-May 2010, the T-bond market exploded to the upside, decisively penetrating both the left and right shoulder highs of what had been a possible H&S top on the weekly chart (see Figure 12.12). This is exactly the type of redefinition alluded to throughout the book. The price target now becomes a test of the early 2009 high around 141-00.

FIGURE 12.12 H&S Failure on the Weekly T-Bond Chart.

Sugar: Still Hope for the Bulls?

This is the final market I will feature as I look toward the future. As shown in Figure 12.13, the rally in late 2009 completed a multidecade base. The recent sharp decline in sugar has dug deeply into this base. Yet no long-term damage has been done to the bull story—yet.

The market has a good chance of holding the 1600–1700 area and launching a giant bull advance into the 60-cent range.

Sugar prices subsequently sliced easily through the 1600–1700 zone, declining all the way to 13 cents. While the long-term bull market in sugar may not be dead, it was seriously injured.

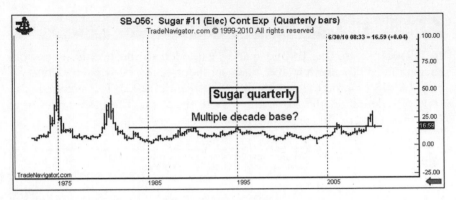

FIGURE 12.13   30-Year Base on the Quarterly Sugar Graph.

Summary

I concluded journaling my trades for the purpose of writing this book on April 20, marking-to-the-market the two open trades as of that date (November soybeans and USD/CAD). Seven trading events were entered during April, of which five closed at a loss and two at a profit (see Table 12.1).

TABLE 12.1   April Entry Signals by Category

Signal Category	Amended Benchmarks	April Trade Entries (# and % of total)
Major patterns		
Completions	4.0 (29%)	3
Anticipatory	1.5 (11%)	1
Pyramid	1.5 (11%)	0
Minor patterns	4.0 (28%)	2
Instinct trades	2.0 (14%)	0
Miscellaneous trades	1.0 (7%)	1
Total	14.0 (100%)	7

This ends the trade-by-trade diary portion of the book. Part IV will be a wrap-up of the period concluded, providing a statistical summary and analysis of the performance and a look-ahead based on lessons learned.

The Wrap-Up

P art IV is a discussion and statistical analysis of the trading from December 7, 2009 through April 15, 2010 followed up by a Best Dressed List. The Best Dressed list represents the best examples of classical charting principles during the trading period.

It is my sincere hope that the discussion of the 21-week period of trading and the examples of the best the charts had to offer can aid you as a trader in the future.

CHAPTER 13

Analysis of Trading Performance

I had two hopes when I began writing this book. The first was that the commodity and forex markets would trend in a way consistent with my trading plan. Some of the markets I trade have trended, but the trends have been with the type of backing and filling inconsistent with my trading rules.

The charts of five different markets are shown, indicating the price behavior from December 7 (date of the first trade in this book) through April 15 (date of the last trade). These charts are gold (Figure 13.1), the Mini Nasdaq (Figure 13.2), sugar (Figure 13.3), the Commodity Research Bureau (CRB) Index (Figure 13.4), and the British pound (Figure 13.5).

These markets were selected to represent precious metals, U.S. stocks, softs, raw material commodities, and forex. One look at these charts confirms the difficulty most commodity traders (including myself) have encountered in recent months. Markets have generally traded on both sides of the line connecting the early December to mid-April price trend.

The second hope was that the global stock markets (especially the U.S. stock market) would run out of gas and stop going up. I am a very conservative trader at this stage in my career. My goal is to perform consistently at about 18 percent annual rate of return with limited capital volatility (see performance disclaimers in the Author's Note).

The idea of an 18 percent annual return is pretty dull when the U.S. stock market from March 2009 through April 2010 put in one of its best performances in history. As shown in Figure 13.6, the Standard & Poor's (S&P) 500 Index almost doubled from March 2009 through April 2010. Numerous individual stocks have doubled and even tripled. It's worth noting that stocks experienced a severe correction after this section in May.

Seeking a low double-digit return in futures and forex seems boring by comparison. In hindsight, I would have been better off applying the

FIGURE 13.1   Gold Chart, December 2009–April 2010.

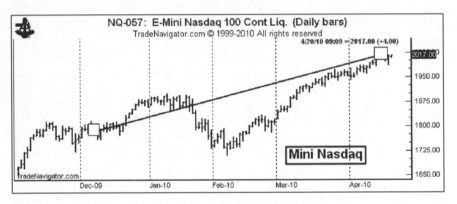

FIGURE 13.2   Nasdaq Chart, December 2009–April 2010.

FIGURE 13.3   Sugar Chart, December 2009–April 2010.

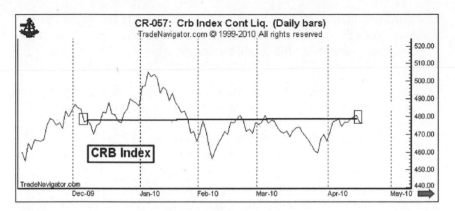

FIGURE 13.4   CRB Index, December 2009–April 2010.

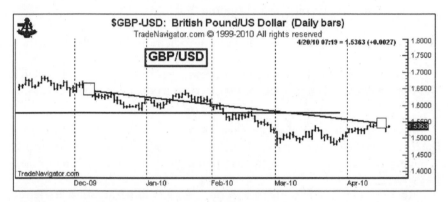

FIGURE 13.5   GBP/USD Chart, December 2009–April 2010.

FIGURE 13.6   S&Ps from March 2009 to April 2010.

Factor Trading Plan to shares of individual stocks during the five months of this diary. Yet I trade commodities and forex, not stocks.

The basic premises of this book remain steadfast.

- Commodity futures and forex markets can be traded in a conservative manner that provides a consistent rate of return with a minimum of capital volatility.
- The principles of classical charting are timeless and can provide a mechanism for driving all trading decisions. Yet classical charting represents a trading tool, not a means to forecast prices.
- Charting provides a slight edge to a trader. The consistent and prolonged execution of a trading plan to exploit the advantage of that edge is the best a trader can expect to achieve.
- The result of any given trade or short series of trades is irrelevant to consistently profitable trading operations.
- Successful market speculation involves many facets and components. Risk and trade management are far more important than trade selection.
- Managing the human emotions of fear, greed, hope, and confidence (too much or too little) are central to consistent speculative success.

Undertaking this book project has been the most educational and enlightening experience of my trading life. I thought that I knew myself as a trader and, relative to most market participants, I did have a lot of self-knowledge.

Keeping a journal of trades and writing about them forced me to define, examine, and analyze my trading paradigm and algorithm like never before. I had to systematically think through what it is I do in my trading operations and why. I had to carefully recall the steps I took to reach my current approach to trading. I reaffirmed myself in many of my trading practices. In some areas, however, I now believe I have the opportunity to make my trading plan more efficient and effective.

I am more certain than ever that no two consistently profitable traders can or should operate exactly the same way. No two traders think the same way. Successful trading is about building upon one's personality and character strengths, and overcoming or managing one's personality and character deficiencies. What works for me will not work for another trader, and vice versa.

I cannot tell other traders what they need to do to improve their trading effectiveness. These issues must be dealt individually by each trader. A consistently successful trading plan is a reflection of the person who develops and executes it.

We'll now analyze the performance of my trades from December 2009–April 2010 in three parts:

1. How the Factor Trading Plan performed in the five-month period covered by the book—a statistical analysis and discussion.
2. What I learned about the Factor Trading Plan (and myself) by critically implementing and analyzing the plan on a trade-by-trade and order-by-order basis during the past five months; and,
3. What my best practices should be going forward.

How the Trading Plan Performed

The Factor Trading Plan had 68 entry signals during the 21 weeks covered by this book. A number of these entry signals were part of the same trading campaign (e.g., short GBP/USD or short T-bonds.)

Table 13.1 compares the signals from the Factor Trading Plan during the period December 7, 2009 through April 15, 2010 to the goals of the plan.

TABLE 13.1   December 2009–April 2010 Trading Signals by Category

Signal Category	Amended Goals Per Month		Dec. 2009–Apr. 2010 Signals (# and % of total)		Dec. 2009–Apr. 2010 Signals (avg. per month)		Variance (# signals per month)
Major patterns							
Completions	4.0	(29%)	23.0	(34%)	5.0	(33%)	+1.0
Anticipatory	1.5	(11%)	9.0	(13%)	2.0	(14%)	+ .5
Pyramid	1.5	(11%)	2.0	(3%)	0	(0%)	−1.5
Minor patterns	4.0	(28%)	22.0	(32%)	4.0	(32%)	0
Instinct trades	2.0	(14%)	4.0	(6%)	1.0	(9%)	−1.0
Miscellaneous trades	1.0	(7%)	8.0	(12%)	2.0	(10%)	+1.0
Total	14.0	(100%)	68.0	(100%)	14.0	(100%)	

As shown in Table 13.1, the Factor Trading Plan compared favorably with the goals of the plan in terms of signal generation. Figure 13.7 provides the month-by-month details of the data shown in Table 13.1.

However, it was in the area of actual performance that the trading operations of the plan varied more significantly from expectations, as shown in Table 13.2.

Factor LLC

Trade entries by category

Signal category	Amended benchmarks (# and % of total)		Dec. 2009 trade entries (# and % of total)		Jan. 2010 trade entries (# and % of total)		Feb. 2010 trade entries (# and % of total)		Mar. 2010 trade entries (# and % of total)		Apr. 2010 trade entries (# and % of total)		Total Dec. - Apr. trade entries (# and % of total)		Dec. Apr. Variance (Pct. Pts.)
Major patterns															
Completions	4	29%	6	46%	8	50%	4	25%	2	13%	3	43%	23	34%	5%
Anticipatory	1.5	11%	0	0%	2	13%	2	13%	4	25%	1	14%	9	13%	3%
Pyramid	1.5	11%	0	0%	1	6%	0	0%	1	6%	0	0%	2	3%	–8%
Minor patterns	4	29%	4	31%	3	19%	6	38%	7	44%	2	29%	22	32%	4%
Instinct trades	2	14%	1	8%	1	6%	1	6%	1	6%	0	0%	4	6%	–8%
Insane/misc. trades	1	7%	2	15%	1	6%	3	19%	1	6%	1	14%	8	12%	5%
Total	14	100%	13	100%	16	100%	16	100%	16	100%	7	100%	68	100%	
Win ratio	35%		38%		69%		44%		19%		29%		41%		
# Winners	5		5		11		7		3		2		28		
# Bottom liners	1.4		1				0		0		0		2		
% Bottom liners	10%		8%		6%		0%		0%		0%		3%		

FIGURE 13.7 Month-by-Month Breakdown of Trades.

TABLE 13.2 Factor Signals—Performance Data (December 2009–April 2010)

Performance Measures	Plan Goals (five month totals)	Dec. 7, 2009–Apr. 20, 2010 (actuals)	Variance (percentage points)**
Percent profitable trades	35% or approximately 1 in 3	41%	+6% points
Percent unprofitable trades	65% or approximately 2 in 3	59%	−6% points
Annualized ROR	18%	12.9%	−5.1% points
Worst month-ending drawdown*	(8%)	(5.8%) est.	
Ratio of $ size of profits to $ size of losses	2.6 to 1	1.8 to 1	
# of net bottom liners and % of total trades	7 (10%)	2 (3%)	−5 trades

*Actual account, marked-to-market VAMI calculation; see disclaimers in the Author's Note for other data.
**Dec. 2009–Apr. 2010 vs. Plan Goals.

Clearly, the Factor Trading Plan performed in a subpar manner during the past five months, underperforming the goal by nearly 5 percentage points for the period.

This underperformance, on its surface, is not alarming because commodity and forex trading is not an annuity or T-bill with amortized income. As I have stated in this book, there are losing trades, weeks, months, and even years in the life of a commodity trader.

The major factor contributing to the less-than-goal performance is the absence of the "net bottom liners," those trades that have historically established my net trading profitability. As a general rule, about 10 percent of my trading events have been net bottom liners, trades that:

- Break out of a clearly defined pattern without hesitation with little or no retesting of the boundary or ice line
- Trend steadily to the implied target
- Provide a rate-of-return of about 2 percent of assets

On average, I have had one or two bottom liners per month over the years. In fact, I need one to two bottom liners to make the Factor Trading Plan work.

During the course of this book, from December 2009 through April 2010, the Factor Trading Plan produced a total of two net bottom liners. Not having bottom liners is an important factor, but I am equally interested in other factors that may have negatively impacted performance. Greater understanding produces greater insight.

Table 13.3 shows the performance of the Factor Trading Plan during the past five months based on the type of entry signal.

TABLE 13.3   Factor Trading Plan Performance by Signal Category (December 2009–April 2010)

Signal Category	# Trades	Total P/L*
Major patterns		
Completions	23	$6,089
Anticipatory	9	$4,003
Pyramid	2	($336)
Minor patterns		
Continuation	10	$884
Reversal	12	($1,658)
Instinct trades	4	$471
Miscellaneous trades	8	($3,960)
Total	68	$5,473

*Per $100,000 trading unit.

Clearly, major patterns provided the most profitable trading results during the period. Minor reversal patterns and the category of miscellaneous trades were significant negative contributors to the net bottom line. A number of these minor reversals were of shorter duration than my guidelines and were, therefore, "outside" the orthodoxy of the Factor Trading Plan. Better management of these trades in the future represents a challenge and opportunity.

I also wanted to take a look at trading performance through several other filters. Table 13.4 displays the performance based on the duration or length of the dominant chart pattern.

As shown, the category of one- to four-week patterns, related to major pattern, contributed more than $4,644 to the total net, just as shorter patterns not connected with major patterns were the largest contributors to negative performance. This speaks volumes in understanding shorter-term patterns within the context of longer-term chart construction. Major pattern breakouts of 14 to 18 weeks in duration were the next greatest contributor to net profits.

TABLE 13.4 Factor Trading Plan Performance by
Duration of Patterns (December 2009–April 2010)

Daily Pattern Length	Total P/L*
1–4 weeks—not connected to a major pattern	($2,157)
1–4 weeks—connected to a major pattern	$4,644
5–8 weeks	$1,274
9–13 weeks	($1,254)
14–18 weeks	$1,996
More than 18 weeks	$991

*Per $100,000 trading unit.

Next, Table 13.5 analyzes performance based on the exit strategy employed.

TABLE 13.5 Factor Trading Plan—Performance
by Exit Strategy (December 2009–April 2010)

Exit Strategy	# of total trades*	Total P/L
Intervening pattern	3	$156
Last Day Rule	25	($10,411)
Last Hour Rule	2	($935)
Quick Profit	4	$4,701
Retest Failure	17	($3,225)
Target	9	$10,959
Trailing stop	10	$6,448

*Some trades counted more than once because of split
exit strategies. Statistics are per $100,000 trading unit.

On the surface, these results are self-evident. There is nothing surprising in any of these line items. Trades that ended by being stopped out at the Last Day Rule by definition will be losers just as trades reaching their targets by definition will be profitable. A further analysis of modified exit strategies relative to the signal category yields some very useful fruit.

I have strongly expressed my disdain for optimizing short-term trade entry signals based on technical indicators. I am far more interested in underlying themes and lessons on trade and risk management than in trade identification.

On the theory that aggressive money management in taking profits would improve bottom-line results and decrease asset volatility, I back-tested the following scenario against the actual trading signals from the period covered by the book.

- Miscellaneous trades would have been eliminated.
- All other trades would have used the protective stop placement as actually employed.
- A predetermined dollar profit would have been taken for all trades (different for major breakout signals versus other signals).

This risk and trade management modeling would have increased profitability from approximately 5.5 percent (as reflected by the diary) to 21.3 percent. This is a hypothetical performance result and subject to all of the limitations of hypothetical results. There is no guarantee that these modifications going forward would produce a similar change in performance.

Of course, taking relatively quick profits would have worked well in the past five months, but would have left major chunks of money on the table in 2007 and 2008.

Given more time to complete this manuscript, I would have looked at several other optional trade and risk management strategies—and will do so in the future. These include:

- What would be the longer-term result of eliminating all minor signals (particularly reversal signals) less than six to eight weeks in duration?
- What would be the result of reestablishing positions previously exited at the predetermined quick profit points if retests of the initial price entry points were subsequently experienced?
- What would be the result of holding a partial position (perhaps 50 percent) of major breakout signals using a "Last Day Rule OCO Target" strategy?
- What would be the long-term impact on performance of standardizing leverage on all trades? Presently, I vary leverage based on a number of factors.

On the last point above, I back-tested all trading signals from the period covered by the book, comparing the wide range of risks I actually assumed (from 0.3 percent to 1.2 percent of assets) against a constant risk per trade of 0.7 percent (based on the initial protective stop used).

A constant risk of 0.7 percent on each and every trade would have improved the net performance for the period from +5.5 percent to +8.2 percent. The message in this comparison is that I am not a good subjective judge of whether a trade will be profitable, or at least I was not a good judge during the period covered by the book.

How the Plan (and the Trader) Evolved

I not sure how many completely new lessons I learn in the markets each year. I think it is more a matter of learning new layers, nuances, and dimensions of lessons previously learned (and, in many cases, relearned again and again).

Lessons learned about one's trading operations are equal to lessons learned about one's self. The practices of a trader reflect the trader's personality and character—the good, the bad, and the ugly. To confront deficiencies in a trading plan, a trader must confront deficiencies in his or her character. To build on the strong points of a trading plan, a trader must recognize and build on the strong points of his or her character. There is a very true adage that if a person wants to really know themselves they just need to become speculators.

Importantly, a trader also must be careful not to modify a trading plan based on what rules or guidelines would have increased the bottom line in the last trade, short series of trades, or previous month or two. I am not a believer in optimization, especially in the area of using price derivative indicators for the purpose of trade identification.

The foundational concepts or building blocks of a trading approach can have flaws that require continual updating and improvement. It is my experience that these concepts deal with money management issues or with the actual implementation of a trading plan.

As traders, we must seek to understand the past, even if we cannot change it. So the questions we ask ourselves are:

- What factors attributed to performance?
- What modifications to a trading plan, rules and guidelines would have improved the performance?
- Do these modifications simply reflect an optimization of recent months, or do they have the potential to improve future performance?

I believe that three factors negatively affected overall performance from December 2009 through April 2010, one of which is outside of my control.

1. *Lack of "Best Dressed List" chart patterns.* This is the uncontrollable factor. As to be discussed in Chapter 14, there were only three Best Dressed List chart patterns during the trading period covered by this book (December 2009 through April 2010). I completely missed one of these. Historically, between five and seven Best Dressed List trades occur during an average five-month period.

2. *Misallocation of trades by category*. I had too many trades in signal categories that were too short term in duration. I also pursued too many trades that were based on diagonal signals.

3. *Faulty trade management techniques*. The primary trade management techniques I use—the Last Day Rule, the Trailing Stop Rule, the Retest Failure Rule, the Intervening Pattern Rule—were developed and refined over years of trading. The primary purpose of these techniques has been to prevent winning trades from becoming losing trades. And these techniques have generally served me well. There have been times when these techniques were right on, and times when they stunk up my trading room.

During the past five months, I have had the wonderful opportunity to examine these trade management techniques under a microscope—and have come to a much deeper understanding of each technique relative to market behavior. I have come to some conclusions about these rules. Specifically, I conclude that these techniques are not equally appropriate for all signal categories.

In the introduction to Part III, I expressed the concern that writing this book could bring me into much closer contact with the markets than I would prefer, removing a detachment from day-to-day and especially intraday price fluctuations that could negatively impact my performance.

Looking back at the process, I believe the concern was legitimate. In fact, I believe the contact with the markets necessary for the book might have cut in half my profitability. I have regained an acute appreciation for my need to limit myself to a very brief exposure to market activity. As a trader, I need to enter my orders and shut off all further unnecessary contact with price behavior.

Summary: Best Practices Going Forward

There is a danger in modifying future trading operations based on what would have worked best in recent months. Modifications that would have improved past performance could be quite counterproductive in the future.

Given this caveat, the Factor Trading Plan will incorporate four lessons learned in recent months.

1. Eliminate all patterns less than six weeks in duration unless the patterns have a direct bearing on larger chart developments, particularly the construction or completion of weekly configurations.

2. More critically appraise diagonal patterns, especially trend lines and channel patterns.

3. Give breakouts of weekly chart configurations much more leeway to develop a successful trend. In fact, potential Best Dressed List trades should retain the Last Day Rule as its only risk management technique.
4. Take quick profits within several days of entry on all trades other than those based on major breakout signals. (This is the most radical change relative to my trading history.)

During the past five months, I have had too many initially profitable trades turn into losses. While it is not possible to grab the optimum profit a market offers, it is possible to adjust trading operations to take profits much more quickly on trades other than major breakout signals.

These modifications may complicate the execution of the trading plan because different signal categories will be managed with different trade management techniques. But, in the final analysis, this is a tactical consideration and is only a matter of trade management. I believe that these modifications will improve long-term profitability while reducing asset volatility.

Trading to the Right Side of Chart

A wise old sage at the Chicago Board of Trade offered me the best advice I have ever been given. This highly successful chart trader said, "Trade to the far right of the chart page."

In other words, the best decisions in chart trading are those that are delayed . . . delayed . . . delayed . . . delayed! Do not anticipate what a chart might become. Make a chart prove itself. Do not lead a breakout. Do not determine what a chart will do; instead, make the chart do it.

Whether a trade will be a profit or loss should not be a chartist's concern. Rather, waiting for a chart's "appointed time" should be the focus of a chart trader.

Sage advice, indeed!

I've created a list of best practices based on my recent trading performance, but I suspect it would apply to many other chart traders out there, whether they're just starting out, struggling with bad performance, or just looking for ways to improve an already successful trading operation.

Practices that I—and other chartists—could focus on in the future are:

- Look at the weekly chart of a specific market no more than once each week. Look at the daily chart of each market no more than once each day. Do not pay any attention to intraday charts unless it is to set money management protective stops on entry orders that were executed.

- Predetermine orders prior to the late afternoon opening. Use good-til-canceled (GTC) open orders wherever feasible. Avoid resting orders in thinly traded overnight electronic trading sessions, such as the grains, meats, or fibers.
- Do not modify the protective stop level on trades based on major breakout signals more than once each week.
- Do *not* chase a missed signal. There will be trading opportunities next week, next month, and next year. Chasing signals can lead to other serious breaches of trading practices.
- Have limited exposure to intraday market volatility.
- Be more aggressive in taking profits on trades other than major breakout signals.
- Enter profit-taking orders in advance. Once a profit is taken in a market, avoid that market for several days.
- Never take a losing trade home over a weekend. If a trade is a loser on a Friday, get out.
- Do not become too attached to trading a given market or obsess over missed opportunities. There is always another day and another chart pattern in a different market.
- Do not pay attention to what other traders/analysts are saying or doing. Work your own program.
- Trade to the right-hand side of the chart (see the sidebar earlier in this chapter).
- Maintain and review a one-year daily continuation chart for all markets traded. Any pattern considered for trading should be among the five best examples of classical charting principles during the past year.
- Avoid all patterns of less than six to eight weeks in duration.

I eagerly look forward to many years of trading based on the experiences and lessons I gained preparing and writing this book. While this book required far greater time and devotion than I would have ever anticipated, I believe I will be a better trader in the future as a result.

I hope that you—the reader—gained even a small proportion of education from reading this book that I gained from writing it.

CHAPTER 14

The Best Dressed List

This chapter presents the Best Dressed List for the period January 2009 through April 2010. The Best Dressed List represents the best examples of classical charting principles. The criteria for inclusion on the Factor Best Dressed List include the following:

- "No question about it" classical chart pattern on the weekly chart of at least 10 to 14 weeks in duration.
- Corresponding and supporting chart structure on the daily charts for the same market.
- A decisive breakout of the pattern boundary or ice line with little or no pattern reentry.
- A sustained trend to the price target implied by the classical chart configurations.

Whether the Factor Trading Plan participated in whole or in part of the trends represented by the Best Dressed List is not a conscious criterion. However, the Factor Trading Plan and its long-term profitability are predicated on a certain level of actual participation in the trends represented by the Best Dressed markets.

Markets included in the Best Dressed List for the period January 2009 through April 2010 are shown in Table 14.1.

TABLE 14.1 Best Dressed List, January 2009–April 2010

Chart Patterns	Market	Breakout Date	Date Target Reached	Magnitude of Target*
Weekly and daily: seven-month double bottom	AUD/USD spot	April 30 and May 1, 2009	July 28	941 pips
Weekly and daily: 14-month triangle and nine-month descending triangle	EUR/CHF spot	December 18, 2009	March 23	676 pips
Weekly: nine-month trend line and six-month wedge Daily: Same plus five-week channel	EUR/USD spot	December 4 and 7, 2009	February 4	1052 pips
Weekly and daily: 16-week horn bottom	GBP/USD spot	May 8, 2009	June 3	1448 pips
Weekly and daily: four-month-plus H&S bottom	NZD/USD spot	May 19, 2009	September 7	1015 pips
Weekly and daily: six-month ascending triangle failure	USD/CAD spot	April 24, 2009	May 29	1122 pips
Weekly and daily: eight-month H&S bottom	S&Ps	July 23, 2009	Target of 1246 remains unmet;	
Weekly and daily: 14-month triangle and three-month triangle Daily: six-week running wedge and three-month triangle	Sugar	May 1 and December 14, 2009	August 6 and January 6	784 points
Weekly and daily: seven-month symmetrical triangle	Gold	September 2, 2009	November 4	$112 per oz.
Weekly and daily: Series of continuation patterns	Copper	Varies	Varies	N/A
Weekly and daily: 23-week H&S bottom	Oct. crude oil	May 6, 2009	June 10	1280 points

*Measured move implied by completed pattern.

A Seven-Month Double Bottom in AUD/USD

The advance in late April completed a double bottom on the weekly and daily charts (Figures 14.1 and 14.2). The daily chart is best described as a compound fulcrum, a phrase borrowed from point and figure charting. In classical charting principles, a compound fulcrum bottom resembles a complex H&S top pattern that breaks out to the upside. The market had a premature breakout in mid-April, but was finally resolved by the advance on April 30 and the close on May 1. The target of 8289 was met on July 28. The consolidation in June and early July was tricky, but was resolved with a fishhook pyramid buy signal on July 14.

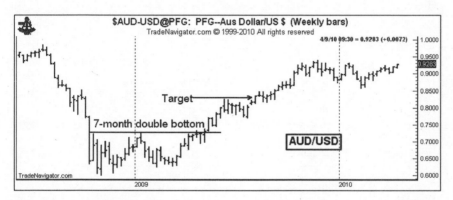

FIGURE 14.1   Double Bottom on the Weekly AUD/USD Graph.

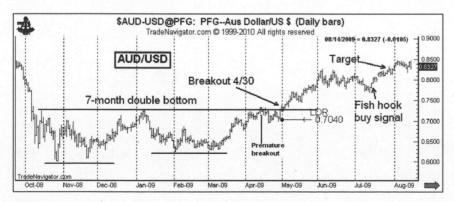

FIGURE 14.2   Double Bottom on the Daily AUD/USD Graph.

A 14-Month Coil and Nine-Month Descending Triangle in EUR/CHF

In December 2009 the EUR/CHF chart simultaneously completed two classical chart developments—a 14-month six-point triangulation or coil (labeled A–F) and a nine-month descending triangle. The initial target was reached in late March. Figure 14.3 shows the weekly graph, and Figure 14.4 is the daily chart. I completely missed this trade, seeing the chart after the move had begun.

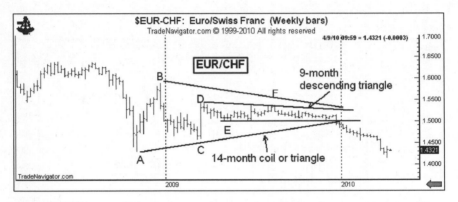

FIGURE 14.3   Descending Triangle and Symmetrical Triangle on the Weekly EUR/CHF Chart.

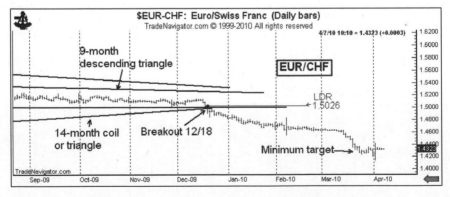

FIGURE 14.4   The Breakout and Run to the Target on the Daily EUR/CHF Chart.

A Six-Month Wedge in EUR/USD

The decline in early December simultaneously violated a nine-month trend line and completed a six-month wedge on the weekly chart (Figure 14.5) and completed a five-week channel on the daily graph (Figure 14.6). The target was met on February 4, 2010. The March through December advance was tricky, and several false and premature breakouts occurred before this decline came to fruition. For full disclosure, I personally took profits way too early in this trend, using the target of the five-week channel rather than the six-month wedge.

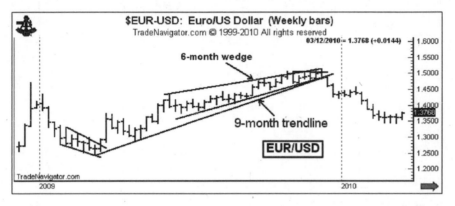

FIGURE 14.5   Weekly EUR/USD Graph Displays Major Trend Line and Rising Wedge.

FIGURE 14.6   The Breakout and Run to the Initial Target on the Daily EUR/USD Graph.

A 16-Week Horn in GBP/USD

Following the prolonged decline in the GBP/USD in 2008, the market formed a rare 16-week horn bottom that was completed on May 8. See the weekly chart in Figure 14.7.

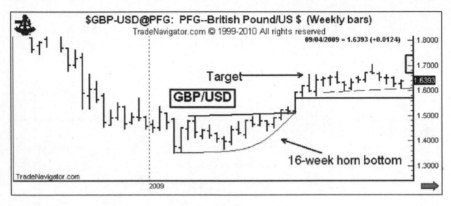

FIGURE 14.7   A 16-Week Horn on the Weekly GBP/USD Graph.

The daily chart (Figure 14.8) shows that the breakout hovered at the ice line of the pattern for several days without challenging the Last Day Rule before trending steadily to the target, reached on June 3.

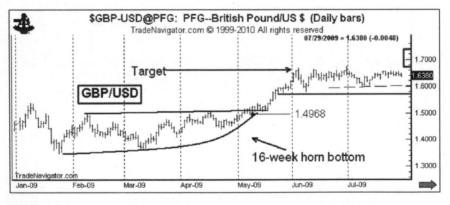

FIGURE 14.8   The Breakout and Run to the Target on the Daily GBP/USD Graph.

A Four-Month H&S in Bottom NZD/USD

The advance on May 19 in this forex pair completed a four-month-plus H&S bottom on the weekly graph, as shown in Figure 14.9. Notice that the right shoulder was quite abbreviated relative to the left shoulder. While symmetry is desirable, abbreviated right shoulders are generally much more trustworthy than are extended right shoulders.

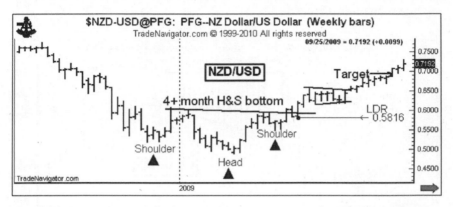

FIGURE 14.9 H&S Bottom and Continuation Triangle on the Weekly Chart of NZD/USD.

Notice on the daily chart (Figure 14.10) that the first breakout attempt on May 8 and 11 pulled back briefly below the neckline. However, the close on May 19 confirmed the deal, and the target was reached on September 7.

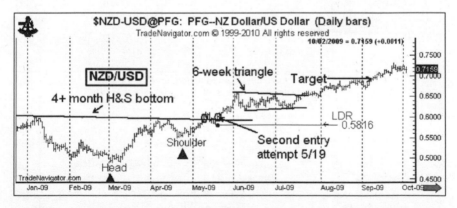

FIGURE 14.10 Daily Chart of the H&S Bottom in NZD/USD Displays a Stutter at the Breakout.

After the initial thrust in late May, the market paused to form a six-week continuation triangle. This offered an opportunity to pyramid the initial position.

A Six-Month Ascending Triangle Failure in USD/CAD

This market situation was shown earlier in the book in Chapter 4. In April, the forex pair completed an ascending triangle failure on the weekly graph, as shown again in Figure 14.11.

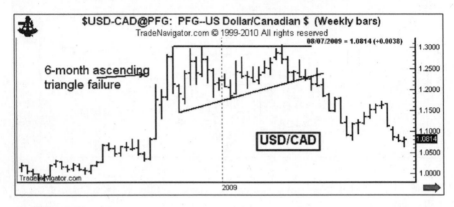

FIGURE 14.11 Downside Breakout of Ascending Triangle on the Weekly USD/CAD Chart.

I term this as a *failure* pattern because the natural bias of a right-angled triangle is to break out through the horizontal boundary. The daily chart, as shown in Figure 14.12, experienced a premature breakout on April 14, followed by a move back into the pattern. On April 24, the market experienced the second and final pattern completion. The target was reached on May 29.

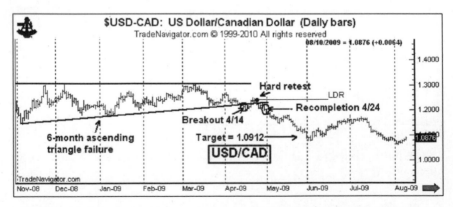

FIGURE 14.12 Daily USD/CAD Graph Shows Initial Breakout Failure Followed by Pattern Recompletion.

An Eight-Month H&S Bottom in the S&Ps

There is always at least one chart each year that I refuse to believe. I usually lose money attempting to fade the trend produced by these patterns. In 2009 (and 2010 to date), it has been the Standard & Poor's (S&Ps). In real time, I saw the eight-month weekly chart H&S bottom in the Mini S&Ps, as shown in the weekly chart in Figure 14.13A.

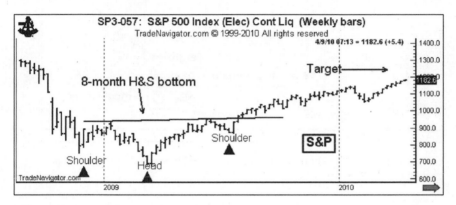

FIGURE 14.13A   H&S Bottom on the Weekly Graph Reverses the 2008 Meltdown in the S&Ps.

The Last Day Rule of the July 23 breakout was never remotely challenged (see Figure 14.13B). The target of this pattern has not yet been met, and it is anyone's guess if it will be met.

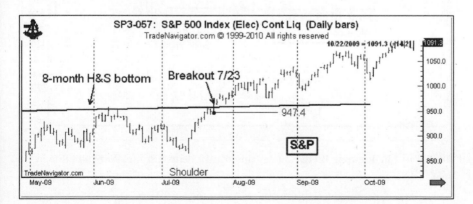

FIGURE 14.13B   Daily S&P Chart Shows Clean Breakout of H&S Bottom.

A 14-Month Symmetrical Triangle in Sugar

The dominant pattern in this market was the 14-month symmetrical triangle on the weekly graph, completed on May 1, 2009 (see Figure 14.14).

FIGURE 14.14 2007–2009 Bull Market on the Weekly Sugar Chart: A Study in Classical Chart Patterns.

The pattern objective was met on August 6. There were several smaller pyramid opportunities during this trend (not shown). The counterpart pattern on the daily graph was a running channel or wedge, as shown in the weekly chart version of the May 2010 contract in Figure 14.15.

FIGURE 14.15 Running Wedge and Symmetrical Triangle Propel 2009 Bull Run in May Sugar.

Both the weekly and daily charts developed a well-defined continuation pattern, completed in mid-December 2009. The target was quickly met on January 6.

A Seven-Month Triangle in Gold

The gold market for most of the year epitomized the concept of pattern redefinition, as daily chart patterns formed, failed, and then became part of larger chart construction. This happened from February through early September. Figure 14.16 shows this period of congestion on the weekly graph. I detailed the constant redefinition of the daily gold charts in 2009 as a case study in Chapter 6.

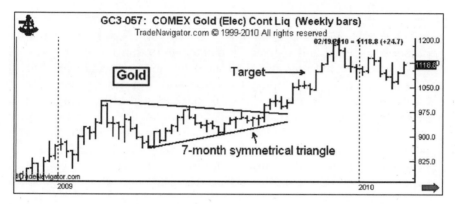

FIGURE 14.16   Seven-Month Symmetrical Triangle on the Weekly Gold Chart.

This congestion took the form of a seven-month symmetrical triangle. On September 2, the market completed the symmetrical triangle with a daily advance of $22 per ounce (see Figure 14.17). After seven months of being burned by buying strength and selling weakness, it was difficult to go long on top of a one-day rally of $22. Yet purchases made at the close of the breakout day were never put into harm's way.

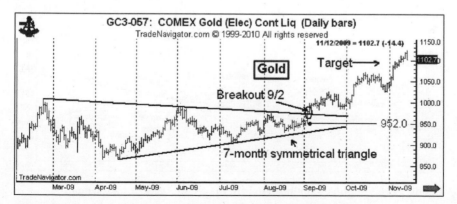

FIGURE 14.17   Symmetrical Triangle Breakout on the Daily Gold Chart.

The markets have a way of breaking down a trader's patience during the course of a prolonged congestion to the point that it is easy to doubt the real move when it comes. There are numerous examples over the years of markets that picked my pocket with premature breakouts, and I never became fully committed to the real breakout when it came.

The Goal of the Markets Is to Separate You from Your Money!

A trader much wiser and more profitable than I once said that the real purpose of capital and speculative markets is to transfer wealth from the many to the few, and that the speculative markets would cease to exist if over the long term they failed to deliver on this purpose. The practical implication of this, if true, is that the goal of the markets is to separate me from my money. Of course, the markets are not setting out in some coordinated and conscious way to do this. The markets do not represent a single cogent entity. Yet I believe that markets behave in an organic manner that can accomplish the same end.

A Series of Continuation Patterns in Copper

Figure 14.18 is presented once again as a wonderful example of how a major trend can occur through a series of small continuation patterns on the daily chart. In the case of copper, five individual patterns averaging seven weeks in length all formed above the dominant 10-month trend line. To be

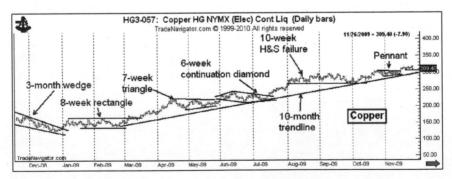

FIGURE 14.18   Multiple Continuation Patterns on the Daily Copper Graph.

perfectly honest, I believe that a sequence of patterns such as displayed on this chart is much more easily seen after the fact. While I admire the beauty of this trend after the fact, the trend itself was a very difficult one for me to trade.

An H&S Bottom in Crude Oil

As a general rule, the best weekly charts to use are those that track the nearby contract month (also referred to as the active month) either through the first delivery notice date or through the expiration of the contract. I monitor both weekly charts.

I also look at the life-of-contract weekly chart of the most actively traded contract month. This can sometimes provide valuable information. Finally, there are times when the weekly chart of a specific deferred contract will show the clearest pattern. This was the case in crude oil in 2009. Figure 14.19 is the weekly chart of the October 2009 contract. The advance in early May completed a 23-week H&S bottom pattern.

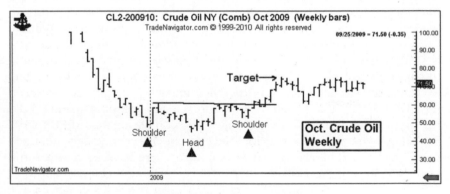

FIGURE 14.19   H&S Bottom on the Weekly Chart of October 2009 Crude Oil.

The daily chart of the October contract, as shown in Figure 14.20, displays the closing price line. Often, a closing price chart can provide insight into the timing of a breakout because it eliminates the intraday noise. The market completed its H&S bottom on May 6, hesitated for a week, then trended directly to reach the target on June 10. Remember, the closing price is the most significant price of the day. Everything else is noise. I all too often let the noise confuse me.

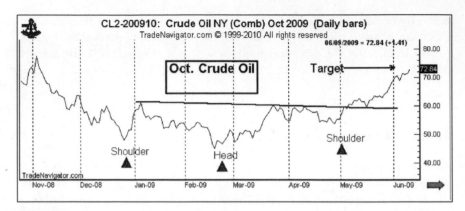

FIGURE 14.20   Daily Close-Only Chart Defines H&S Bottom in October 2009 Crude Oil.

Summary

Some years have more qualified candidates for the Best Dressed List than do other years. For example, the charts in 2008 were loaded with great weekly chart patterns offering strong breakouts and trends, especially in the traditional raw material commodities. The Factor Trading Plan depends on these types of classical charting situations to produce profitability. Without catching some of these chart situations, my trading tends to tread water.

There have been relatively few Best Dressed List market situations in the five months covered by this book. In fact, the only Best Dressed trading events since December that have met their implied price targets have been the EUR/USD, EUR/CHF, and the final thrust in the sugar bull market. I did not fully exploit EUR/USD, caught sugar, and completely missed EUR/CHF.

Some years are better years for the charts and for chart traders, but there is one reality that all chartists must embrace. There have been wonderful chart situations in the past and there will be wonderful chart situations in the future. The most important asset that a trader has is his or her trading equity. It is vital that trading equity be protected during those times when the charts are not providing excellent opportunities, or when a trader just can't get in step with the rhythm of the markets.

Remember, it is easy to make money in the commodity and forex markets when the charts are working and trends are sustained, but the challenge is to keep the profits during the tough times.

Postscript

The last regular entry into the trading journal was made on April 20, 2010. It is now very early June 2010, my last chance to add content to the book, and I'd like to take this opportunity bring you up to date on the Factor Trading Plan.

Final Performance

May was my best month by far in 2010. I closed out the *Diary of a Professional Commodity Trader* on April 20 with a cumulative gain of 5.4 percent. You will recall that my optimistic goal for the period covered by the book was a gain of 10 to 15 percent.

From April 20, the end of the diary, through May 31, the Factor Trading Plan experienced some excellent trades, and the six-month gain from December 7, 2009 (the first trade of the diary), through the end of May stands at 9.6 percent. This is the actual gain by the fund traded by Factor LLC. Of course, who knows what the future will bring. Specifically, the profits in the past five weeks have come from two markets.

The Stock Market Turns Down

As shown in Figure PS.1, the June Dow Jones Industrial Average completed a small H&S top on May 4. I shorted the completion of this top. The target of 10630 was quickly met and far exceeded. The retest rally through May 13 took the form of a rising wedge and offered the opportunity to again trade the stock indexes from the short side.

As of this writing, a multi-month H&S top looms large and the bears appear to be in control.

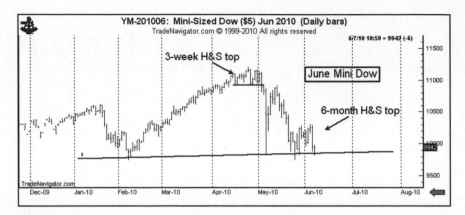

FIGURE PS.1 A Small H&S Pattern Created a Top in DJIA.

The Trading Range in AUD/CAD is Resolved

You may recall from Chapter 11, Figures 11.5 and 11.6, the severe whiplashing I endured when the daily AUD/CAD chart worked its way too far toward the apex of a triangle. I went from short to long to short, each trade being a loss.

Figure PS.2 shows that the trading range in this forex pair was finally resolved. The decline on May 11 confirmed a 14-week rectangle and a possible six-month descending triangle. This chart has already qualified for the 2010 Best Dressed List. The downside target has been met.

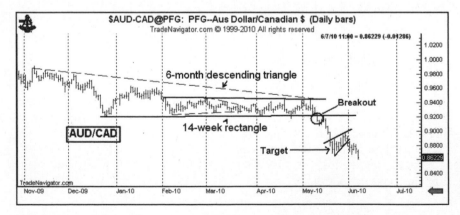

FIGURE PS.2 Major Sell Signal in AUD/CAD.

Performance Compared to Other Benchmarks

It has been a tough six months for commodity traders. Table PS.1 compares the performance of the actual commodity/forex pool traded by Factor LLC in accordance with the diary in this book against some benchmarks commonly used by the futures and forex industry. The benchmarks are the Lyxor CTA Index, the Barclay Hedge NewEdge CTA Index, and the S&P 500. Lyxor and Barclay track the commodity trading advisors (CTAs) managing large assets in the forward commodity and forex markets.

TABLE PS.1   Factor Trading Plan (Actual) versus Industry Benchmark Comparisons, December 2009–May 2010

Asset	Past Month (May 2010)	Past Six Months (December 2009–May 2010)
Factor Trading Plan	**+7.8%**	**+6.2%**
Factor Goal of 18% annual rate of return	+1.5%	+9.0%
S&P 500	(9.2%)	(0.5%)
BarclayHedge NewEdge CTA	(1.4%)	(1.3%)
Lyxor ST & LT CTA Index (equal weight)	(0.2%)	(2.38%)

Note: Proxy for Factor Trading Plan is the Factor Classic Fund, all fees included.
Sources: SPX closing price; Factor internal audit; www.BarclayHedge.com; www.LyxorHedgeIndicies.com.

No representation is made that this relative performance would hold true for any period of time other than the time covered by the diary of the book. The Factor Trading Plan could underperform or outperform industry benchmarks during any other floating periods of time.

Putting it in Perspective

Five or six months is a microcosm in the life of a trader. Frankly, six months, or even a year, really do not matter very much. I want to end this book by placing the past six months into the perspective of my career as a trader.

Figure PS.3 shows the trading performance of the period covered by this book into the context of my trading from 1981 through May 2010. This is a graph of the Value Added Monthly Index (VAMI) representing the growth of $1,000 without factoring in additions or withdrawals. Note that the period of the book is marked on the graph.

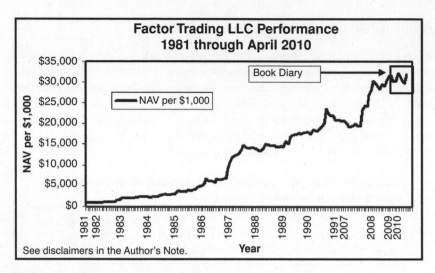

FIGURE PS.3   Factor Trading LLC Performance, 1981 through April 2010.

This graph makes a pro-forma adjustment to reflect the fact that I am currently trading with about one-third of the leverage I used from 1981 through 2008. So, the VAMI is constructed using monthly rates-of-return that are only one-third of the actual monthly returns in my proprietary accounts from 1981 through late 2008. The VAMI beginning in 2009 is based on actual performance, reflecting the lower leverage currently being used.

APPENDIX A

Factor Trading Plan Signals

Table A.1 contains the signals and trades of the Factor Trading Plan from December 7, 2009, through April 20, 2010. The results of the trades open as of April 20 are marked-to-market. Please read the disclaimers in the Author's Note for a complete explanation of the performance reporting.

TABLE A.1

Factor Classic LLC 2009 Trading Log

Pro-Forma Record Per $100,000 of Capitalization

*Currency cross trades expressed in quantity of primary (first listed) currency unit

Part of split exit

Final as of Apr. 20, 2010

Date	Market	Month	L or S	Entry price	Contracts per $100k*	LDR	Initial stop	Initial risk as % of NAV	Targets	Signal type	Pattern length	Daily pattern	Weekly pattern	Other	Date stops moved	Exit date	Exit price	Net P/L per $100,000	Net P/L per round lot	Exit rule used
7-Dec	EUR/USD	Spot	S	1.4796	−35000	1.5092	1.5096	1.1	1.4446& 1.3972	MjC	5-wk	Channel	9-mo channel		12/9 to 15009	12/17	1.4446	$1,215	$0	Target
9-Dec	GBP/USD	Spot	S	1.6228	−65000	1.6376	1.6386	1.0	1.5668	MnR	9-wk	H&S top				12/16	1.6386	($1,037)		LDR
11-Dec	Sugar	Mar	L	2371	0.5	2312	2298	0.7	3500	MjC	14-wk	Channel		6-wk H&S	12/21 to 25.29	12/22	2528	$874	$1,748	Trl stop
11-Dec	Sugar	Mar	L	2371	0.5	2312	2298	0.7	2736	MjC	14-wk	Channel		6-wk H&S	12/24 to 2496	12/28	2736	$2,039	$4,078	Target
14-Dec	Cotton	Mar	L	7522	1.0	7381	7378	0.8	7880	Misc	3-wk	Pennant			12/21 to 7423	12/22	7421	($515)		Retest fail
15-Dec	Soybean Oil	Mar	L	4037	0.7	3958	3949	0.7	Open	MjC	17-wk	Sym tri	Possible 12-mo fulcrum	Retest of 11/13 BA gap	12/17 to 4004	12/17	4003	($150)	($214)	Retest fail
16-Dec	AUD/USD	Spot	S	0.8989	−45000	9140	9142	0.7	8486	MjCr	11-wk	H&S			12/17 to 9021; 12/24 to 8871	12/28	0.8872	$517		Trail stop
16-Dec	DAX	Mar	L	5870.5	0.5	5759	5757	0.7	6390	MjC	5-wk	H&S cont	3+-mo cont diamond		12/21 to 5933	1/21	5833	($665)	($1,330)	LDR
17-Dec	GBP/USD	Spot	S	1.6224	−40000	16342	16281	0.5	1.5668	MnR	9-wk	H&S top		2nd completion	12/29 to split prices	12/30	1.5987	$938		Other

17-Dec	Soybean Oil	Mar	S	3929	0.7	4080	4016	0.4	3743	Instinct	5-wk	H&S top		12/23 to 3971	12/28	3971	($176)	($262)	Retest fail
17-Dec	Soybeans	Mar	S	1024	1.0	1071	1042	1.0	956	Misc	5-wk	H&S top		12/21 to 1041	12/28	1041	($860)		LDR
21-Dec	Mini Nasdaq	Mar	L	1821	0.5	1803	1802	0.3	1876	MnC	3-wk	Asc tri			12/28	1876	$683	$1,365	Target
29-Dec	USD/CAD	Spot	S	1.0378	-40000	1.0446	1.0454	0.5	1.0106	MnR	9-wk	Desc tri			12/30	1.0456	($308)		LDR
31-Dec	AUD/USD	Spot	S	0.8939	-120000	9012	9022	1.0	8486	MjC	11-wk	H&S top	Retest		1/4	0.9024	($1,140)		LDR
4-Jan	Sugar	July	L	2324	1.0	2270	2269	0.6	Open	MjC	2-wk	Running wedge	4-mo rectangle	1/8 to 2297	1/11	2297	($312)		LDR
4-Jan	Corn	Mar	L	425.2	1.0	415	414.4	0.6	468	MnC	10-wk	Asc tri			1/4	414.2	($560)		Intervening LDR
12-Jan	USD/JPY	Spot	S	91.69	-30000	9243	9271	0.4	87.55	MnR	5-wk	Rising wedge	Major down trend	1/20 to 9207; 2/1 to 9101	2/3	91.02	$211		LDR
12-Jan	Mini Nasdaq	Mar	S	1862.25	1.0	1883.8	1884.5	0.6	1831	Misc	2-wk	Broadening top	Retest		1/13	1884.5	($566)		Retest fail
13-Jan	T-Bonds	Mar	S	116-19	0.5	118-14 (12/21)	117-25	0.5	112-02	MjC	17-wk	Double top		1/14 to 107-07	1/15	107-07	($318)	($635)	Trail stop
14-Jan	Corn	Mar	S	3802	0.5	3924	397	0.5	3310	MjC	12-wk	Sym tri	Break-away gap	2/4 to 3702; 2/12 to 3664	2/16	3664	$339	$678	Trail stop
15-Jan	Wheat	Mar	S	512	0.5	5256	526	0.4	461	MjC and 432	13-wk	H&S top		1/29 to 5052; 2/8 to 4964	2/10	4966	$376	$753	Target
15-Jan	EUR/JPY	Spot	S	130.74	-30000.0	132.41	132.51	0.5	127.4	MjA	3-wk	H&S top	Possible 11-mo H&S top	1/21	1/21	127.52	$1,058		LDR

(Continued)

TABLE A.1 (Continued)

Factor Classic LLC 2009 Trading Log

Pro-Forma Record Per $100,000 of Capitalization

*Currency cross trades expressed in quantity of primary (first listed) currency unit

Part of split exit

Final as of Apr. 20, 2010

Date	Market	Month	L or S	Entry price	Contracts per $100k*	LDR	Initial stop	Initial risk as % of NAV	Targets	Signal type	Pattern length	Daily pattern	Weekly pattern	Other	Date stops moved	Exit date	Exit price	Net P/L per $100,000	Net P/L per round lot	Exit rule used
19-Jan	Mini S&Ps	Mar	S	1126.5	1.0	1137	1140.25	0.7	Open	MjC	13-wk	Rising wedge	10-mo trend-line			1/19	1140.5	($710)		Trail stop
19-Jan	Sugar	May	L	2716	0.5	2660	2654	0.4	Open	MjP	2-wk	Pennant			2/2 to 2763	2/3	2763	$258	$516	Quick profit
20-Jan	Mini Gold	Apr	S	1117.1	0.5	1143	1144.4	0.5	1096	Instinct	3-wk	H&S top	Possible 3-mo failure top			1/21	1096	$343	$686	Quick profit
20-Jan	Mini Gold	Apr	S	1117.1	0.5	1143	1125.1	0.1	1079	Instinct	3-wk	H&S top	Possible 3-mo failure top			1/28	1079	$619	$1,247	$ mgmt
20-Jan	Mini Gold	Apr	S	1117.1	0.5	1143	1133.6	0.3	1033	Instinct	3-wk	H&S top	Possible 3-mo failure top		1/28 to 1125.2; 2/1 to 1124.3	2/3	1124.4	($125)	($251)	Quick profit
21-Jan	Mini S&Ps	Mar	S	1125	0.5	1139.3	1140.25	0.4	1086	MjC	3-wk	H&S top	13-wk wedge			1/26	1086	$970	$1,940	Trail stop
21-Jan	Mini S&Ps	Mar	S	1125	0.5	1139.3	1140.25	0.4	1024	MjC	3-wk	H&S top	13-wk wedge		2/4 to 1103; 2/12 to 1084	2/16	1084.25	$1,014	$2,028	Retest fail
21-Jan	Mini S&Ps	Mar	S	1125	0.5	1139.3	1140.25	0.4	1024	MjC	3-wk	H&S top	13-wk wedge		2/5 to 1120.5	3/5	1120.5	$108	$215	Trail stop
21-Jan	GBP/JPY	Spot	S	146.16	−20000	149.11	148.12	0.6	140.12	MjA	3-wk	Sym tri	Possible 4-mo desc tri		2/1 to 147.41	2/4	140.22	$1,324		Trail stop

26-Jan	EUR/JPY	Spot	S	126.42	−20000	128.37	128.47	0.6	116.52	MjC	43-wk	Rounding top	Same		2/4 to 126.52; 2/23 to 125.36; 3/3 to 122.67	3/5	122.68	$819	$3,078	Trail stop
27-Jan	Copper	Mar	S	323.95	0.3	335.7	332.1	0.6	311.60 & 295.05	MjC	3-wk	Horn	10-mo channel			2/11	311.6	$769		Target
29-Jan	GBP/USD	Spot	S	1.6069	−30000	16180	16187	0.4	15828	MnC	1-wk	Pennant	Possible 9-mo double top			2/4	1.5828	$714		Target
2-Feb	Soybean Oil	Mar	L	3670	0.5	3600	3573	0.3	3838	Instinct rev 5/8	43-wk	Sym tri			2/10 to 3694	2/10	3838	$499	$999	Retest fail
4-Feb	Mini Gold	Apr	S	1067.4	1.0	1111.8	1087.2	0.7	927	MnR	9-wk	Desc tri		Poor fill	2/10 to 1085.1	2/11	1085.2	($597)		LDR
5-Feb	GBP/USD	Spot	S	1.5661	−30000	1.5776	1.5806	0.4	1.463	MjC	39-wk	Double top				2/17	1.5806	($445)		Retest fail
12-Feb	Mini Crude Oil	Apr	S	73.95	0.5	75.8	76.225	0.6	58.2	MjC	52-wk	Fan principle	Same			2/16	76.25	($580)	($1,160)	Rev. LDR
18-Feb	GBP/USD	Spot	S	1.5583	−40000	1.5688	1.5701	0.6	1.463	MjC	8-wk	Flag	9-mo double top	Hikkake	3/16 to 15439; 3/15 to 1.5061	3/30	1.5062	$2,074		Retest fail
18-Feb	T-Bonds	June	S	115-17	0.5	116-10	116-19	0.6	113-17	MjA	3-wk	Broadening top	Possible 8-mo H&S top	1-wk flag	2/22 to 116-12	2/23	116-12	($427)	($854)	Quick profit
18-Feb	Mini Gold	Apr	L	1099.7	0.5	1094	1089.4	0.2	1124	MnC rev	11-wk	Wedge	H&S bottom 9/09	Breakaway gap	2/18 to 1096.3	2/19	1124	$396	$792	Retest fail
18-Feb	Mini Gold	Apr	L	1099.7	0.5	1094	1089.4	0.2	1223	MnC	11-wk	Wedge	H&S bottom 9/09	Breakaway gap	2/18 to 1096.3	2/24	1096.2	($63)	($126)	LDR
18-Feb	10-Yr T-Notes	June	S	116-01	0.5	116-14	116-15	0.3	114-24	Misc	3-wk	H&S top		Too tight of an entry stop		2/23	116-15	($224)	($448)	Other

(Continued)

253

TABLE A.1 (Continued)

Factor Classic LLC 2009 Trading Log

Pro-Forma Record Per $100,000 of Capitalization

*Currency cross trades expressed in quantity of primary (first listed) currency unit

Part of split exit

Final as of Apr. 20, 2010

Date	Market	Month	L or S	Entry price	Contracts per $100k*	LDR	Initial stop	Initial risk as % of NAV	Targets	Signal type	Pattern length	Daily pattern	Weekly pattern	Other	Date stops moved	Exit date	Exit price	Net P/L per $100,000	Net P/L per round lot	Exit rule used
23-Feb	GBP/JPY	Spot	S	139.36	−30000	141.68	141.23	0.8	128.1	MjC	22-wk	Desc triangle	Same		2/26 to 13976; 3/11 to 137.49	3/12	137.62	$565		Target
23-Feb	Sugar	Oct	S	2103	0.5	2155	2161	0.4	1976	MnR	8-wk	Rectangle	Retest of major top	Hourly chart		3/2	1976	$706	$1,412	LHR
23-Feb	Copper	May	S	321.4	0.5	334.35	326.7	0.6	280	Misc	3-wk	Channel				2/26	326.8	($680)	($1,360)	LDR
25-Feb	Soybean Oil	May	L	3956	2.0	NA	3898	0.4	4069	MnC	2-wk	Flag	Possible 10-mo triangle			2/25	3897	($728)		LDR
25-Feb	Mini S&Ps	June	S	1085	1.0	1098.3	1098.5	0.7	Open	MnR	3-wk	H&S top	Retest of major top	3-wk channel		2/26	1098.5	($685)		LDR
25-Feb	Mini Dow	Mar	S	10234	1.0	10355	10367	0.6	Open	Misc	2-wk	H&S top	Retest of major top			3/1	10368	($680)		Target
25-Feb	EUR/GBP	Spot	L	0.8861	35000.0	0.8773	0.8769	0.4	9062	MjA	17-wk	Channel	Possible 14-mo H&S bottom	5-wk horn		3/1	0.9062	$1,045		Target
26-Feb	Soybean Oil	May	L	3954	1.0	3924	3906	0.3	4069	MnC	2-wk	Flag	Possible 12-month asc triangle			3/10	4069	$680		Intervening
1-Mar	OJ	May	L	14485	1.0	14070	14045	0.6	158	MnC	9-wk	Sym tri	Same		3/8 to 14360; 3/16 to 14475	3/18	14455	($55)		Retest fail
2-Mar	Mini Gold	Apr	L	1133.6	1.0	1115.1	1114.8	0.7	1195	MnR	9-wk	H&S top	Mnthly H&S unmet target		3/5 to 1124.8	3/8	1124.7	($304)		Rev LDR

Date	Instrument	Month		Entry	Size				Value	Code	Period	Pattern	Comment	Exit range	Exit	Price	P/L		Note
3-Mar	USD/CAD	Spot	S	1.0352	−50000	1.0444	1.0451	0.5	9720	MjA	22-wk	Desc tri	Same	3/10 to 1.0351; 3/22 to 1.0332; 3/25 to 1.0301	3/26	1.0301	$238		Retest fail
4-Mar	Soybeans	May	S	938.4	0.5	963	962.4	0.7	899	Misc	3-wk	H&S top	Possible 19-wk triangle	3/5 to 950.2	3/8	950.2	($304)	($598)	Retest fail
12-Mar	USD/CAD	Spot	S	1.0198	−70000	10322	10326	0.8	9720	MjC	22-wk	Sym tri	20-wk triangle	3/22 to 1.0256	3/24	1.0256	($406)		Retest fail
12-Mar	Mini Crude Oil	May	S	81.35	0.5	83475	8295	0.8	7740	MjA	7-wk	Rising wedge	Possible fan	3/16 to 8255	3/17	8255	($305)		LDR
19-Mar	AUD/CAD	Spot	S	0.9258	−100000	9381	9326	0.8	Open	Instinct	4-wk	Triangle	Possible 3-mo triangle		3/19	0.9327	($688)		Trail stop
19-Mar	EUR/USD	Spot	S	1.353	−30000	1.3627	1.3741	0.6	1.3132	MnC	6-wk	H&S fail	May down channel	3/27 to 1.3436	3/29	1.3474	$158		LDR
22-Mar	Mini Gold	June	S	1096.8	1	1109.6	1111.2	0.5	1052	MnR	6-wk	H&S top	Possible 3+-mo H&S fail		3/26	1111.3	($489)		Retest fail
24-Mar	T-Bonds	June	S	117-08	0.5	117-22	117-24	0.3	Open	MjA	12-wk	Asc tri failure	Possible 12-mo H&S	4/11 to 116-01	4/12	116-02	$589	$1,178	LDR
24-Mar	GBP/USD	Spot	S	1.4916	−40000	15049	15061	0.3	1.441	MjP	4-wk	Flag	Dbl top		3/30	1.5062	($594)		LDR
25-Mar	Wheat	May	S	470.4	0.5	478.2	479	0.3		MnC	New lows	New lows			4/7	479	($218)	($435)	Retest fail
25-Mar	Corn	May	S	358.2	1.0	366.4	367	0.3		MnC	New lows	New lows		4/8 to 360.2	4/14	3604	($123)		Quick profit
29-Mar	USD/CAD	Spot	S	1.0192	−30000	1.0273	1.0287	0.5	9720	MjCs	22-wk	Sym tri		Books closed 4/20 MTM	4/20	0.9984	$615	2nd completion	LDR
31-Mar	AUD/CAD	Spot	S	0.9332	−30000	0.9382	0.9402	0.2	0.8812	MjA	14-wk	Sym tri	Same	4/5 to 9327	4/7	0.9327	$5		LHR

(Continued)

TABLE A.1 (Continued)

Factor Classic LLC 2009 Trading Log

Pro-Forma Record Per $100,000 of Capitalization

*Currency cross trades expressed in quantity of primary (first listed) currency unit

Part of split exit

Final as of Apr. 20, 2010

Date	Market	Month	L or S	Entry price	Contracts per $100k*	LDR	Initial stop	Initial risk as % of NAV	Targets	Signal type	Pattern length	Daily pattern	Weekly pattern	Other	Date stops moved	Exit date	Exit price	Net P/L per $100,000	Net P/L per round lot	Exit rule used
31-Mar	Soybeans	Nov	S	906.4	0.5	930	931.4	0.6	872/857	MnR	8-wk	Sym tri	Same		3/31 to 916.4	3/31	916.4	($255)	($510)	Retest failure
1-Apr	Mini Gold	June	L	1126.2	0.5	1112.1	1110.8	0.4	Open	MjA	4-wk	Channel	Possible 4-mo H&S bottom		4/7 to 1131.8; 4/12 to 1141.9	4/16	1141.3	$477	$954	LDR
5-Apr	AUD/CAD	Spot	S	0.9238	−100000	9320	9311	0.8	8862	MjC	15-wk	Sym tri	Same			4/7	0.9312	($745)		Retest failure
5-Apr	EUR/GBP	Spot	L	0.8844	25000	8814	0.8812	0.2	9124	Misc	22-wk	H&S bottom	Same	Retest		4/6	0.8812	($131)		LDR
7-Apr	Mini Gold	June	L	1151.1	1	1133.1	1131.8	0.7	1230	MjC	17-wk	H&S bottom	Same			4/16	1131.4	($660)		LDR
7-Apr	EUR/JPY	Spot	S	124.61	−20000	126.16	126.31	0.5	112.27	MjC	43-wk	Rounding top	Same	Secondary completion	4/9 to 125.41	4/9	125.41	($182)		LDR
9-Apr	AUD/CAD	Spot	L	0.9361	20000.0	9282	9279	0.3	0.9608	MnR	15-wk	Sym tri	Same	End-around	4/11 to 9319	4/12	0.9319	($94)		Quick profit
15-Apr	Soybeans	Nov	L	953	0.5	9414	940.6	0.4	998	MnR	10-wk	Asc tri	Same	Books closed 4/20 MTM		4/20	963.2	$256	$513	

Split exit strategy

Trades assigned to month of entry

Totals	Z-J $5,386
Dec	$1,413
Jan	$6,330
Feb	$857
Mar	($2,135)
April	$256

PAST PERFORMANCE IS NOT NECESSARILY INDICATIVE OF FUTURE RESULTS.
READ COMPLETE DISCUSSION OF PERFORMANCE IN AUTHOR'S NOTE.

Quick Reference to Charts

The following tables are intended to be a quick reference guide to the charts in this book. The tables list various elements of classical charting principles, trading signals, and trade management techniques used by the Factor Trading Plan and where they can be found in the book.

Table B.1 lists the charts in the book according to which classical chart pattern they illustrate.

Table B.2 lists the charts in the book based on the type of signal generated and the appropriate trade management strategy.

TABLE B.1   Charts by Pattern

Figure #	Market	Wedge	Sym triangle	Flag	Trendline	Channel	Diamond	H&S	Right angled triangle	Double top or bottom	Broadening or fishhook	Rounding	Rectangle	Pennant	Horn	Bull or bear trap	Secondary completion	False/premature breakout
		Diagonal						**Horizontal**								**Other**		
2.2	Swiss Franc	■																
3.2	GBP/USD								■									
3.3	GBP/USD								■									
3.4	Platinum								■									
3.5	Lnd Sugar		■															■
3.6	Sugar	■																
3.7	Cocoa						■											
3.8	DAX																■	
3.9	S&Ps															■	■	
3.10	Gold												■					
3.11	EUR/USD				■													
3.12	Gold	■																
3.13	Crude Oil							■										
3.14	Silver								■				■					■
3.15	S&Ps								■									
3.16	Rice	■							■									
3.17	USD/CAD								■									■
3.18	Soybeans		■													■		
3.19	Sugar																	
3.20	GBP/USD								■									
3.21	AUD/USD			■						■				■				
3.22	AUD/USD					■	■											
3.23	DJIA																	
3.24	GBP/USD							■								■		
3.25	Sugar		■													Weekend Rule		
3.26	Sugar		■													Weekend Rule		
3.27	Bean Oil															Market Run		
3.28	Gold															Market Run		
3.29	USD/JPY							■										■
4.1	Copper								■									
4.2	AUD/USD	■																
4.3	Bean Oil	■	■															
4.4	Bean Oil									■								
4.5	Sugar		■															
4.6	USD/CAD								■	■	■							
4.7	Silver								■				■			■		■
4.8	Russell 1000							■								■		
4.9	KC Wheat												■					
4.10	KC Wheat												■					
4.11	Crude Oil		■											■				
4.12	DJ Util							■										

TABLE B.1 (*Continued*)

Figure #	Market	Diagonal						Horizontal								Other		
		Wedge	Sym triangle	Flag	Trendline	Channel	Diamond	H&S	Right angled triangle	Double top or bottom	Broadening or fishhook	Rounding	Rectangle	Pennant	Horn	Bull or bear trap	Secondary completion	False/premature breakout
4.13	EUR/USD		■							■								
4.14	EUR/USD		■															
4.15	EUR/USD			■						■								
4.16	GBP/JPY	■					■							■				
4.17	GBP/JPY		■											■				
4.18	AUD/JPY		■															
4.19	AUD/JPY		■															
4.20	GBP/CHF	■							■				■					■
4.21	Sugar		■															
4.22	Sugar	■																
4.23	AAPL							■										
4.24	Gold										■							
4.25	Gold			■			■											
4.26	Copper					■	■							■				
4.27	USD/CAD								■									■
4.28	USD/CAD								■								■	■
4.29	DJTI											■						
4.30	Brent Sea													■				
4.31	S&P 500								■									
5.2	GBP/USD									■								
5.3	GBP/USD							■									■	
5.4	GBP/USD			■	■			■						■				
5.5	GBP/USD				■			■										
6.1	DJIA							■								■		■
6.2	DJIA							■										
6.3	Gold				Multiple Trades													
6.4	Gold																	
6.5	Gold		¡															
6.6	Gold																	
6.7	Gold																	■
6.8	Gold																	
6.9	Gold																	■
6.10	Gold		■															
6.11	Gold																	
6.12	Gold							■										
6.13	Gold							■										
6.14	Gold									■								
6.15	Sugar		■															
6.16	Sugar				Multiple Trades													
6.17	Sugar		■												New Highs			
6.18	Sugar												■					
6.19	Sugar	■																

(*Continued*)

TABLE B.1   (*Continued*)

Figure #	Market	Diagonal						Horizontal								Other		
		Wedge	Sym triangle	Flag	Trendline	Channel	Diamond	H&S	Right angled triangle	Double top or bottom	Broadening or fishhook	Rounding	Rectangle	Pennant	Horn	Bull or bear trap	Secondary completion	False/premature breakout
6.20	Sugar		■															
6.21	Sugar	■									■			■				
6.22	Sugar						■							■				
6.23	Sugar													·			Impulse buys	
6.24	Sugar						■		■									
8.1	EUR/USD				■													
8.2	EUR/USD					■											■	
8.3	GBP/USD								■									
8.4	GBP/USD															Hikkake		
8.5	GBP/USD															Hikkake		
8.6	GBP/USD								■		Hikkake							
8.7	GBP/USD								■									■
8.8	Sugar						■											
8.9	Cotton													■				
8.10	Bean Oil		■															
8.11	Bean Oil								■									
8.12	AUD/USD								■									
8.13	DAX								■									
8.14	Soybeans								■									
8.15	Nasdaq								■									
8.16	CAD/USD									■								
9.1	GBP/USD								■									
9.2	SPX	■				■												
9.3A	T-Bonds								■									
9.3B	T-Bonds								■									
9.3C	T-Bonds								■									
9.4	Gold								■									
9.5	Sugar											■						
9.6	DJIA								■									
9.7	Sugar	■											■					
9.8	Corn								■							■		■
9.9	Corn								■									
9.10	USD/JPY																	
9.11	USD/JPY	■																
9.12	Nasdaq										■					■		■
9.13	T-Bonds									■	■							
9.14	Corn		■															
9.15	Wheat								■									
9.16	EUR/JPY												■					
9.17	EUR/JPY																	
9.18	S&P 500	■																
9.19	Sugar					■								■				

TABLE B.1 (*Continued*)

Figure #	Market	Diagonal: Wedge	Sym triangle	Flag	Trendline	Channel	Diamond	H&S	Horizontal: Right angled triangle	Double top or bottom	Broadening or fishhook	Rounding	Rectangle	Pennant	Horn	Other: Bull or bear trap	Secondary completion	False/premature breakout
9.20	Gold							■										
9.21	Gold								■							■		
9.22	Gold	■																■
9.23	Gold																	
9.24	Gold							■								■		
9.25	Gold						■	■										
9.26	GBP/JPY		■						■									
9.27	Copper				■										■			
9.28	GBP/USD			■												Hikkake		
10.2	GBP/USD									■								
10.3	GBP/USD			■												Hikkake		
10.4	GBP/USD																	■
10.5	Crude Oil									■						Fan Lines		
10.6	Crude Oil									■								
10.7	Crude Oil				■													■
10.8	T-Bonds			■							■							
10.9	T-Notes							■										
10.10	GBP/JPY			■					■									
10.11A	Sugar												■					
10.11B	Sugar												■					
10.12	Bean Oil							■										
10.13	Bean Oil																	
10.14A	Bean Oil													■				■
10.15	S&P 500							■								■		
10.16	DJIA							■										
10.17	EUR/GBP					■		■										
10.18	EUR/GBP							■										
11.1	USD/CAD												■					
11.2	USD/CAD							■									■	
11.3	Soybeans							■										
11.4	Crude Oil	■																
11.5	AUD/CAD		■															
11.6	AUD/CAD		■															■
11.7	EUR/USD			■					■									
11.8	EUR/USD								■									
11.9	T-Bonds								■									
11.10	Wheat																	
11.11	Corn								■									
11.12	Soybeans		■						■							■		
11.13	Copper			■	■													
11.14	OJ		■															■
12.1	Gold							■										

(*Continued*)

TABLE B.1   *(Continued)*

Figure #	Market	Wedge	Sym triangle	Flag	Trendline	Channel	Diamond	H&S	Right angled triangle	Double top or bottom	Broadening or fishhook	Rounding	Rectangle	Pennant	Horn	Bull or bear trap	Secondary completion	False/premature breakout
			Diagonal							Horizontal							Other	
12.2	Gold					■		■										
12.3	EUR/GBP													■				
12.4	EUR/JPY											■					Retest	
12.5	EUR/JPY					■												
12.6	Soybeans		■															
12.7	Soybeans		■															
12.8	DJIA					■		■										
12.9	DJIA							■										
12.10	T-Bonds						■											
12.11	T-Bonds							■										
12.12	T-Bonds							■										
12.13	Sugar											■						
14.1	AUD/USD							■										
14.2	AUD/USD									■								
14.3/4	EUR/CHF		■					■										
14.5/6	EUR/USD	■			■													
14.7/8	GBP/USD														■			
14.9/10	NZD/USD		■					■										
14.11/12	USD/CAD							■										■
14.13A/13B	S&P 500							■										
14.14	Sugar		■															
14.15	Sugar	■																
14.16/17	Gold	■																
14.18	Copper	■	■		■		■				■		■					
14.19	Crude Oil								■									
14.20	Crude Oil							■										
PS.1	Dow Jones							■									Retest	
PS.2	AUD/CAD								■						■			

TABLE B.2 Charts by Signal Category and Trade Management Technique

Figure #	Market	Completion	Anticipatory	Pyramid	Continuation	Reversal	Instinct	Misc	Last Day Rule	Retest Failure	Trailing Stop Rule	Target	Other
		Major Pattern			Minor Pattern								
2.2	Swiss	■										■	
3.2	GBP/USD	■										■	
3.3	GBP/USD	■										■	
3.4	Platinum	■										■	
3.5	Lnd Sugar	■							■				
3.6	Sugar	■							■				
3.7	Cocoa	■							■				
3.8	DAX	■											
3.9	S&Ps	■											
3.10	Gold	■										■	
3.11	EUR/USD	■											
3.12	Gold					■			■				
3.13	Crude Oil	■							■				
3.14	Silver				■				■				
3.15	S&Ps												■
3.16	Rice	■											
3.17	USD/CAD	■							■				
3.18	Soybeans									■			
3.19	Sugar											■	
3.20	GBP/USD											■	
3.21	AUD/USD	■			■								
3.22	AUD/USD											■	
3.23	DJIA										■		
3.24	GBP/USD											■	
3.25	Sugar											■	
3.26	Sugar											■	
3.27	Bean Oil						■						
3.28	Gold											■	
3.29	USD/JPY	■							■				
4.1	Copper	■										■	
4.2	AUD/USD	■										■	
4.3	Bean Oil		■										
4.4	Bean Oil	■				■							
4.5	Sugar	■										■	
4.6	USD/CAD				■							■	
4.7	Silver	■							■				

(Continued)

TABLE B.2   *(Continued)*

Figure #	Market	Completion	Anticipatory	Pyramid	Continuation	Reversal	Instinct	Misc	Last Day Rule	Retest Failure	Trailing Stop Rule	Target	Other
4.8	Russell	■				■			■			■	
4.9	KC Wheat	■										■	
4.10	KC Wheat	■										■	
4.11	Crude Oil			■									
4.12	DJ Util	■											
4.13	EUR/USD	■											
4.14	EUR/USD	■											
4.15	EUR/USD	■			■								
4.16	GBP/JPY	■		■									
4.17	GBP/JPY	■		■									
4.18	AUD/JPY	■											
4.19	AUD/JPY	■											
4.20	GBP/CHF	■		■					■				
4.21	Sugar	■											
4.22	Sugar	■										■	
4.23	AAPL	■										■	
4.24	Gold	■											
4.25	Gold	■			■								
4.26	Copper				■								
4.27	USD/CAD	■							■			■	
4.28	USD/CAD	■							■				
4.29	DJTI	■											
4.30	Brent Sea	■											
4.31	S&P 500	■											
5.2	GBP/USD	■											
5.3	GBP/USD	■	■										
5.4	GBP/USD				■								■
5.5	GBP/USD				■								
6.1	DJIA					■			■				
6.2	DJIA		■									■	
6.3	Gold												
6.4	Gold		■										
6.5	Gold										■		
6.6	Gold										■		
6.7	Gold					■				■			
6.8	Gold					■				■			
6.9	Gold					■				■			

TABLE B.2 *(Continued)*

Figure #	Market	Signal Type							Trade Management Strategy				
		Major Pattern			Minor Pattern								
		Completion	Anticipatory	Pyramid	Continuation	Reversal	Instinct	Misc	Last Day Rule	Retest Failure	Trailing Stop Rule	Target	Other
6.10	Gold	■											
6.11	Gold			■									
6.12	Gold				■								
6.13	Gold											■	
6.14	Gold												■
6.15	Sugar												
6.16	Sugar	Multiple trades											
6.17	Sugar	■			■				■				
6.18	Sugar												
6.19	Sugar												
6.20	Sugar												
6.21	Sugar	■			■								
6.22	Sugar			■					■				
6.23	Sugar							■					
6.24	Sugar	■										■	
8.1	EUR/USD	Major trendline										■	
8.2	EUR/USD	■										■	
8.3	GBP/USD		■		■				■				
8.6	GBP/USD				■								
8.7	GBP/USD				■								
8.8	Sugar	■											
8.9	Cotton						■						
8.10	Bean Oil	■								■			
8.11	Bean Oil					■				■			
8.12	AUD/USD	■									■		
8.13	DAX	■					■						
8.14	Soybeans						■						
8.15	Nasdaq				■							■	
8.16	CAD/USD					■			■				
9.1	GBP/USD	Example of double top											
9.2	SPX	Example of channel											
9.3A	T-Bonds	Example of channel											
9.3B	T-Bonds	Example of H&S top											
9.3C	T-Bonds	Example of H&S top											
9.4	Gold	■											
9.5	Sugar	Example of multiyear base											
9.6	DJIA	Possible H&S top											

(Continued)

TABLE B.2   (*Continued*)

Figure #	Market	Completion	Anticipatory	Pyramid	Continuation	Reversal	Instinct	Misc	Last Day Rule	Retest Failure	Trailing Stop Rule	Target	Other
		Major Pattern			Minor Pattern				Trade Management Strategy				
9.7	Sugar	■							■				
9.8	Corn				■				■				
9.9	Corn								■				
9.10	USD/JPY	Multidecade triangle											
9.11	USD/JPY					■							■
9.12	Nasdaq							■	■				
9.13	T-Bonds	■											
9.14	Corn	■									■		
9.15	Wheat	■									■		
9.16	EUR/JPY		■										
9.17	EUR/JPY		■								■		
9.18	S&P 500												■
9.19	Sugar			■									
9.20	Gold					■							
9.21	Gold					■				■			
9.22	Gold								■				
9.23	Gold					■			■				
9.24	Gold								■				
9.25	Gold	■							■				
9.26	GBP/JPY	■										■	
9.27	Copper						■		■			■	
9.28	GBP/USD				■				■				
10.2	GBP/USD								■				
10.3	GBP/USD					■							
10.4	GBP/USD	■			■				■				
10.5	Crude Oil												
10.6	Crude Oil	Possible H&S top											
10.7	Crude Oil	■							■				
10.8	T-Bonds		■										
10.9	T-Notes							■					
10.10	GBP/JPY	■									■		
10.11A	Sugar					■						■	
10.12	Bean Oil	Ascending triangle											
10.13	Bean Oil					■						■	
10.14A	Bean Oil				■				■				
10.14B	Bean Oil				■				■				
10.15	S&P 500					■			■				

TABLE B.2 (*Continued*)

Figure #	Market	Major Pattern — Completion	Major Pattern — Anticipatory	Major Pattern — Pyramid	Minor Pattern — Continuation	Minor Pattern — Reversal	Instinct	Misc	Last Day Rule	Retest Failure	Trailing Stop Rule	Target	Other
10.16	DJIA							■	■				
10.17	EUR/GBP		■									■	
10.18	EUR/GBP		■										
11.1	USD/CAD		■										
11.2	USD/CAD		■								■		
11.3	Soybeans						■		■				
11.4	Crude Oil												
11.5	AUD/CAD												
11.6	AUD/CAD		■			■							
11.7	EUR/USD				■						■		
11.8	EUR/USD				■						■		
11.9	T-Bonds		■										
11.10	Wheat								■				
11.11	Corn								■				
11.12	Soybeans								■				
11.13	Copper	Missed trade											
11.14	OJ										■		
12.1	Gold												
12.2	Gold		■						■				
12.3	EUR/GBP						■						
12.4	EUR/JPY						■						
12.5	EUR/JPY						■						■
12.6	Soybeans					■							
12.7	Soybeans	■									■		
12.8	DJIA	Signal Pending							Pending				
12.9	DJIA	Signal Pending							Pending				
12.10	T-Bonds	Signal Pending							Pending				
12.11	T-Bonds	Signal Pending											
12.12	T-Bonds												
12.13	Sugar								Pending				
14.1	AUD/USD	■										■	
14.2	AUD/USD	■										■	
14.3/4	EUR/CHF	■										■	
14.5/6	EUR/USD	■										■	
14.7/8	GBP/USD	■										■	
14.9/10	NZD/USD	■										■	
14.11/12	USD/CAD	■										■	

(*Continued*)

TABLE B.2   (*Continued*)

Figure #	Market	Signal Type							Trade Management Strategy				
		Major Pattern			Minor Pattern								
		Completion	Anticipatory	Pyramid	Continuation	Reversal	Instinct	Misc	Last Day Rule	Retest Failure	Trailing Stop Rule	Target	Other
14.13A/13B	S&P 500	X										X	
14.14	Sugar	X										X	
14.15	Sugar	X										X	
14.16/17	Gold	X										X	
14.18	Copper				X							X	
14.19	Crude Oil	X										X	
14.20	Crude Oil											X	
PS.1	Dow Jones					X						X	
PS.2	AUD/CAD	X										X	

APPENDIX C

Recommended Resources

Barrie, Scott, *The Complete Idiot's Guide to Options and Futures*, 2nd ed. New York: Alpha Books, Penguin Group (USA), 2006.

Brandt, Peter L. (with Bruce Babcock), *Trading Commodity Futures with Classical Chart Patterns*. Sacramento, CA: Commodity Traders Consumer Reports, 1990.

Chicago Board of Trade, *Commodity Trading Manual*. New York: AMACOM, 1999.

Edwards, Robert D., and John Magee, *Technical Analysis of Stock Trends*, 8th ed. Boca Raton, FL: CRC Press, 2001. [*Note:* The author uses the fifth edition of this book for personal use.]

Elder, Alexander. *Trading for a Living: Psychology, Trading Tactics, Money Management*. New York: John Wiley & Sons, 1993.

Kiev, Ari, *The Mental Strategies of Top Traders: The Psychological Determinants of Trading Success*. Hoboken, NJ: John Wiley & Sons, 2009.

Kiev, Ari, *Hedge Fund Masters: How Top Hedge Fund Traders Set Goals, Overcome Barriers, and Achieve Peak Performance*. Hoboken, NJ: John Wiley & Sons, 2005.

Lewis, Michael. *Liar's Poker: Rising Through the Wreckage on Wall Street*. New York: W.W. Norton & Company, 1989.

Lewis, Michael. *The Big Short: Inside the Doomsday Machine*. New York: W.W. Norton & Company, 2010.

Murphy, John, *Technical Analysis of the Financial Markets*. New York Institute of Finance, Prentice Hall Direct, 1999.

National Futures Association, *Opportunity and Risk, An Educational Guide to Trading Futures*, 2006, PDF download at www.nfa.futures.org/NFA-investor-information/publication-library/opportunity-and-risk-entire.pdf.

Schabacker, Richard W., *Technical Analysis and Stock Market Profits: The Real Bible of Technical Analysis*. Hampshire, UK: Harriman House, 1998.

Schwager, Jack D., *Market Wizards: Interviews with Top Traders*. Columbia, MD: Marketplace Books, 2006.

Schwager, Jack D., *New Market Wizards: Conversations with America's Top Traders*. New York: John Wiley & Sons, 1992.
Schwager, Jack D., *Market Wizards*. New York: HarperBusiness, 1993.
Teweles, Richard J., and Frank J. Jones, *The Futures Game: Who Wins, Who Loses, & Why*. New York: McGraw-Hill, 1999.

In addition to the extremely insightful and informational books cited previously, I recommend a few services that provide web-based trading platforms, price quotes, charting capabilities, and other research.

FactorTrading.com: This is the official web site of Factor LLC. The web site attempts to identify and report on the best examples of classical chart patterns in the commodity and forex markets. Periodic chart stocks are also featured.

Mercenarytrader.com: This quirky and brilliant web site is written for professional traders by a couple of skilled professional speculators (using pseudonyms). Mercenarytrader provides unusual macro analyses of markets and global economics that break the mold of conventional wisdom. The authors/traders frequently blow holes through the sacred cows of Wall Street. Loaded with great insight on the things that really matter to be profitable.

Trade Navigator: By Genesis Financial Technologies, Colorado Springs, CO (800) 809-3282. For the money this is the best and most user-friendly quote and charting platform available. Actual trading can be executed from the platform through selected futures commission merchants (FCMs). Live customer support is readily available and extremely knowledgeable.

Commodity Research Bureau: I grew up as a trader with CRB products and services. CRB has been serving the commodity industry with excellent resources for more than 70 years. CRBtrader.com provides a multitude of valuable market research and quote and charting functions.

Barchart.com: This is a free web site with quote and charting capability. When I am on the road without my own computer I stay in contact with the charts through Barchart.com. I weekly print off the charts for the markets I will be closely monitoring from Barchart.com, using the "Classic Style Chart" setting. I then keep these charts up to date throughout the week by hand.

Author's Note

This book is educational and not intended to promote any product or service of Factor LLC now or in the future.

Monthly performance data for the period covered by the book represents a combination of data and not the trading activity of any specific account. The combination of data includes:

- An exempt commodity pool managed by Factor LLC
- Periodic trades in a proprietary account
- Management of trading signals according to the rules and guidelines specified by the Factor Trading Plan

Because no specific account has fully reflected the signals and trades reported in Part III of this book, the performance data reported herein should be considered as hypothetical. However, the performance reported in the diary portion of this book in Part III closely mirrors the trading performance of the actual exempt commodity pool managed by Factor LLC. Past performance is not necessarily indicative of future results.

Factor LLC traded proprietary accounts from October 1981 through April 1995. From October 1981 through March 1991 the proprietary accounts were controlled solely by Factor LLC under the trading program or early versions of the trading program represented by this book (see the performance capsule of Factor LLC in Figure AN.1).

From time to time throughout this period, the accounts were capitalized in part by notional funds. The notional funds were included in the calculation of performance. Performance data is reported in accordance to format and Value Added Monthly Index (VAMI) specified by the Commodity Futures Trading Commission (CFTC). Neither the CFTC nor the National Futures Association (NFA) has reviewed this material.

From April 1991 through April 1995, I granted a power of attorney over my proprietary accounts to another trader. However, because I made periodic trading decisions during this time, the performance of this trading period is included herein. The drawdowns of this period are not included in a table reporting the size and duration of drawdowns in Factor LLC's

Factor LLC

Actual Proprietary Performance Capsule (Triple Leverage Program)

Month	1981	1982	1983	1984	1985	1986	1987	1988	1989	1990	1991	1992	1993	1994	1995	2007	2008
January	–	–18.74%	71.18%	–12.62%	3.32%	14.59%	122.98%	–3.41%	8.79%	–1.20%	–11.05%	–2.55%	–1.62%	–1.24%	0.00%	–1.25%	14.05%
February	–	2.71%	2.43%	–4.77%	74.99%	29.54%	43.48%	–7.22%	–9.91%	–8.20%	–2.23%	0.89%	2.29%	–0.78%	–0.66%	–7.86%	24.59%
March	–	–7.11%	–7.08%	15.37%	–2.06%	65.64%	32.31%	–5.79%	31.26%	19.03%	–1.22%	–2.66%	–1.91%	0.24%	–0.73%	–11.76%	–5.95%
April	–	12.27%	–0.49%	0.47%	–14.07%	–20.57%	9.25%	–3.07%	–11.58%	–2.41%	–1.50%	0.50%	3.95%	–3.59%	2.91%	1.41%	–9.53%
May	–	44.08%	6.96%	7.00%	16.17%	–7.39%	3.60%	11.10%	38.89%	–4.67%	–1.58%	–0.93%	0.51%	–2.70%	–	3.00%	–5.36%
June	–	32.65%	–5.88%	19.37%	–18.69%	1.02%	11.65%	23.90%	2.26%	14.50%	6.44%	1.90%	–0.46%	–3.14%	–	7.64%	13.31%
July	–	–26.33%	16.75%	29.72%	40.30%	–8.82%	16.04%	–3.65%	4.84%	2.35%	22.00%	–0.07%	–1.58%	0.80%	–	–9.48%	–4.61%
August	–	6.64%	24.08%	10.85%	–11.87%	34.56%	27.55%	3.06%	1.73%	17.92%	–1.10%	0.68%	–0.04%	–1.00%	–	–1.30%	14.21%
September	–	–4.07%	12.33%	–1.34%	9.21%	–3.72%	–12.27%	–7.92%	5.64%	51.85%	–1.41%	4.31%	0.07%	0.53%	–	62.94%	12.18%
October	4.34%	9.09%	–1.06%	–11.54%	3.06%	0.14%	–2.69%	4.66%	–4.56%	–16.25%	2.27%	–3.19%	0.11%	5.06%	–	15.37%	–
November	21.77%	106.46%	12.37%	6.19%	39.14%	1.65%	–0.45%	–10.22%	2.90%	–8.81%	4.64%	–1.51%	–0.01%	–1.72%	–	–1.37%	–
December	–14.50%	8.90%	–1.73%	6.78%	15.18%	3.20%	4.73%	–1.58%	5.28%	–0.55%	6.86%	–2.44%	–0.14%	–0.89%	–	30.48%	–
Year	8.64%	207.48%	190.20%	75.29%	220.57%	126.70%	604.67%	–4.74%	88.22%	60.06%	–0.95%	–5.21%	1.04%	–8.36%	1.49%	95.12%	58.84%
Worst D.D.	–14.50%	–26.33%	–7.54%	–16.79%	–18.69%	–32.26%	–15.02%	–18.16%	–11.58%	–24.06%	–16.73%	–6.98%	–2.07%	–10.93%	–1.39%	–19.71%	–19.47%

PAST PERFORMANCE IS NOT INDICATIVE OF FUTURE RESULTS

FIGURE AN.1 Factor LLC Performance, October 1981–September 2008.

272

proprietary trading in Table 9.1. I retired from the trading business from April 1995 through the end of 2006. During this period I pursued some non-profit political and social endeavors. In January 2007, I once again began trading a proprietary account using the program represented by this book. In September 2008, I withdrew funds from the proprietary account to below the level required to implement the trading program described in this book. However, I took very selected trading signals for my proprietary account in 2009 and experienced a profitable year.

The performance of the proprietary trading record from 1981 through 2008 was at a leverage of three times that currently employed by Factor LLC.

Index